D0307160

MEMOIRS OF A RAILWAY ENGINEER

MEMOIRS OF A RAILWAY ENGINEER
Edgar J Larkin, OBE, CEng, FIMechE

MECHANICAL ENGINEERING PUBLICATIONS LTD
LONDON

ISBN 0 85298 388 3

Typeset by Galleon Photosetting, Copdock, Ipswich

Printed by The Burlington Press (Cambridge) Limited,
Foxton, Royston, Herts. SG8 6SA

Bound by Mansell (Bookbinders) Limited, Witham, Essex

To my daughter, Anthea Jean, and my son, John Garth.

CONTENTS

FOREWORD

by Roland C. Bond, CEng, FICE, FIMechE
Formerly Chief Mechanical Engineer of British Railways and subsequently
General Manager of British Railways Workshops Division
Past President of the Institution of Mechanical Engineers

More than 50 years have passed since Edgar Larkin and I first met. He was in the Locomotive Drawing Office of the London, Midland and Scottish Railway at Derby. I was a pupil in the Locomotive Works. As a close friend and colleague in the railway service ever since, I am particularly pleased to have been asked to write a Foreword to Edgar Larkin's autobiography. It gives me the opportunity, which I welcome, to pay my tribute to him.

We both had the good fortune to receive our practical training as mechanical engineers under Sir Henry Fowler, KBE, the Chief Mechanical Engineer of the Midland Railway, and later after the grouping of the railway companies in 1923 of the LM and S Railways. Sir Henry held strong views, more liberal and democratic than those commonly held at the time, on the training of young men aspiring to become professional engineers. As a consequence, the scope and variety of the training offered to the engineering apprentices and pupils at Derby was very good indeed. Indeed, though some brought up in other famous establishments may hold other views, long experience confirms me in my opinion that the training we received at Derby was second to none at any of the locomotive works of the old railway companies.

Nevertheless there were some weaknesses in the system – notably in the planning of moves from shop to shop to ensure a balanced course of training. His appointment as Superintendent of Apprentices at Derby Locomotive Works – the first in which he had direct personal responsibility – gave Edgar Larkin the opportunity, of which he took full advantage, to demonstrate his flair for original thought and innovation. The Progressive System of Workshop Training, in which the sometimes conflicting interests of training on the one hand and works production on the other were successfully reconciled, which Edgar Larkin established at Derby was the forerunner of the system at all the Locomotive and Carriage and Wagon Works of the LMS Railway, and, in more recent years, throughout the workshops of British Railways. The training of young engineers, and more senior people also, remained a dominant interest throughout Edgar Larkin's professional life.

Important though it is, training in all its forms is only one of the many aspects of the art and practice of works management, a fact of which Larkin himself soon became aware in the managerial appointments to which he was promoted in Derby Works. The organizations for the control and progress of locomotive repairs at Derby and the outstation shops of the Midland Division, developed over many years, were already highly efficient when Edgar Larkin was given charge of this side of the works activities. The possibilities of further improvement resided more in matters of detail than in fundamental principles. The situation was less satisfactory in respect of new locomotive building. In this important field Edgar Larkin was given free rein to apply his knowledge of sound production engineering principles in setting up a comprehensive organization, amalgamating in one office under his personal control, sections hitherto separate, dealing respectively with manufacturing specifications, material ordering and progressing, rate fixing and cost control. Full production planning was introduced for the first time.

With more than ten years' experience in works management successfully behind him, Edgar Larkin may well have expected soon to be given a works of his own to manage. But it has always seemed to me that in appointing him next as his headquarters staff assistant, C. E. Fairburn showed his unerring judgement in recognizing where Edgar Larkin's talents really lay, apart altogether from the advantages which would accrue from having, for the first time, an engineer in charge of the staff office. This was an appointment which gave great satisfaction particularly to the Works Managers, who felt that here was a man who spoke their own language and understood their problems.

It was during the years which followed that Edgar Larkin's influence extended into all the works of the LMS Railway and, after nationalization, to those of the other Regions of British Railways. His continuing concern for the improvement of training facilities was demonstrated by the establishment, first at Derby and later at all main works, of Apprentice Training Schools. They are, and will remain, a lasting memorial to Larkin's work.

In the wider field of works organization, Edgar Larkin made his mark in the reports of committees, of which he was chairman, set up by R. A. Riddles soon after nationalization, to examine in detail the arrangements at all the works and recommend a standard pattern of organization for the future. The impact of these reports led on to further special assignments, this time on Productivity throughout the railway service, culminating in his appointment to the new post of Director of Work Study.

This was not an easy job. Many of those detailed for training in the new techniques were at first rather sceptical of their practical value. Such doubts, however, were soon dispelled. And when he moved up once more to familiar ground as Deputy General Manager of the newly formed Workshops Division, Edgar Larkin left behind him a work study organization of significant value to management in the better utilization of manpower and equipment.

I am not a fisherman, nor do I excel at swimming. I cannot, therefore, add anything to Edgar Larkin's own account of his principal off-duty preoccupations. Fishing clearly demands great patience, and swimming stamina and precision, qualities which Larkin possesses to a marked degree. Above all, this autobiography reveals a man of the highest principles and integrity, one who is at ease with all manner of men, concerned at all times to give help where help is needed. Edgar Larkin is one of the few among the many railway engineers I have known and worked with, who can be positively identified as having done the original thinking and planning of important new projects for which, of course, the Head of the Department carried the ultimate responsibility.

Finally, I acknowledge with gratitude the unfailing support and wise advice which Edgar Larkin gave me during our last year together in charge of the British Railways Workshops Division. To all who know Edgar, and to many others, I commend this book as a fascinating story, simply told, of a full and rewarding life of service in many directions.

Roland C. Bond
October 1978

PREFACE

It was several years after my retirement from British Railways that I decided to write these Memoirs. I was eventually prompted to do so because, in retrospect, I felt I had a story to tell. My career had taken somewhat contrasting turns and had covered a wide spectrum of railway working. Additionally I had played an active part in various other spheres of activity involving both statutory and voluntary organizations. My narrative – some of which reveals my home and social life – extends over a period of more than three-quarters of the twentieth century.

I take this opportunity of expressing my indebtedness to colleagues who so readily co-operated in supplying me with information to help document my autobiography. In particular I proffer my sincere thanks to my only employers, British Railways and their predecessors, for their courtesy in providing me over the years with many of the photographs which illustrate bygone days.

80 Brim Hill
Hampstead Garden Suburb
London N2

Edgar J. Larkin
October 1978

CHAPTER 1

FAMILY BACKGROUND

I was born in Derby on 11 February, 1900, eleven months before the end of Queen Victoria's epoch-making reign of sixty-four years.

Towards the end of the nineteenth century, my mother and father were living in a modest corner house in Arnold Street, Derby, a short thoroughfare just off the Ashbourne Road and about a mile from Derby Market Place, and it was here that I was born. It was an area consisting mainly of terraced houses with a few larger properties in the vicinity, housing a mixture of lower and upper middle class families.

I was christened Edgar John at the parish church of St Barnabas, Derby. I remember my mother telling me that she chose the name Edgar from a book of Christian names which gave it the meaning of 'brave and true'. It is certainly a very old name. Edgar, the Saxon king of England who reigned, before the Norman Conquest, from 958 to 975, was a monarch with enlightened ideas who was known as Edgar the Peaceable. I am no historian, but I like to believe that a peaceable disposition has been a trait in my own character over the years, and maybe I have also been brave and true. I'm not at all sure that I've lived up to that definition, but my large circle of friends and countless others I have met will be the best judges.

My mother, Ada Annie Hoon, was born on 1 March, 1873, in the village of Longdon, Staffordshire, and my father, William Larkin, was born in the delightful city of Chester on 9 July, 1871. My mother was the second child of a family of no less than fourteen children. Her father, Thomas Hoon, was the son of Samuel and Sarah Hoon (née Robotham), and was born in Armitage, Staffordshire, on 27 August, 1842. He was a farmer and the family lived in Armitage and Brereton, Staffordshire, and later in Hilton, Derbyshire. Her mother, Eliza Watkiss, and

father were married at Armitage Parish Church, Staffordshire, on 27 February, 1871. I understand that it was the occasion for a double wedding – a brother and sister marrying a sister and brother. The Christian name of both the brides was Eliza, and so Eliza Watkiss became Eliza Hoon and Eliza Hoon became Eliza Watkiss. The ceremony took place at 6.00 am! I gather that in the farming community of those days it was the customary practice to have early morning weddings to enable all concerned to get on with their daily tasks as soon as the celebrations were over.

My mother's mother, Eliza Hoon, née Watkiss, was born at Brereton, Staffordshire, on 2 January, 1846. By an odd coincidence she had, in chronological order, two girls, two boys, two girls, two boys, two girls, one boy, one girl and two boys – a total of fourteen children, none of whom was a twin, and with an interval of only about a year between each birth. The three youngest children – only one of whom, Frederick, was christened – died in infancy, and the eldest child, Sarah Anne, died at 24 years of age. This left my mother as the eldest living child of ten, all of whom I remember as mature men and women. All of them married except Florence Watkiss, my mother's eldest sister, who was a trained nurse. My mother's youngest sister, Katherine Eliza, who married an American farmer, John Baker, and lived in Wisconsin, also trained as a nurse before emigrating. Such large families were of course commonplace in those days, hence the very rapid increase in the indigenous population at that time. We were always a closely linked family and since all my mother's generation have passed on, we have continued to maintain close links as a family. Some of our cousins have visited us from the United States.

The longest living of the fourteen children of my mother's family was her sister Frances Lily,

1

Fig. 1.1   The author's mother (second from left) with her four sisters (from left: Florence, Cecil, Lily and Kathleen) in 1913

who was the ninth child, and who remained quite capable of looking after herself until a short time before her death in 1977 at the grand old age of 95. Her hearing, in particular, was always one hundred per cent. She trained as a nurse in Glasgow and later worked as a theatre sister in the world-famous Mayo Brothers' Hospital in Rochester, Minnesota, USA. In 1915, during the early days of the First World War, she returned from the States to join Queen Alexandra's Military Nursing Service, taking charge of the officers' hospital in the desert near Cairo; for this strenuous work she was awarded the Royal Red Cross. Whilst still in Egypt she was given the option of going to the Palace or receiving her award from Field Marshal Viscount Allenby. She chose the latter because she had met the Field Marshal at the officers' hospital. It was in Cairo that she met her future husband, Captain Eric J. R. McAnsh, MC, whilst he was one of her patients, and throughout almost all of their married life they lived at 2, Priory Walk, Kensington, London. I was best man at their

wedding, which took place at St Mary's Church, Redcliffe Square, Kensington, on 26 April, 1923, the same day as the wedding of their Royal Highnesses the Duke and Duchess of York, later to become King George VI and Queen Elizabeth.

My mother's mother died at the early age of 48 on 6 June, 1894, only a matter of weeks after my parents' marriage on 16 April, 1894. My mother described her own mother as a 'saint' and there is no doubt that she was a profound influence in the development of my mother's loving and gentle character.

My mother's father, Thomas Hoon, was born in Armitage, Staffordshire, on 27 August, 1842. He was largely self-educated – amongst other things he taught himself Pitman's shorthand and to my own knowledge he regularly used a Pitman's shorthand prayer book at church – and could play several musical instruments, including violin, trombone, harmonica and Jew's harp, with a fair degree of competence. Although he made enough money as a farmer to keep his large family in reasonable comfort, he was apparently a good spender on unprofitable ventures, especially property. He died a relatively poor man at Milwich, Staffordshire, in 1917, during the First World War, and is buried in the churchyard of Milwich parish church. I can well remember his funeral. The coffin was carried to the church on a horse-drawn farm cart, as was the village custom, and the family mourners, including my mother and I, followed behind on foot.

As a boy I was told by my mother that my father became an orphan at an early age. It was not until I came to write these memoirs that I took steps to obtain a few facts to this end and I paid a number of visits to Somerset House in the Strand and subsequently to St Catherine's House, Kingsway, perusing register after register. I well remembered that my father died on 13 May, 1908, at the early age of 36. This enabled me to trace a William Larkin born in the Chester Cathedral District of the City of Chester on 9 July, 1871. His father was John Larkin, in business as a tailor in St Martin's Fields, Chester, and his

Fig. 1.2 William Larkin, the author's father

mother was Jane Elizabeth Larkin, née Wilkins. My father had an elder brother Harry whom I never met, and a twin brother who died at birth. Sadly my father's mother died on 10 November, 1876, at 40 years of age, when my father was only 5 years old, and my father's father died seven years later on 7 July, 1883, at 46 years of age. I learned from my mother that my father was a pupil at the famous Blue Coat School, Chester, where the boys who attended were easily recognized by their knee-length blue coats.

My enquiries concerning the Blue Coat School at Chester elicited some interesting information from the City's Archivist, Annette M. Kennett. The admission register of the Blue Coat School (Ref CR36/26) shows that William Larkin was admitted to the Green Cap section of the school, which was for day pupils only, on 2 May, 1881, and that on 17 April, 1884, he was admitted to the Blue Coat section which was for boarding pupils. His parents' address is given as 5, Long Edge, Chester. He left the school on 2 April, 1885.

The school was founded in 1700 by public subscription under the patronage of Nicholas Stratford, Bishop of Chester from 1689 to 1707, to provide an education for poor boys. The school's premises in Upper Northgate Street, which still stand today, were built in 1717 on a site previously occupied by St John's Hospital and conveyed to the school's trustees by Chester Corporation. There is a small forecourt in front, with a central archway leading to a quadrangle behind the façade, and over this central archway there is a niche in which the figure of a Blue Coat scholar still stands. In 1790, Dr John Haygarth, a trustee of the Blue Coat Hospital, established the day boys, known as 'green caps' from the colour of the caps which they wore. The blue coat boys, whose number never exceeded forty, were chosen from amongst the 'green caps'. The Green Cap School closed in 1901, and the Blue Coat School in July 1949. Today the premises are used as a careers office and a young people's club.

The Chester City Record Office has a fine collection of records from the school, dating from 1700. These include material relating to the period of my father's schooldays, and are available at the office for research purposes.

For generations the Larkin family lived and worked in the cathedral city of Lichfield, Staffordshire, the home and birthplace of Dr Samuel Johnson (1709–84). Most of the Larkins were businessmen or tailors in the city and it is apparent from various sources that they were much respected by the local citizens.

On the death of my paternal great-grandfather, William Larkin, in 1890, one of his sons, George Larkin, who was also in business as a tailor, took over the responsibility for bringing up my father. On his fourteenth birthday my father became an indentured apprentice with the well-known Staffordshire firm of those days, Holmes & Co. of Lichfield, builders of high-class horse-drawn coaches. The actual Indenture, the text of which is reproduced below, is hand-written on parchment and its drafting reflects the Victorian concern for moral duty and obligation:

> 26 Nov 1885
> William Larkin to Mr Herbert Holmes
> Indenture of Apprenticeship
> 7 years from 9 July last

This Indenture Witnesseth that William Larkin, son of John Larkin deceased, Grandson of William Larkin of Tamworth Street in the Parish of Saint Mary in the City of Lichfield, Tailor, a poor Inhabitant, with the consent of his said Grandfather and at the sole charge of a certain Public Charity then called Mousley's Charity and with the authority of the Trustees thereof being the Trustees of the Municipal Charities and estates of Charities of the said City, Doth put himself apprentice to Herbert Holmes of the said City, Coach Manufacturer, to learn their art and after the manner of an apprentice to serve from the ninth day of July last unto the full end and term of seven years thence next following to be fully complete and ended, During which term the said Apprentice his Master faithfully shall serve, his secrets keep, his lawful commands every where gladly do, he shall do no damage to his said Master nor see to be done of others but to his power shall tell or forthwith give warning to his said Master, he shall not waste the goods of his said Master nor tend them unlawfully to any, he shall not commit Fornication nor contract Matrimony within the said term, he shall not play at Cards or Dice Tables or any other unlawful games whereby his said Master may have any loss with his own goods or others during the said term without License of his said Master, he shall neither buy nor sell, he shall not haunt Taverns or Playhouses, nor absent himself from his said Masters service day or night unlawfully, but in all things as a faithful Apprentice he shall behave himself towards his said Master and all his during the said term, And the said Herbert Holmes for the consideration aforesaid their said Apprentice in the art of Coach Painter, which they use by the best means that they can, shall teach and instruct or cause to be taught and instructed, Paying unto the said Apprentice the following weekly sums during the said term, that is

to say, three shillings a week during the first year, three shillings the second year, four shillings the third year, five shillings the fourth year, six shillings the fifth year, seven shillings the sixth year, and eight shillings for the last year.

And for the performance of all and every the said Covenants and Agreements either of the said parties bindeth himself to the other by these Presents.

In Witness whereof the parties above named to these Indentures interchangeably have put their hands and seals the twenty sixth day of November in the forty ninth year of the Reign of our Sovereign Lady Victoria by the Grace of God of the United Kingdom of Great Britain and Ireland, Queen, Defender of the Faith, and in the year of our Lord one thousand eight hundred and Eighty five.

Signed, sealed and delivered
by all the parties in the   William Larkin
presence of Charles Simpson,   Wm Larkin
Steward and Treasurer to   Herbert Holmes
the said Trustees

This is in striking contrast to the streamlined documents which I, and others, have devised in more recent years.

The house where my father lived with his Uncle George was 49, Tamworth Street, Lichfield, and I understand this house remained in the family until the 1960s. After all these years it is still a distinctive property, with its Georgian bow windows. I remember visiting the house only once, with my mother and sister, soon after my father died on 13 May, 1908.

Over the years the Larkins have moved away from Lichfield. Alfred Larkin, who died in August 1974, was a prominent businessman who had three separate establishments in the city. The Larkin home at 7, John Street, where Alfred was born and where his widow, Pauline, still lives has been in the family for many generations. Alfred Larkin, Philip Larkin, CBE (the eminent poet and novelist who is Librarian at Hull University) and I are the three grandsons of three of six brothers who were born at 49, Tamworth Street, Lichfield; hence, Alfred, Philip and I are second cousins.

As a boy my father was a chorister at St Chad's Church, Lichfield; for special services he was a member of the augmented choir which sang in Lichfield Cathedral. I have never had the inclination to follow in my father's footsteps in this respect. My only sister, Winifred Annie, however, had music lessons and sang solos at local concerts in Derby before she was married, and my brother William James was a choir boy for several years at St John's Parish Church, Derby.

In the churchyard at St Michael's Parish Church, Lichfield, there is a sizeable area known as 'Larkin's Corner' containing the graves in which are buried many of my ancestors. The oldest record at present available is of Edmund Larkin, born at Lichfield in 1720. The accompanying genealogical diagram (Fig 1.3) indicates the relationship of those I have mentioned as well as others; the centralized records of births, deaths and marriages go back only to the first half of the nineteenth century following the establishment of the office of Registrar General by the Births and Deaths Registration Act of 1836, and so one has to delve elsewhere if it is desired to go back further. For much of the information in my chart I am indebted to the late Alfred Larkin.

My father was of medium height and of slight build. I have the original wedding certificate which shows that he married my mother on 16 April, 1894, at St Michael's Parish Church, Lichfield. They continued to live in Lichfield where my sister, Winifred Annie, was born on 12 December, 1895, and moved to Derby some time before the birth of my elder brother Harry, who was born in Derby on 14 September, 1898, but who died at the age of 11 months, a few months before I was born. There was evidence that my father was not a robust man and, owing to illness, was forced to have lengthy periods away from work. He and my mother had come to the conclusion that his health might improve with a new job and a different environment; hence the move to Derby. My mother's two eldest brothers William and James, with whom my father had always been on good terms, had come to work in Derby as teenage boys, and my father joined William for a short while before taking up alternative employment. We moved from Arnold Street to a corner house in nearby Langley Street. Unfortunately my father's health did not improve and he died after a short illness on 13 May, 1908. Four months elapsed and my brother William James (named after my father and after my mother's two eldest brothers) was born on 13 September, 1908. Thus my parents had three sons and a daughter. My mother had four sisters, three of whom married, and two had children. It is a coincidence that both had the same number of children as my own parents: three sons and a daughter.

With the death of my father my mother became the bread-winner. Years later she told me that my father had left only £36 in the bank, an indication of the extent to which his money had been eroded as a result of long spells of illness. But my mother rose to the occasion and she became both mother and 'father', and brought up the three of us (my sister, my brother and me) in a manner that could be compared favourably with many a family considered to have a good income. Small in stature, my mother was one who never sought any limelight; she lived only for her family and put all her energies into any task which came her way. My sister, my brother and I held her in the highest esteem, and in our different ways she has had a great influence on our respective behaviour and mode of living. She passed peacefully away on 9 March, 1949, at the age of 76. I had been privileged to be with her the day before at my sister's home in Broadway, Derby, and I received the sad news at the Industrial Court in London where I was giving evidence in a case. She was buried in my father's grave, No. 46753, in Nottingham Road Cemetery, Derby.

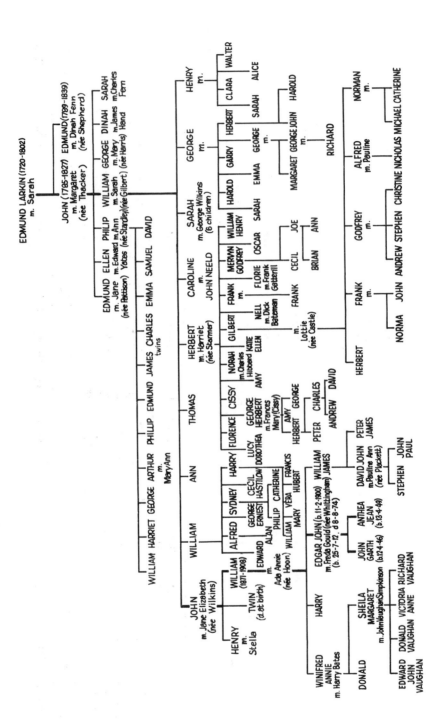

Fig. 1.3(a)   Paternal genealogical chart – the Larkin family

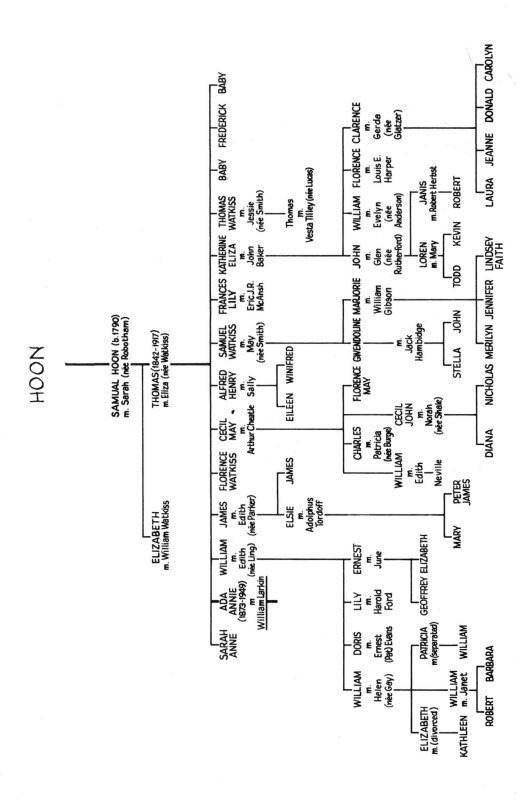

Fig. 1.3(b) Maternal genealogical chart – the Hoon family

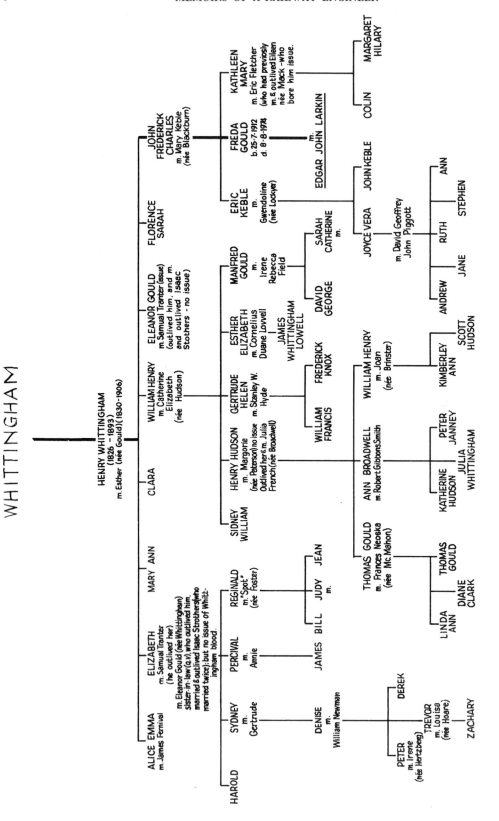

Fig. 1.3(c)   Wife's paternal genealogical chart – the Whittingham family

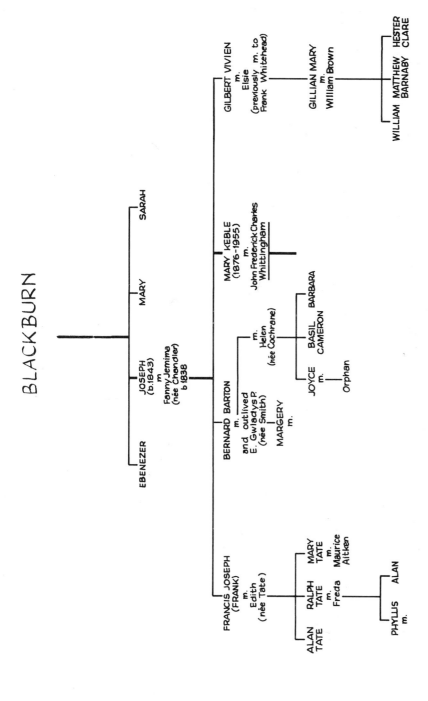

Fig. 1.3(d) Wife's maternal genealogical chart – the Blackburn family

CHAPTER 2

HOME AND SOCIAL LIFE TO 1943

During the whole of my bachelor years to 1943, and the early years of my married life from 1943 until 1956, my life centred around my home town of Derby, now a city. Located in the Midlands – 90 miles from the east coast and 110 miles from the west coast – Derby is an industrial city of considerable importance. Currently it has a population of around 220 000, equivalent to a quarter of the population of the county of Derbyshire. The county has only one other major town, Chesterfield, and that is much smaller with about 70 000 people. The history of Derby goes back to Roman times and it is doubtful whether any other town or city, comparable in size, in the British Isles today can lay claim to so many well-established industries with an international reputation. Since 1840 Derby has played a key role in the development of the railway industry and has become the home of the Advanced Passenger Train and the High Speed Train. British Rail's technical and research departments in the city combine to make it a centre for railway activity without equal in the world. With the advent of the motor-car industry, Derby became the traditional home of the world-renowned Rolls-Royce company. Perhaps one of Derby's most famous concerns is Royal Crown Derby Porcelain, with its origins in the eighteenth century. Other important companies include British Celanese, a part of the Courtaulds group; Aiton and Company, producing high and low pressure pipework, heat exchangers and fluid agitators; International Combustion, well known for their developments in burners for steam generators, oil burners and multiple fuel firing techniques; Qualcast, who have produced over fourteen million lawnmowers since the early 1920s, and many more. A famous old silk mill, built in Derby by Thomas Cotchett in 1702 and now an industrial museum, was Britain's earliest textile mill and is generally accepted as being the first factory to be established in this country in the sense that it had machinery driven by water power and employed a regular work force.

With my father's untimely death in 1908 at the early age of 36, my mother decided to try and start a small business in ladies' and children's clothes, millinery and haberdashery. I came home from school one day and told her I had seen an empty shop on Ashbourne Road not far from my school. My mother followed it up and took the premises on a monthly rental. We moved in around 1910 and she eventually worked up a very good business.

My mother was given a dispensation by the Derby Education Authority for my sister, Winifred Annie – four years older than I – to leave the Derby Practising School (a school run in conjunction with the Derby Teacher Training College) when she was 13 years of age instead of the normal leaving age of 14 years. My sister was well reported on at school but my mother found it necessary for her to look after my baby brother, William, whilst she herself ran the business. Not only did my mother run the business but, having been trained as a tailoress and being an accomplished needlewoman, she made all the clothes for the family. Whether it was dresses, costumes and coats for herself and my sister, little boy's clothes for my brother or suits and overcoats for me, she produced them all. There were times when she took on similar work for a few of her regular customers. It was a very hard struggle. She was always working and, even for relaxation, produced faultless and exquisite crotcheting.

After a few years at 4, Ashbourne Road some premises diagonally opposite, at 70, Friar Gate – an impressive thoroughfare containing several Georgian houses and always spoken of as Derby's Harley Street because of its preponderance of physicians' and surgeons' consulting rooms and residences – became vacant and we moved into them in 1914. Around the corner was Vernon Street, with the Diocesan School for Boys at the Friar Gate end, and HM Prison at the other. Opposite to us was Friary House School, a well-established private boarding school for girls. The Church of St Werburgh is located at the Wardwick end of Friar Gate and has a register recording the marriage in 1735 of Dr Samuel Johnson to Elizabeth 'Tetty' Porter.

I attended Ashbourne Road Boys' School, a mere quarter of a mile from home, which consisted of a substantial building, with the Girls' School on the same site, and which has for some years now been used as a junior school known as Ashgate School, still retaining all the old school's original character. I enjoyed my schooldays. We had excellent teachers and I can look back on them all as being dedicated men and women. In the junior school we were taught by women and in the senior school by men; they were greatly respected and truancy was almost non-existent.

I never recall any boy going to my school without boots or shoes, although in some parts of the town it was commonplace at that time to see lots of boys and girls running about barefooted and often in ragged clothes. This kind of poverty has not been seen since the end of the First World War and it is a clear indication that the standard of living of even the poorest families has appreciably improved over the years. Of course, the size of the average family has fortunately become smaller since that period, and this fact in itself must have been of material assistance.

Many long years ago the Railway Servants' Orphanage was built by the Midland Railway next to my school on Ashbourne Road. It was later renamed St Christopher's Home for Children and as recently as 1977, the Queen's Silver Jubilee Year, a new building was constructed to take the place of the older one and was appropriately opened by Queen Elizabeth The Queen Mother. Thanks to generous benefactors its invaluable work continues unabated.

During my schooldays, horse-drawn tramcars gave way to electric trams. Motor-cars were few and far between and pedestrian crossings and automatic signals had not been invented. Living on a main road, I looked forward every Tuesday and Friday to seeing cows being herded along the Ashbourne Road into the centre of the town through Friar Gate, the Wardwick and Victoria Street on their way to the cattle market. Usually

there were about a dozen or so cows in a herd, but sometimes as many as fifty, under the care of a couple of herdsmen and a dog. It always amused me if a cow or a bullock took a dash down one of the side streets and remained at large for a while.

My first success at school occurred in the junior school when I was 8. The teacher promised threepence of her own money to the boy who could best read the newspaper to her and to the class. Threepence in those days was usually a silver coin and to any of us at that age it was a sum of money well worth having and I wondered whether I should be able to compete. It was my good fortune to be selected and I was one of the six finalists who the teacher named and lined up in front of the class. In turn we each read aloud a different paragraph which the teacher had selected and at the end of this contest I was declared the winner. It was very encouraging to me and I understand that some time later the head teacher spoke to my mother and said I showed considerable promise.

In my first year in the senior school I was chosen to take part in an historical pageant. All the Derby schools were involved and the pageant took place in the Drill Hall, Derby's largest covered building, which was frequently used for exhibitions and concerts. My own school gave a performance depicting the early Britons and I wore a bear skin and a wig with a huge beard. Despite all our rehearsals and the combined, untiring efforts of our teachers I can imagine it was all a very amateurish show. It certainly stands out as my only attempt at acting because I have spared everyone in subsequent years.

We had only two non-academic subjects: handicraft work and physical training. Handicraft work was only taken in the last two years at school, but it was a subject which I thoroughly enjoyed and it was an invaluable introduction to hand tools which has always served me well. We had a morning or afternoon session each week and after we had successfully completed set test pieces, mostly in wood, we were allowed some freedom of choice, for which we were taught to set out an orthographic projection. My final and most memorable effort was a four-wheeled trolley with a pivoted front axle to facilitate steering. I decided to give the trolley as a present to my younger brother, and on the day I anticipated finishing it I arranged for him to meet me outside school at four o'clock. He was not disappointed and still tells a vivid story of how he sat himself firmly on the trolley and how I whisked him along the pavement to our home a quarter of a mile away. The trolley was a great success and the forerunner of many varied items I have built in my spare time over the years, some in metal, some in wood and some in both. For firing my enthusiasm I owe a great deal to the handicraft masters at school, John Adnams (the senior master) and Richard Bennett (the junior master).

To the best of my knowledge, only my last teacher, Leonard Holme, was still alive when I eventually left Derby to move to London early in 1956. Apart from his being an outstanding teacher he was an accomplished violinist and also did an enormous amount of charity work in connection with the Derbyshire Children's Home at Skegness, Lincolnshire. I had not seen him around for a few years and I took the opportunity of visiting him at his home in Littleover, Derby, on the eve of my departure. He was then in his 80s, and it gave me a great deal of pleasure to see him and recall some of my boyhood days. Within a week or so of my having called I received a most moving and appreciative letter from him.

I was always happy at school, except perhaps when I had the cane on both hands for some minor disobedience such as talking in class. It was an extremely painful experience and I was downright sorry for those who had to suffer a couple of strokes on each hand. Happily for me caning was a rare occurrence. I like to think that a more civilized punishment, equally salutary, has been substituted over the years.

The school day normally ended at four o'clock and was marked by the singing of a hymn, usually 'The day Thou gavest, Lord, is ended'. My family have always said with a wry smile that this was my favourite hymn. For myself, I'm not sure; there are other hymns which continue to give me equal satisfaction and food for thought.

I had some private piano lessons, and succeeded in playing a duet with my sister, but whereas she continued to make progress I fell by the wayside, and whatever I may have learned I have regrettably forgotten. All I can say now is that I have enjoyed listening to most types of music, other than so-called 'pop' music, especially comic opera, military and brass bands such as the Bands of the Royal Marines and the Brigade of Guards, and not least the commendable Salvation Army.

My mother was always a staunch churchgoer and a woman of the highest principles, and she tried to bring up her family in the same worthwhile manner. For several years I regularly attended St John's Church and Sunday School. The Sunday School was a morning and afternoon session, with the morning session being followed by matins in the church, with the children leaving before the customary sermon. We were required to learn the Collect at home and repeat it before the Sunday School teacher. For the most part I found this exercise a tedious one, but on looking back I accept that it was a discipline which is perhaps little encountered today but which did me much more good than harm. I received many book prizes over the years, for attendance and progress.

Each Whitsuntide it was the practice in Derby, as in Manchester and other northern towns, for Whit Tuesday to be a public holiday during which the different Sunday Schools had an early tea party after which they paraded, led by a band, to a nearby field. St John's were lucky because a farmer always kindly loaned them a large field located in beautiful surroundings. Each class had a sprint race and I was lucky enough to win the first prize every year I competed – usually a handsome pocket knife. As a boy I was of athletic build, tall and slim, and I finished growing at five feet ten and a half inches.

There were only two other occasions in my life when I was a competitor in athletics. The more important was when I was chosen to represent my school in the individual furlong race and also in the four-a-side team race in the Derby Schools Championships. But I had no success in either. My other athletic experience was at a Garden Fete held in Markeaton Park, Derby, the home at that time of the Mundy family, but subsequently acquired by Derby Corporation from a legacy. There were several thousand visitors enjoying the amenities because the Park was seldom open to the public. No car park was required because cars scarcely existed and a high proportion of those present had either come by tram or had walked. I was thirteen years of age and my sister accompanied me. It was my first visit to this delightful park and I was tremendously impressed with its lawns, its gardens and extensive greenhouses and perhaps even more with its lovely lake. Sprint races were organized for juniors and seniors and I was chosen for the latter category. For the seniors the distance was 100 yards and once again I was fortunate enough to win the first prize. Although I had met with success in my very limited experience of athletics, my interest in swimming was already developing – mainly confined to my weekly visits to the swimming baths with my school. Even at this early age I had learned that athletics and swimming did not mix and I decided to concentrate on the latter.

As a boy I played the occasional game of football or cricket with my friends on the local recreation ground. I preferred football but was not very good at either game. I have continued to take a modicum of interest in league football, especially my home city team, Derby County, who won the FA Cup at Wembley in 1949 and the First Division League Championship in 1971 and again in 1974. I can never hope to win the football pools for the reason that I have no wish to fill in a coupon. To me it's a case of what you never have you never miss! To others it may well mean a fortune.

By the year 1925 the time had come when my mother felt she could no longer carry on her business. At this time I was a draughtsman on the London Midland and Scottish Railway and my brother was at the Bemrose Grammar School. Two years earlier, on 5 September, 1923, my sister married Harry Bates, who was working with his father, Joseph Bates, in a family hardware and timber business in the centre of Derby; my sister and her husband had set up home in Longford Street, Derby, and later built a house on Broadway, Derby, a wide thoroughfare which was opened by King George V and Queen Mary not long after the First World War. My mother had a genuine desire to live in the country; after all she was a farmer's daughter and was accustomed to the land, to driving and riding horses and having her own garden even as a girl. My mother and I looked around and in 1925 she bought a plot of building land of eighteen hundred square yards on the Kedleston Road at Allestree some two miles short of Kedleston Hall, the former home of Lord Curzon, onetime Foreign Secretary and later Viceroy of India. In co-operation with a drawing office colleague of mine who owned the adjacent plot, we arranged for a pair of semi-detached houses to be built on the two plots and my mother, brother and I moved in during 1926. There was much gardening to be done and we jointly set about it and converted what had been part of a field into a very desirable garden with a lawn, rockery, a small fruit orchard and a sizeable kitchen garden. Several years earlier, during the First World War, when food was in short supply,

my mother had run a garden allotment of three hundred square yards on the Ashbourne Road, nearly half a mile from where we were living; she did the whole of the work herself and it was a model of a kitchen garden. On Wednesday afternoon, which was her well-earned half-day closing, she would dig and hoe away and bring home appetizing vegetables.

Until we moved into the country in 1926 I had been using a cycle to travel to the office but now that I was further away as well as being slightly better off I bought myself a 2¼ horsepower BSA motorcycle. Petrol was only eleven old pence per gallon and the machine gave me excellent service and ran for about ninety miles on one gallon.

During 1920 I became a radio enthusiast and like many others of my age I built several radio sets, each one being an improvement on its predecessor. It was a 'do it yourself' exercise at its best! The wiring diagrams were obtainable through the wireless magazines of the day. How we have advanced since those pioneering days, and how we now take so much of it all for granted!

During 1924 when I was employed as a draughtsman in the Locomotive Drawing Office of the LMS, Derby, and holding office as the first Honorary General Secretary of the Derby LMS Swimming Club, of which I was co-founder, I met a girl named Elsie Village, the Secretary of the Ladies Section of the Club. Her father had recently retired from the position of Passenger Commercial Superintendent of the Midland Division of the LMS Railway. We became friendly and were engaged in 1926. Two years later I bought a plot of building land in Constable Drive, Littleover, and I designed a small detached house to our liking and drew up the building specification for the house which was built there in 1930. We planned to get married in October 1930, following my heavy commitment with the Liverpool and Manchester Railway Centenary Celebrations which were centred in and around Liverpool, and to a lesser extent in Manchester, in September 1930. I had arranged for a much respected friend of mine, the Reverend L. G. Appleton, who had been a curate at St John's Church, Derby, to perform the marriage ceremony in Derby. He was then a padre in Toc H in London, and introduced me to the Reverend 'Tubby' Clayton, rector of All Hallows, London and founder of Toc H in 1922. The banns were read and we had reached the stage of having the house furnished and I had managed to erect the boundary fence and a sectional garage, as well as plan the garden.

To my great sorrow my fiancée was taken ill a month before the date of the wedding and although she had every possible medical attention, including a long period at the Windsor Clinic, she became progressively worse and eventually passed away a year later on 17 September, 1931, at the age of 28. It was the most bitter experience of my life and for many long years the tragedy was ever-present in my mind. She was a Derbyshire County hockey player and a finalist in our tennis club championship and was well recognized as an accomplished sportswoman in local circles. The vicar of St Peter's Church, Littleover, the Reverend C. R. Brown, kindly volunteered to recognize Elsie as a parishioner and allow her to be buried at St Peter's. Her parents were in full agreement with this proposal and Elsie was laid to rest in the churchyard there.

There were times when I thought I would never get over my loss. I realized, however, that I had to take hold of my future and I continued to apply myself to my new job as Superintendent of Apprentices. It was in my private life that I had to make changes and it was at this period that I began to devote more of my spare time to work in the world of swimming. This took the form of coaching, writing and lecturing. I took further interest in the Derby Railway Engineering Club and also became a Committee Member of the Derby Society of Engineers as well as accepting an invitation to serve on the Council of the Derby Railway Institute with its varied and wholesome interests.

At that time I was the owner of a fully furnished, newly built detached house which was standing empty. Elsie and I had put so much effort into this new home that I gave a great deal of thought as to what action I should take with it. In the end I decided to let the property and following my advertisement in a local newspaper my tenants were a young married solicitor with the Derby Corporation, and his wife. This worked out very satisfactorily except that at the end of six months the solicitor obtained a post as Assistant Town Clerk in Norwich, and I again found myself with an unoccupied home. My mother and I were still living in her house at Allestree and I asked her whether she would let her own home in which we had lived for a number of years and join me in my new home at Littleover. The latter was a larger house and I

thought the change would be good for both of us. Happily my mother agreed and so we moved home, and my mother had no difficulty in finding a tenant for her own house.

On 19 May, 1932, my mother and I moved into my house in Constable Drive, Littleover, Derby. Whilst it had been under construction Elsie and I had decided to call it 'Westwood' because one of her school friends, Winifred Dix, daughter of the then Headmaster of Heanor Grammar School, Derbyshire, and herself a school teacher, had married an Anglican clergyman, Reverend Harold Sanders, and they were living at Westwood Parsonage near Heanor.

The early thirties were years of economic depression, and at this period my brother was one of many hundreds of young craftsmen in Derby who encountered frustrations at a relatively early stage in their careers, many of them moving elsewhere as an alternative to being unemployed. Thus, within a decade of his having left school in 1924 to become an apprentice at the renowned Rolls-Royce works, my brother found it necessary to consider his options. Most of his apprenticeship experience at Rolls-Royce had fortunately been spent on repairing customers' cars rather than working on new cars, a much wider experience for him than would otherwise have been the case, and this was a factor when in 1930 he was successful in obtaining a position as a maintenance engineer at a garage on the south coast. In his spare time he became a prominent member of the Bexhill Football Club as well as of the Bexhill Swimming Club water polo team, and he gained medals with each. Whilst living in Bexhill he struck up a friendship with Nancy Slator from Tunbridge Wells, to whom he became engaged before returning to Derby in the mid-thirties. He became the manager of the Littleover Garage situated on the main road linking Derby and Burton-on-Trent. On 18 August, 1937, he married Nancy at St John's Church, Tunbridge Wells. I was best man for the third and last occasion in my life, the previous occasions being on 26 April, 1923, at the wedding of Captain Eric McAnsh and my aunt, and on 4 January, 1930, at the wedding of Dr Archie Steele to Winifred Lewin who was a school teacher and a close friend of Elsie Village. In 1942 my brother joined the Royal Naval Volunteer Reserve and appointed sub-lieutenant engineer. The following year he was transferred from duties in British coastal waters to Bombay where he was promoted to lieutenant engineer in 1945. After the war was over he served for a short period in Germany before returning to England on completion of his naval career.

A few years before the war, in November 1936, when I was still at Derby locomotive works, I had my first experience of jury service when I was sworn in as a juror at the Derbyshire Assizes in a case of alleged manslaughter. During the two-day proceedings before Mr Justice Atkinson, the judge said to the defendant, 'I understood you to say in answer to your Counsel a moment ago that you were an experienced car driver'. The reply came, 'Yes, my Lord'. The learned judge went on, 'Now you have just said in reply to a further question 'I was baffled by the lights of an oncoming car'. The defendant replied, 'Yes, my Lord'. The judge commented, 'An experienced driver doesn't gaze at the lights of an oncoming car. If he can't see the road for any reason, surely he proceeds very slowly or applies his brakes and pulls up.' The jury subsequently found the defendant guilty of manslaughter.

The first winter of the 1939–45 war was one of the most severe for many years, and towards the end of January 1940 we experienced the heaviest fall of snow I remember. Several inches fell on the 27th, more fell on the 28th and 29th, and then again still more snow on the 1st and 2nd of February. Almost everything, everywhere throughout the country, was at a standstill, and the snow was several feet deep in many places. We certainly didn't need to be at the beginning of the Second World War to make everyone feel distraught and almost helpless.

Derby experienced its first air raid by bombers of the German Luftwaffe on 24 June, 1940, when the circular leaded light in our front door at Westwood, Littleover, caught a bomb splinter and had to be replaced. It could have been much worse. Along with our neighbours we were finding it prudent when the air raid sirens went into action to take refuge in a nearby air raid shelter erected by the county council, on the Burton Road. During the night of 19 August, 1940, I was on fire warden duty with my neighbour, Charles Ashton, the Town Clerk of Derby, in his house opposite to ours when, following the thud of heavy bombs exploding, I received a telephone message from my Works Manager, James Rankin, to say that Derby railway station had been attacked and that he

Fig. 2.1 *Freda Gould Whittingham, 1942, married to the author on 9 July 1943*

would pick me up and we would go and inspect. On arrival at the works we found that the only damage in the works was to my own office, which was a veritable shambles. The station roof, about fifty yards away, had however received several direct hits and the station was out of action. It was the debris from this and the permanent way which had caused all the damage to my own office. Later it was learned that eleven bombs had been dropped at Derby station but luckily only two of these had exploded. Unhappily several passengers were killed on this occasion. The nine unexploded bombs were safely recovered within the next week or so, but it was some time before Derby station was functioning normally again. Mother and I were spared, and we moved back to her own house, Hazeldene, in Allestree on 7 February, 1942. Hazeldene had become vacant and as it was a smaller house than Westwood my mother thought it was an opportunity she should take. I was perfectly happy to go with her and, as I thought Westwood might be subject to further bombing, I decided to sell it even though the property market was understandably at a low ebb.

Before the beginning of the War I had a personal typist at the office for whom I had considerable regard. She was Freda Gould Whittingham. She had ability and integrity of a high standard. A reorganization took her elsewhere on the railway. At a later date, my personal typist Barbara Cramp was selected for promotion to the post of secretary to the first Principal, Brigadier L. Manton, at the newly completed and well equipped LMS School of Transport, Derby, which was opened in 1938. The railway architect had won the Royal Institute of British Architects' award of the year for this design. At this stage I was successful in arranging for Freda Whitting-ham to return to me as my personal typist. In 1942, however, I left the locomotive works to take up a senior position in the headquarters office of the Chief Mechanical and Electrical Engineer of the LMS at Derby. By this time I was conscious of the fact that I had formed a strong attachment to Freda. I realized too that my feelings were reciprocated and we began to meet regularly and visit each other's homes. The friendship developed and we decided to get married in 1943, a year after I had left the works in which Freda continued to be employed. We fixed the wedding date for 9 July, 1943, and the marriage took place at All Saints Parish Church, Mackworth, where I was vicar's warden for a period of five years. Because the war was still on, with all its uncertainties, we hesitated to purchase a property and after discussion with my mother it was decided we would live with her until more normal conditions prevailed. Actually we stayed with her for three years when, in anticipation of the birth of our first child, we began to look around for our own accommodation.

CHAPTER 3

TRADE APPRENTICESHIP AND PRIVILEGED APPRENTICESHIP

I owe my start on the railway to the late Henry Sheppard, a director of Marley Tiles. His wife had been cared for during an illness by my mother's eldest sister, Florence Hoon, a trained nurse who in later years, and until she retired, was companion to the Hon. Mrs Skeffington Craig at Carlton Hall, Newark-on-Trent, Nottinghamshire, the mother of the novogenarian Viscountess Masserene and Ferrard, both of whom I met on several occasions.

My aunt was my godmother and she took a lively interest in all my activities. She had told Henry Sheppard that my mother was a widow and was having to make a living for herself and her three children. As a young man he had shared accommodation with James E. Anderson, a Scot and a draughtsman in his day who became the Chief Draughtsman of the locomotive drawing office at Derby and was at that time the Works Manager at the Derby locomotive works. He was to become the first Chief Motive Power Superintendent of the entire London Midland and Scottish Railway network on amalgamation in 1923. Henry Sheppard kindly wrote to James Anderson and told him that I was anxious to become a draughtsman and he inquired whether there were any possibilities open to me. I was just recovering from diphtheria and my mother had been making enquiries about sending me, at some financial sacrifice, to the Diocesan School, a well-known private day school situated nearby in Friar Gate. The headmaster at the school had been a teacher at the school when both he and we lived in Langley Street and we knew him well. In due time I was called for interview at the Derby locomotive works when it was explained to me that to become an engineering draughtsman it was first necessary to serve an apprenticeship to a craft grade and that possible promotion to draughtsman depended entirely on good workshop reports

coupled with success in technical examinations. There was no guarantee. I had no idea of industry nor did I realize, believe it or not, that Derby contained such a vast railway centre. Whenever I had travelled by train as a boy I was taken to the small Friar Gate station of the Great Northern Railway. Our home was in Friar Gate and this station was only a few hundred yards away, whereas the Derby Midland station was nearly two miles distant and was the centre of a rail complex of which at that time I knew literally nothing.

I went along for my interview wondering what the immediate future held in store for me. I was interviewed by George Woolliscroft, Superintendent of Apprentices. He was a Whitworth Scholar, a graduate of Manchester University, a former Mayor of Ilkeston, Derbyshire, in which town he still resided, a Justice of the Peace and Chairman of the Heanor and District Water Board. To me at that time he was a venerable, kindly gentleman whose knowledge seemed profound. He asked me a number of questions one of which at least I can still recall. He said, 'Can you distinguish between a passenger engine and a freight engine?' I replied by saying, 'A passenger engine is painted red and a freight engine is painted black.' Although that was true he was clearly not impressed. He asked with a faint smile, 'Can't you tell me any more than that?' I thought deeply and then I said, 'A passenger engine has large wheels and a freight engine has small wheels.' 'Why?' said he, after an ominous pause, and I hesitatingly replied, 'I think it is because large wheels give greater speed and small wheels give greater pulling power.' By this time I was nervously wondering what would come next, but to my great relief he asked me to spell a mixed bag of words such as 'essential', 'necessary', 'spherical', 'possession' and 'received'.

These presented me with no problem, nor did any of his oral questions on fractions ('What is one third plus one quarter?'), percentages, decimals ('What is 0·125 of a gallon expressed in pints?'), and tables of weight, length and liquid measure. He asked 'How do you find the area of a circle?' and this too was no problem. Indeed, I think I left school with a goodly dose of 'the three R's' and possibly not much else. Perhaps this was not surprising because I had been absent from school at some time or other with most, if not all, of the infectious diseases to which children were prone. And because my mother was running a business there was no alternative but for me to go into hospital each time. I was in hospital with scarlet fever when I was eleven and I missed the scholarship entrance examination. I was again in hospital with diphtheria on my fourteenth birthday and as a result I never went back to full time day school. There was no question in those days of having to finish only at the end of the school year. Happily these and many other infectious diseases are no longer the scourge which they were in my boyhood days. It may be that I had so many that they fortified me.

In spelling and arithmetic in particular I always felt reasonably sure of myself. On the occasion of my interview, however, when I was standing on my own feet, so to speak, for the first time in my life I felt my temperature was unusually high. I can well imagine that the colour of my cheeks and my neck were very different from normal. I did at least survive! At the end of the interview I was only promised that my application for an apprenticeship would be considered and that I should be notified of the company's decision in writing. I came away from my interview feeling inwardly somewhat apprehensive. Yet a fortnight later I was requested to present myself at the staff office for employment in the locomotive drawing office of the Midland Railway as a trade apprentice on 5 May, 1914. Clearly, I was starting as the office boy but I have certainly never regretted this turn of events and my not attending the Diocesan School.

I was employed as the office boy in the locomotive drawing office for a period of twelve months. Throughout this time I was kept usefully occupied either in the office or in conveying drawings and correspondence in and around the large office block and the works. I was learning all the time – not least how to get on with people. The Chief Draughtsman was Sandham James Symes, OBE, who followed J. E. Anderson as Works Manager. He was an outstanding railway officer of Irish descent, respected by all, and who, ultimately, became Principal Assistant to Sir William Stanier, FRS, the Chief Mechanical Engineer of the LMS Railway. He finished his distinguished railway career as Chief Stores Superintendent of the LMS Railway. He lived to be 92 years of age and he wrote to me only a year before he passed away and reminded me of the drawing board at which I worked when I became a draughtsman on completion of my apprenticeship.

The drawing office employed about fifty draughtsmen, some male tracers and some clerical office staff. Without exception they were all very helpful to me and from them I learned a great deal about drawing office practice and routine. I also learned Pitman's shorthand from one of the clerical officers, John W. Croxall, and thirty and more years later I never had any difficulty in reading my wife's telephone messages written in shorthand. We all worked a five-and-a-half-day week and my own wages were fixed at five shillings and eight pence per week. It seems quite incredible nowadays when one stops to think of this meagre rate of pay which was usual for an apprentice of my age.

I was transferred to the locomotive workshops at 15½ years of age and I was placed in the Machine and Fitting Shop. In this shop nearly a thousand men and boys were employed and there were approximately five hundred machine tools of various types. Structurally it was a very impressive shop indeed, and it was a hive of activity. I immediately came on to the standard fifty-four-hour week and was placed on a nut tapping machine. We started at 6.00 am and we worked until 8.15 am when we stopped for breakfast. We resumed at 9.00 am and continued until 1.00 pm. We had an hour for lunch and the afternoon shift went on until 5.30 pm. Saturday was a half day and we finished at 12.00 noon. It took me many months to become accustomed to three working periods a day – before breakfast, after breakfast and after the luncheon break. For a long time I used to think that the breakfast break was the midday break. What an awakening! It was a nine-and-three-quarter-hour day from Mondays to Fridays, with five-and-a-quarter hours on Saturday mornings for good measure. My wages had now increased to eight shillings a week. On top of these long hours, however, I attended evening classes on three evenings a week and

Fig. 3.1   Section of the machine shop, Derby Locomotive Works, to which the author was allocated during his apprenticeship in 1916. (At that time, and until the late 1920s, a whole group of machines was powered by a single large electric motor and line shafting, with individual driving belts operating each machine)

there were times when I had some difficulty in keeping awake. It was tough going and I am very glad indeed that the apprentice of today working forty hours including one whole day at day classes is not called upon to do the same as I and thousands more did. Although I found it difficult enough, goodness knows what the working hours would have been if I had lived 100 years earlier. The Factories Act of 1874 introduced a fifty-six-and-a-half-hour working week and raised the minimum age for work to nine years. By comparison I was very lucky.

There was an odd practice which prevailed throughout the works. We could only visit the toilet once a day, for a maximum period of fifteen minutes. We first had to obtain a ticket from a clerk in the Shop Office. The clerk inserted the time of day, the lavatory attendant franked the ticket and we had to return the ticket to the Shop

Office before we resumed our work. I can't imagine how employees would react to such a practice these days!

Even in my early days as an apprentice, the Derby locomotive works – the oldest locomotive works on British Railways, having been started by the North Midland Railway in 1840 – had gained a high reputation for training engineers, many of whom had gone on to acquire distinction both inside and outside the railway service.

Although I was only engaged on the nut tapping machine for a few weeks I must have produced several thousand nuts and in doing so came home every day, despite my taking every precaution, with very greasy overalls, trousers and shirt. I was much relieved when I was transferred to a nut facing machine, and then a bolt screwing machine, both of which were relatively clean jobs. I progressed to other machines including several months on centre and capstan lathes where I made a large variety of steel and cast iron parts for locomotives. It was all very valuable experience.

For some months I was employed in the Brass Machining and Fitting Shop, operating first a milling machine and then a turret lathe and later working on the bench as an apprentice fitter. I recall the occasion when the chargehand gave a thread making tap and a wrench to a 'privileged apprentice' and asked him to tap a hole through a regulator gland to accommodate a set screw. Shortly afterwards, and to everyone's amusement – including mine – the apprentice took up his hammer and drove the tap right through the gland. He had no use for the wrench which of course should have been used for turning the tap in a hole in the regulator gland and forming a Whitworth thread! Seeing our reactions the unfortunate apprentice concerned could only say that he had been asked to tap it through and this was precisely what he had done. The young man concerned was clearly not in his element and not many months elapsed before he left the company to become a bank employee in which capacity I hope he was much more successful.

During my apprenticeship days electric trams had taken the place of horse-drawn trams. Initially, however, the upper decks of the electric trams were not covered, and many a time in the winter I was unable to cycle to the works because of a heavy fall of snow and had to ride on a tram which had been left in the open overnight. As the inside seats were full by the time I boarded the tram, it was a case of having to ride on the upper deck, and as the seats would be thick with snow, I had no alternative but to stand for the journey to the railway works. Not so palatable at 5.30 am with a long day's work ahead! Only once or twice throughout my apprenticeship did I not start work until 9.00 am instead of at 6.00 am. One of these occasions was on 1 February, 1916, when a German zeppelin dropped bombs in Derby during the night – there was no sleep that night! No fewer than eighteen bombs were dropped on the locomotive works but fortunately most of them fell in open yards and caused minimum damage. Sadly there were two men in the works on the night shift who took shelter in a yard underneath a locomotive tender and the shrapnel from a nearby bomb killed them both outright. I found a jagged segment of bomb in the works and kept it for almost twenty years before deciding to dispose of it.

So far I have referred mainly to my practical training. But to become a professional engineer, or even a draughtsman, theoretical training is equally important.

Soon after leaving my day school I was supplied with a card which I was to hand to the headmaster of the Ashbourne Road Evening Continuation School if I decided to continue with my studies in September 1914. The Ashbourne Road Evening Continuation School offered a preliminary course of three evenings per week which, if successfully completed by March 1915, would take me to a higher course at Abbey Street Evening Continuation School for the 1915–16 session. I worked out that, if I first did a session at Ashbourne Road School, I should be about a year behind boys of my own age or slightly older who had attended a secondary school and gone direct to Abbey Street School and then into the works without first being an office boy. Accordingly, of my own volition, I took my card to the headmaster of the Abbey Street Evening Continuation School to see whether I could go straight into his school. This headmaster was William Fearn who in the day time was the mathematics master at the Abbey Street Grammar School for Boys (later the Bemrose School) and who ultimately became head of the mathematics department at the Derby and District College of Technology. He was the most brilliant lecturer it was my good fortune to know, and I benefited enormously from his knowledge when I later became a student at the college. At this first meeting he asked me some random questions and then told me he would be pleased to accept me if my former headmaster at Ashbourne Road School would be willing to alter the card accordingly. The latter was W. B. Scott, a thoroughly dedicated headmaster, and when he heard my story he immediately supplied me with a new card and endorsed it. I do not think I let anyone down because at the end of the session I won two prizes awarded by the Derby Education Committee and I also won the Chief Mechanical Engineer's Prize for the best railway student at the school. I still treasure these prizes which may have been instrumental in my gaining promotion to privileged apprentice in 1916. The main qualification for this upgrading was the annual internal examination for which I sat, coupled with my Workshop Supervisor's reports and my time keeping record.

Besides trade apprentices who became skilled

craftsmen, there were two higher grades of trainees, namely the graduate pupil and the privileged apprentice. The graduate pupil was a young man who had been to university for three years and had obtained an honours degree in mechanical engineering. His works pupillage was for a minimum period of two years which conformed to the regulations of the Institution of Mechanical Engineers, and he covered a well-planned course of practical training including a period in the drawing office and a similar period on the footplate as a locomotive fireman. There were usually four pupils at any one time which meant that normally two were able to start each year.

The privileged apprentice was recruited from grammar school or public school between the ages of 16 to 18 and was required to have matriculated in at least five subjects, two of which were English and mathematics. Alternatively he was a trade apprentice between 16 and 19 who was promoted based on an internal examination, and workshop and evening school reports. There were about forty privileged apprentices at any one time representing rather less than ten per cent of the trade apprentices. Every apprenticeship terminated on the apprentice's twenty-first birthday. Privileged apprentice status provided an all-round practical engineering training as well as two mornings a week for theoretical instruction at the Derby and District College of Technology. The course, both practical and theoretical, was designed to produce professional engineers rather than craftsmen.

A privileged apprentice who started direct from school at 16 years of age undertook a five-year training course. Where a boy remained at grammar or public school until he was, say, nearly 18 years of age, the five-year course had to be shortened to three years to enable the apprenticeship to terminate at 21. In such circumstances certain training had to be omitted completely to avoid having to reduce it to an unsatisfactory period which would have amounted merely to a veneer.

The Chief Mechanical Engineer of the Midland Railway at that time was Sir Henry Fowler, KBE, who laid the trail for part-time day education in this country. Sir Henry was also a pioneer in the training of engineers and in neither of the two grades (graduate pupil and privileged apprentice) was a premium paid by, or on behalf of, the student. For Sir Henry the candidate could only be admitted strictly on merit, and in this respect his policy was different from that which applied in other railway companies where it was the practice for a premium to be paid by, or on behalf of, pupils and privileged apprentices.

In the case of the pupil an allowance of £2.00 per week was paid for accommodation and sustenance. For a privileged apprentice the rate of pay was precisely the same as that of a trade apprentice, in accordance with age. Because of the wider scope of training of the privileged apprentice, compared with the trade apprentice who was learning to become a craftsman in any one of the many trades, there was less opportunity for the former to be placed on a bonus or piecework scheme, although this was done wherever practicable. Looking back over the years I realize that the quality and range of training provided for engineers on the railway takes second place to none within the engineering industry. This is due to the great variety of work undertaken in railway workshops and the high standard of craftsmanship required.

For myself I never liked the designation 'privileged' apprentice – I always had a feeling that it could be misunderstood – and many years later when I was in a senior management position at Headquarters and able to lay down rules for all the LMS Railways works I had great pleasure in altering the title to engineering apprentice – a title which was extended to all the main works of British Railways.

In May 1916 I sat for the annual internal examination for promotion from trade apprentice to the grade of privileged apprentice. Another trade apprentice, Irvine Cathcart Forsyth, who became a lifelong friend, also sat for the examination at the same time. The subjects included mathematics, applied mechanics, heat engines, machine drawing, and an essay. Irvine, who had attended Hastings Street Central School, a higher grade school with a high reputation, topped the list and I came second. The examination result had to be supported with satisfactory reports from the workshop supervisors on attention to duties and ability, and I am glad to say we were both favourably reported on, and were both promoted. It was our first upgrading.

Irvine Forsyth and I remained staunch friends and we customarily sat next to each other. In 1917 we were both awarded free studentships at the college and these were renewed each year until 1922. Each term we usually alternated between being first or second in each subject. I remember

Irvine's book entitled *Calculus Made Easy* by the eminent philosopher and mathematician, Sylvanus P. Thompson, who told the reader in his foreword 'What one fool can do another can!' To this day I'm not sure whether he was right!

Apart from the wider practical training for which the higher grade provided, the privilege of attending the Derby and District College of Technology on two mornings a week for theoretical training in engineering subjects was a tremendous fillip. It avoided two 6.00 am starts at the Works and also took some pressure off evening studies – hence the origin of the 'privileged' apprentice.

Over the next two years I was moved around the workshops on to various contrasting sections of work, learning something beneficial to my career all the time. In turn I worked on the brake gear, motion, regulator and cylinder sections. Training was on a broad front and included valuable experience in associated trades. Discipline was quite rigid and most of our work was hard – locomotive building and repairs has always been classed as heavy engineering – and I recall quite a few occasions when I found myself dozing off during evening classes. They were long days and one really had to organize one's life to ensure a limited amount of leisure and avoid encroaching on theoretical instruction. Moral support from my mother was always available. As I have previously explained she led a busy life, but she made a practice of keeping me company when I was doing my homework or revising for an examination and she would sit in the room, quietly sewing, until late in the evening.

In British Railways workshops the rates of pay of apprentices is now based on a percentage of the craftsmen's basic rate of pay and this arrangement has a great deal to commend it. In my day as an apprentice we started at 14 years of age and completed the apprenticeship at 21, which gave an apprenticeship of seven years' duration. Nowadays, owing to the school-leaving age having been raised from 14 to 16 and with the apprenticeship terminating on the 20th birthday, the apprenticeship is of only four years' duration, the first year of which is spent in the Works Training School. More striking is the comparison between the rates of pay in my own time as an apprentice and the current rates of pay, as shown in the accompanying table.

I continued to attend College on two mornings a week except during vacations when I reported to the Works instead. I also continued to attend evening classes on three evenings a week, two of

TABLE 3.1 COMPARISON OF WEEKLY APPRENTICE RATES OF PAY IN 1915 AND 1978

Age in years	Rate of pay in 1915 (s. d.)	Rate of pay in 1978	
		Fixed percentage of craftsman's rate	Actual amount (£ . p)
14	5/8	—	Still at school
15	8/0	—	Still at school
16	9/0	45	30.55
17	12/0 +2/6 war bonus	48	36.95
18	18/3 +13/0 war bonus	60	43.30
19	20/6 +25/6 war bonus	75	47.65
20	22/9 +30/6 war bonus	100 (Craftsman's rate)	52.05 (Craftsman's rate)
21	50/0 +26/6 war bonus (Craftsman's rate)		

Note. All staff were entitled to one weeks unpaid annual leave, with the exception of privileged apprentices who received two weeks unpaid leave.

  Pay deductions were made if the time card recorded more than two minutes late at starting times.

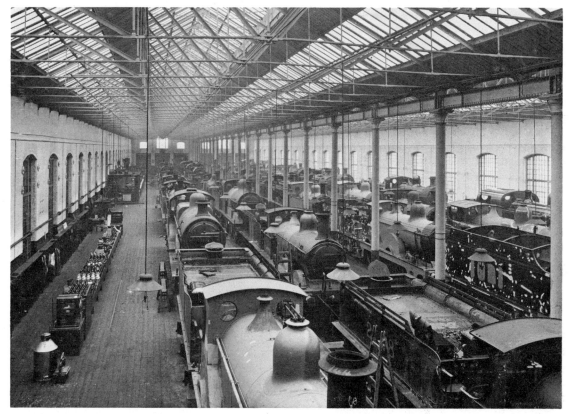

Fig. 3.2 The paint shop in Derby Locomotive Works during the author's apprenticeship (modern British Rail paintshops are much smaller – see Table 3.2)

which were compulsory for part-time day students like me. Some of the work was undertaken in the laboratories.

We were required to sit for the annual examinations of the East Midlands Educational Union which covered Derbyshire, Leicestershire and Nottinghamshire. There were two grades in each subject, Elementary and Higher, and at each level First and Second Class certificates were issued for each subject to successful candidates. I normally sat for all the subjects I had studied, usually three each year, and these included Theoretical and Applied Mechanics, Practical Geometry and Graphics, Heat Engines, Machine Design and Drawing, Practical Mathematics and Theory of Machines and Structures. I managed to avoid any failures but there were times when I had to be satisfied with some Second Class certificates.

A typical question we were required to solve in practical geometry and graphics was as follows:

A rotating cam has to lift a bar with uniform speed through a height of 3 in and then to lower it at a uniform speed one third the speed of ascent while the cam shaft makes one revolution. The diameter of the roller is ⅜ in, the diameter of the cam shaft 1 in, and the least thickness of metal round the cam shaft ½ in. The line of stroke of the bar passes through the centre of the cam shaft. Draw the profile of the cam.

This was a question in the Term Examination in 1917 in which I finished third in this subject. I doubt very much whether I could shape up to such problems these days!

As an extra subject I also sat and passed the examination of the Royal Society of Arts Certificate in English Language and English Literature. In order to achieve this I had to spend an extra evening a week at evening classes for a year, making four evenings in all.

Throughout all my years at the College either Irvine Forsyth or I finished first or second in our age group each term – and it was usually Irvine who was first!

When I returned from my short service in the

RAF there was a privileged apprentice in the works of the name of Graham Sutherland. He was the nephew of a senior experimental draughtsman with whom I later worked, Major Frank L. Sutherland. Graham Sutherland only stayed in the works for about a year because he found that he detested engineering. Today he is a world famous sculptor and artist. In 1972 Dr Parris, his biographer, arranged to see Sir Basil Spence – the architect of, amongst other things, Coventry Cathedral – in Malta, and on his way back arranged to see me at my home in Chiddingfold, Surrey, to glean further information concerning Graham Sutherland's early life as an apprentice at Derby.

With the First World War over I resumed my apprenticeship at the works and was placed in the locomotive erecting shop where over 600 men, a very high proportion of whom were craftsmen, were employed on new locomotives and loco-

motives undergoing heavy repairs. This well-planned workshop of three bays had several overhead travelling cranes of 50 tons capacity each, two of which were required for lifting locomotives and carrying them down the workshop. The work was divided into many sections and I was moved from one section to another. For another period I was attached to the Locomotive Running Shed at Derby carrying out day-to-day repairs on locomotives in service, and for about a month I was required to prepare drawings of the oil fuel tanks and piping in the works.

At about this time the Midland Railway, with its headquarters in Derby, commissioned Sir Edwin Lutyens, the renowned sculptor who designed the Cenotaph in Whitehall, to design a memorial to the employees of the Midland Railway who had lost their lives during the War. This memorial is located on Midland Road, near to Derby railway station. In each workshop there is also a modest

TABLE 3.2   LOCOMOTIVE PAINTING SEQUENCE FOR NEW STOCK

Midland Railway Stock in the 1920s

Day 1	One coat primer
Day 2	One coat brush filler and hard stopping
Day 3	One coat brush filler and hard stopping
Day 4	Face down with rubbing blocks and water
Day 5	Stop up small areas and face down
Day 6	Apply one coat lead colour
Day 7	Apply one coat brown undercoating
Day 8	Apply one coat undercoating for synthetic enamel
Day 9	Synthetic resin enamel to British Standard colour
Day 10	Synthetic resin enamel to British Standard colour
Day 11	Apply lines and transfers
Day 12	Apply one coat of synthetic resin varnish
Day 13	Flat down varnish
Day 14	Apply one coat of synthetic varnish (or oil varnish if locomotive has stood over 24 hr)

Overall time: Three working weeks

British Railways stock in 1978

Stage 1	Apply one coat green primer
Stage 2	Apply filler, using brush
Stage 3	Apply stopping, spreading by knife
Stage 4	Polyester stop as required and touch up
Stage 5	Stop and touch up with undercoat locally, as required
Stage 6	Rub down
Stage 7	Apply one coat undercoat
Stage 8	Apply one coat enamel
Stage 9	Line as required

Overall time: Four to five days

bronze plaque giving the names of those who joined the forces, and there is a cross against the names of those who were killed. My own name appears on the Machine and Fitting Shop plaque and fortunately for me there is no cross against my name.

A few months before the end of my apprenticeship I was placed in the locomotive drawing office at Derby and at 21 years of age I was designated Improver Draughtsman, a title used in the railway service at that time for a junior draughtsman. I was on the threshold of attaining my schoolboy ambition of becoming an engineering draughtsman. It was a splendid feeling and I felt amply rewarded for the long hours of work and intensive studies which I had already undertaken and which were to continue for a considerable time.

On the occasion of my 21st birthday party on 11 February, 1921, I invited three contemporary privileged apprentices, Richard Rowland Beesly, Harold James Castle and Irvine Cathcart Forsyth, all of whom were born in 1900. These three colleagues generously presented me with a set of eight delightfully bound volumes of works written by Robert Louis Stevenson. I still treasure these books, each of which bears the handwritten words 'With every success for the future', followed by their three signatures. Some time later Richard Beesly left the employ of the Midland Railway and joined the famous woollen manufacturing firm of Wolsey in Leicester as a Plant Engineer. Harold Castle emigrated to Rhodesia and ultimately attained to the position of Chief Mechanical Engineer of the Rhodesian State Railways. (His brother, Edgar, whom I knew, was Chief Engineer of the Westinghouse Brake and Signal Co.). Irvine Forsyth, like me, stayed with the Midland Railway and, after a notable career including a long period in the Locomotive Running Department of the LMS and later as Works Manager at Crewe locomotive works, retired in 1965 from the key position at Derby Headquarters of Production Manager in the Workshops Division of British Railways. It has been a great pleasure for me to keep in touch with Irvine and his family over all these years.

CHAPTER 4

RAF CADET PILOT NO. 177461

*Per ardua ad astra – through difficulties to the stars –
the RAF motto.*

In 1918 Great Britain was in the midst of the
First World War – it was called the Great War
then – and I was in the middle of my
apprenticeship at Derby. On 1 April, 1918, the
Royal Naval Air Service and the Royal Flying
Corps, which had been two independent Armed
Services, were amalgamated and became the
Royal Air Force. In retrospect it was a natural
development.

Keen though I was to press on with my
apprenticeship to become an engineer, I had a
strong urge to do something more closely allied to
the war effort. I was conscious of the fact that in
the works in which I was employed, new
locomotive building had ceased for the duration of
the war, and the resultant spare capacity in the
works amounted to possibly 30 per cent of the
total. The remaining 70 per cent was taken up
with normal locomotive maintenance work and
associated activities, and the spare 30 per cent was
rapidly diverted to the manufacture of precision
armaments of various types – a clear indication of
the skill and versatility of railway workshop staff.
Although I was already actively engaged on some
of this vital war work and was therefore in a
reserved occupation, my patriotism asserted
itself. I hated war and violence, but I had a strong
urge to be directly involved, in addition to which
there was something about the newly created
Royal Air Force, with its high technical and
engineering content which had a special appeal for
me. All my contemporaries who had obtained
leave to join the Forces had gone into the Navy or
the Army, and I had no precedent to follow in
seeking to become a pilot, which was my aim.

My attitude had changed completely from two
years previously. Nor was this surprising because

at that time I was only 16 years of age. As an
apprentice I qualified for one free railway pass a
year and I had decided during my holidays to
spend a day in London. I wanted to see the Houses
of Parliament, Trafalgar Square, Buckingham
Palace and other places of interest at close
quarters, and as I walked from Whitehall past
Big Ben and towards Westminster Bridge I saw an
impressive military band with a company of
soldiers and a number of young men dressed in
civilian clothes trailing behind. To my surprise I
was taken by the arm and a recruiting sergeant
said, 'You are just the type of young man we are
looking for.'

I said, 'Looking for what?'

He replied, still holding me firmly, 'To join the
Army and help us win the War!'

I told him I was only 16 and was only in
London on a day's visit. He wasn't to be put off
easily and he did his best to try to get me to join
up there and then. In the end I managed to shake
him off and proceeded to enjoy the rest of the day.

Two years elapsed and twice my application to
get leave of absence from the Works Manager was
declined. It was pointed out that I was carrying
out essential Government work and that not
everyone of my age would be allowed to go. On
the third occasion, however, leave was granted
and I then lost no time in making inquiries about
joining the RAF. I learned that the RAF
Recruiting Office for the East Midlands was
located in Nottingham, only 16 miles from
Derby. I wrote to the RAF and an application
form was sent to me. This was duly returned to
Nottingham together with a certificate from my
employer confirming I had been given leave to
join the Forces. Within a week I was called for an
interview and medical examination in Nottingham. At the conclusion of the interview I was
delighted to be informed that my name would be

forwarded to London for a further interview, but particularly for a series of medical tests. If successful I should be deemed to be in the RAF for the duration of the war, from the day I had to report in London.

A week or so passed and I was instructed to report to an address in Fitzjohn's Avenue, Swiss Cottage, in the London Borough of Hampstead. Here I underwent a whole series of different physical tests with a different medical officer for each classification. After an hour or so of examinations I was given a paper to hand to another medical officer who, having perused it carefully and asking some questions, told me I was suitable for enlistment as a Cadet Pilot. It was a great thrill and I felt I could jump over the moon! It was April 1918.

Along with others, I was taken to another large house in Fitzjohn's Avenue, and told that a small round tent on the lawn would be home for three of us until such time as we were posted to No. 1 Officers' Technical Training Wing (the OTTW) at Hastings St Leonards on the Sussex coast. In

the meantime we would be equipped with uniform and certain equipment in readiness for our departure to our first Training Centre. I stayed ten days at Swiss Cottage and found myself having introductory talks from commissioned and non-commissioned officers. There was also some drill for us in the nearby thoroughfares. Need I add that in those distant days passing cars were very few and far between!

I underwent eight weeks' training on the south coast. It was a gorgeous summer. Our training was largely of a military character, all our officers being military men. Our dress was khaki with a peak cap and white band. Some of the cadets bought tailor-made RAF officers' uniforms for off-duty periods, but I never thought it worthwhile; quite apart from the expense involved, there was always the possibility of my commission not materializing.

At the outset we were all supplied with 'cut-throat' razors for shaving. Most of us used them in those days because the safety type of razor was not so well developed. Whatever our choice it was never a joy because we had the doubtful pleasure of having to be content with cold water!

Our feeding arrangements were generally ample and very good, especially when one considers how everyone was faring at home on strict rations. In the Mess we were efficiently served by members of the Women's Auxiliary Air Force, now the WRAF: off duty there was no fraternizing.

There must have been upwards of 5000 cadet pilots and observers under training at Hastings St Leonards at the time of my period of training there in 1918. Most, but not all of the cadets, had been recruited like myself direct from school or industry. There were others who had already served in some other unit of the Armed Forces and who had been accepted as cadets in the RAF with a view to promotion as Commissioned Officers. Everyone of us seemed to have a different background. One Cadet, I recall, was Frank Foster, formerly Captain of the Worcestershire and England cricket teams.

The Cadet pay for those of us who had come in to the RAF direct was precisely the same as that of a Private in the British Army, the princely sum of one shilling and sixpence (7½p!) a day.

There were several wings constituting the Brigade, each wing comprising four squadrons. I was attached to No. 4 Squadron, commanded by Captain A. E. Worrall, MC. The Commanding

Fig. 4.1   RAF Cadet Pilot No. 177461, taken shortly after the RAF was formed on 1 April 1918

Officer of the Cadet Brigade was Brigadier A. C. Critchley, DSO, an outstanding figure of a man, who after the war became the first Chairman of the newly formed National Greyhound Racing Association. A Canadian by birth and a model of a soldier, he was reported to be the youngest Brigadier in the British Forces. Discipline under him was strict, and it was a case of woe betide any one of us for the slightest deviation from what was laid down in the interests of orderly and exemplary conduct. Our image as RAF Cadets had to be second to none. One of our youngest officers was the 22-year-old Prince Albert, Duke of York, who became King George VI following the abdication of his elder brother King Edward VIII, in 1936.

We had our full share of notabilities visiting and inspecting the Brigade including Lord Weir, the Air Minister. The high spot of all, whilst I was attached to No. 1 OTTW under Colonel R. Cockburn, was the review of the entire Brigade by King George V. It was indeed a memorable occasion and the following extract from the *Daily Telegraph* of 31 August, 1918, recalls the scene:

The King, who is General-in-Chief of the Royal Air Force, inspected the Cadet Brigade yesterday at a popular seaside resort. The programme gave the inhabitants and visitors unusual opportunities of witnessing the events, and they took full advantage of them. The streets were gay with flags, and the enthusiasm which prevailed, added to the holiday mood, infused a gala atmosphere to the day's proceedings. The spirit of the cadets in itself was contagious. The force throbs with vitality. With snatches of joyous song the men marched to the parade-ground, and when the real business of the day was reached they exhibited a keenness and a vigour in their work which was wonderful to behold. It was a tribute to the methods of training and example set by Brigadier-General Critchley and the officers under him, and to the zest with which the Cadets themselves have entered into the realities of their work.

Arriving by special train from Windsor, the King, who was attended by Sir Charles Cust and the Earl of Cromer, was received at the station by the officer in command of the brigade, Brigadier-General Critchley, and the Mayor. In the station yard his Majesty inspected a guard of honour, comprising British, Canadians, Australians, New Zealanders, and South Africans – a fine body of Cadets, most of them 6ft. or more in height. A Canadian band played while the inspection was in progress. Proceeding by motor-car to a stand erected on high ground, his Majesty saw drawn up on parade in a large field, which formed a natural amphitheatre, the main body of the Cadet Brigade – the future pilots and observers of the Air Force in embryo. As the King took up his position the Cadets below sang the first verse of the National Anthem.

On the rising ground immediately beyond, a most picturesque spectacle presented itself to the King's gaze. A huge flag was spread across the hillside, flanked on three sides by the letters R.A.F. At a word of command it began to show signs of life. It was a human flag, the component parts of which were men who have passed through the brigade. With a precision which produced intense effect, the complexion of the flag gradually altered, like some great set piece of fireworks which in pre-war days was to be witnessed at the Crystal Palace, until the alternating colours of blue and red revealed the flag of the Royal Air Force. Then the letters R.A.F., which till then had been of a drab colour, also underwent a change, which was similarly enacted with the most pleasing rhythm, and they stood out in a bold relief of black and white. Next the whole piece of human mechanism began to move to the top of the hill, without any breaking of its regular contours, until it disappeared from sight. It was a strikingly well-executed performance, which immensely delighted the King and the public.

And now the lines of Cadets drawn up on the parade-ground were to give the first demonstration of their soldierly qualities. Looking at the movements of presenting and ordering arms, fixing bayonets, and so forth, from an elevated position, it was possible to appreciate completely the really marvellous clockwork of the whole thing. Not the smallest flaw was to be seen throughout the ranks. It was hard to believe that but a short month or so before many of these men had been working in offices or in some other occupation which engenders no discipline of this kind.

His Majesty, having inspected the Brigade, afterwards drove to a saluting base on the sea front. The March-past in companies was a fine exhibition. To quick music the men swung by with short, rapid steps, their arms swinging to the fullest extent, and the whole movement giving an impression of the utmost vigour. They wore the lightest of uniform, the tunic being khaki drill, and their shorts of a similar material. They walked in shoes, over which their socks were rolled down.

As Prince Albert, who is a captain in rank, appeared at the head of one of the last companies to reach the saluting base, the spectators warmly cheered. The description given of him by one who ought to know that he is "a very smart, keen lad" was not belied by his appearance. Bringing up the rear of the Cadets were the men who had figured in the human flag.

In an adjoining public garden the King next

witnessed a short and intensive display of massed boxing and physical drill by some of the recently joined cadets. This over, his Majesty drove to the various wing headquarters in the town, officers' messes, cadet clubs, instruction school, and other selected centres, proceeding afterwards to the station for the return journey to Windsor.

It is already known to the public that a good many applications to join the Royal Air Force have come recently from Ireland, and it is not surprising to learn that those who have been taken into the Cadet Brigade are such very fine material that the force is anxious to get some more of it from this source, which is capable of being tapped to a much greater extent. As the Allies will have an unlimited number of machines, so will an unlimited number of pilots and observers be required. It takes about six months to procure the finished flying man, and the Cadet Brigade affords the preliminary training.

Following the satisfactory completion of our first eight weeks training, we were transferred from No. 1 OTTW to No. 2 OTTW. The first was located in St Leonards and the second in Hastings, the two areas together forming the Borough of Hastings St Leonards. We were billeted in what were normally large private houses or boarding houses; but for us they only boasted bedboards and blankets with a chair, and a built-in cupboard if you were lucky. For a large bedroom there were usually three Cadets and if you were on your own you could be sure it was a very small room indeed. In No. 2 OTTW there was a greater measure of theoretical tuition: our days were long and studious and none of us could ever get enough rest!

We were inspired by epic stories of many who were already on active service or who had already paid the supreme sacrifice for their valour. One of these was Major Lance Hawker, VC, DSO, the first officer of the former Royal Flying Corps to win the Victoria Cross for air fighting. This was on 25 July, 1915. Sadly he subsequently met his death in an air battle in 1916 at the hands of Rittmeister von Richthoven. Over half a century later I met Colonel Tyrrel Hawker, brother of Major Lance Hawker, when I had the pleasure of fishing on the former's beat of the River Test at Longparish, Hampshire. Life is full of strange coincidences. In Colonel Hawker's home I saw for the first time a copy of the book entitled *Hawker VC* and saw the stained glass window to his brother's memory in the parish church at Longparish.

Whilst at Hastings St Leonards I was one of six Cadets who were allowed to go swimming in the sea at 6.00 am instead of carrying out PT exercises. (The delightful St Leonards swimming pool on the sea front was not constructed until many years after the war had ended.) On one occasion which I well remember, Brigadier Critchley and the CO of No. 2 OTTW, Colonel Grenfell, came along the beach on horseback. I had left the other Cadets and had swum out and round the pier, a total distance I suppose of about half a mile. On my return, as I waded in, Colonel Grenfell came towards me, still on horseback, and said, 'In future you must all keep together. I don't want any fatalities!'

There were other times when the entire Squadron went swimming in the covered White Rock Swimming Baths, measuring 180 feet in length. These were the longest covered Baths in England. On these occasions we were all required to swim in the nude; no members of the public were present.

We had our own excellent magazine appropriately entitled *Roosters and Fledglings*. It came into being when the RAF was formed in April 1918, and replaced *The Fledgling* of the Royal Flying Corps. *Roosters and Fledglings* was the monthly journal of the Royal Air Force Cadets and it was circulated in all Wings of the RAF Cadet Brigade and the several Schools of Aeronautics. Everyone looked forward to reading it each month. Its editor was Second Lieutenant B. Macdonald Hastings, of the King's Royal Rifle Corps. Each Wing had an officer who acted as Assistant Editor or Correspondent and there were eleven altogether. The Administrator was Lieutenant Colonel W. G. Macfarlane of the Canadian Forces, who was attached to the HQ of the Cadet Brigade. The editor and his team did a really sparkling job. For his first copy the editor invited George Bernard Shaw to contribute a message. Shaw replied in typical fashion:

> You know not what you ask. There are in the service now, at a moderate estimate, about 5,000 magazines, and they all want a contribution from me. In addition, every man at the front writes me a personal letter and asks for a personal reply. As I am expected to solve the Irish question and the Russian question and to finish a new play, it really can't be done. I must throw myself on your indulgence. Yours in desperation,
>
> *Bernard Shaw.*

With the signing of the Armistice at the forest of Compèigne in France on 11 November, 1918, the magazine came to an abrupt end, having had a total of only eight editions, and being regarded as a 'winner' from the outset. The final issue was despatched to all RAF Stations in Great Britain shortly before Christmas, 1918. Some 300 bound copies, containing all eight editions, were sold at fifteen shillings each, and I was fortunate enough to purchase one.

Following the successful completion of my course at Hastings St Leonards I was posted to No. 8 School of Aeronautics at Cheltenham. Here the whole of our training, covering a period of eight weeks, was based strictly on flying techniques, in all of which, oddly enough, we remained firmly on the ground. It was a fascinating though daunting course. The various subjects covered were Aerial Navigation, Air Frame Rigging, Airplane Engines, Topography, the Morse Code and Aerial Photography.

Not surprisingly our Manual Instructors were mostly non-commissioned officers. Besides being specialists in their own particular field they were accomplished, hand-picked lecturers and I know that we learned a great deal from them. The individual sessions were seldom long enough because there was such a wealth of knowledge to be crammed into each one. After all there was a war on and nearly everything had to be presented in what I would describe as tabloid form. There was an inordinate amount of private study involved.

Much of our training revolved around the Bristol Fighter (F2B), a two-seater which was used in the war for defensive work and bombing, and the Handley Page Bomber which carried a crew of five, two of whom were pilots. The engines in which we received very complete instruction were the Beardmore 120 hp six-cylinder Water Cooled Aero Engine (stationary type) and the nine-cylinder Air Cooled Clerget Aero Engine of 130 hp (rotary type).

When acquiring a detailed knowledge of aircraft rigging we spent long hours in making adjustments to the various controls on planes which never took to the air. The planes in those days were covered with pure unbleached Irish linen which formed a strong, light, airtight and watertight covering. The planes were certainly museum pieces in the fullest sense imaginable when compared with the sophisticated fighters and bombers of today, or even in comparison with the planes used twenty years later in the Second World War.

The RAF seemed to have taken over the entire town at Cheltenham for its No. 8 School of Aeronautics. There was scarcely any road or thoroughfare where we didn't occupy a goodly proportion of the larger properties. We even took over the Town Hall for our Mess, and I have never forgotten the Australian rabbits which we used to eat – they were nearly as big as foxes!

I found that some of my theoretical training as a railway apprentice at Derby was extremely valuable and in the final qualifying examination in particular, covering all subjects, I was informed that I had done especially well and had been recommended to become a Day Bombing Pilot. I still have my training book giving this information.

It was now the first week in November 1918. My next posting, still as a Cadet Pilot, was to have been to the Armament School, Uxbridge, for a month's course to learn about aerial gunnery and how to use a machine gun. This posting never materialized, however, because my impending transfer coincided with Armistice Day, 11 November, 1918. Within a matter of days, I was sent with the entire Squadron to No. 8 RAF Training Wing at Shorncliffe, near Folkestone. At Shorncliffe we were all billeted under canvas and there was little planned to keep us usefully occupied. It was clearly curtains down. We were simply marking time (not literally!) until a decision had been made on our future, assuming the validity of the Armistice. We were not kept waiting long and within ten days we were all provisionally discharged and sent home. Obviously no time was lost because our training was expensive.

Although it was a great relief to feel that the terrible war which had cost millions of lives was virtually over I was keenly disappointed not to be able to complete my training as a pilot. If the month's aerial gunnery course had been completed I should then have started my real flying training instead of merely making adjustments to aeroplanes which never left the ground. Instead I found myself back in Derby and in the unique position of being the first Serviceman in the town to be demobilized. This was in the third week in November 1918, and I gave the local Ministry of Food office quite a problem in fixing me up with an ordinary ration book for food. My official discharge from the RAF was actually dated 31 December, 1918.

Although my eight months' service in the RAF

as Cadet Pilot No. 177461 temporarily interfered with my apprenticeship with the railway, I shall always regard it as having done me a world of good. After all, I had not been required to leave home previously and, short though my training was, I learned a great deal from it. This included the strictest of discipline, experience in spheres which were good for my training as an engineer, in general knowledge, in organized sport and above all in loyalty and *esprit de corps*. If the war had continued all these would have been of material assistance in helping me to play my part.

I resumed my railway apprenticeship in the Derby locomotive works early in January 1919. Whilst I had been away the normal hours of duty throughout the engineering industry had been reduced from 54 to 47 hours a week. No longer did it mean three sessions a day – just two – and for this improvement I was indeed very thankful.

CHAPTER 5

THE DRAWING OFFICE AND LOCOMOTIVE TESTING

By 1921 I had achieved my ambition to become an engineering draughtsman, for I was appointed an improver draughtsman on my 21st birthday. In my new position as a 'junior' draughtsman in the locomotive drawing office at Derby I was attached to the Experimental Section and was responsible to Herbert Chambers, the head of the Section. He later became Chief Draughtsman and ultimately Technical Assistant to Sir William Arthur Stanier, FRS, Chief Mechanical Engineer of the LMS Railway. For the greater part of my time in the drawing office I remained a member of the Experimental Section. These were exciting days because a great deal of my time was spent on the footplate carrying out important locomotive tests of various descriptions, sometimes as a member of a test team and at other times working on my own. Of course, analysing technical data and helping to draw up the findings was exacting work. There was always something happening a little out of the ordinary, and in this chapter I will relate some of these experiences.

It will be appreciated that during the 1920s and 1930s the steam locomotive was still in the ascendant. The diesel electric locomotive, the diesel rail car and the electric locomotive were not to be seen around for a quarter of a century, and electrification of the main lines was not considered to be a viable proposition. The ambition of the average schoolboy was to become an engine driver; it was a glamorous occupation. Fortunately when the time came to start work not all boys adhered to their first love. Although I never wished to become an engine driver and was not deflected from my own schoolboy ambition to become a draughtsman, my experiences on the footplate were very closely allied to the work of an engine driver – especially when I took over the controls, under supervision – and apart from being highly absorbing at the time, were to prove

valuable experience throughout my working life.

Those of us engaged in locomotive testing usually had long hours to work whilst the tests were being carried out. Overtime pay never entered our heads. Nowadays the thought seems to be ever-present with many people.

On my 21st birthday, 11 February, 1921, I spent most of the day with a very experienced and thoroughly competent senior draughtsman, Major Frank L. Sutherland, carrying out static tests with worsted trimmings of various designs for siphoning oil to various working parts of the locomotive. It was one day in a series of tests carried out with oils of various viscosities at extreme temperatures, both high and low. The Major had served in the Sherwood Foresters during the First World War and had suffered a severe wound in one leg which had left him slightly lame. He was a bachelor affectionately known to all his associates as Uncle Sutherland because of his friendly and gentlemanly nature. As mentioned earlier his nephew was Graham Sutherland.

One of my first jobs in the drawing office was to take delivery of, and to travel with, batches of new 0–6–0 Standard Freight Locomotives. These were being built to Midland Railway design by Armstrong Whitworth of Scotswood, Newcastle-on-Tyne, a firm of great repute more accustomed to building armaments than locomotives. In all there were fifty locomotives for the Midland Railway and five for the Somerset and Dorset Joint Line. It was an order placed by the Ministry of Transport whilst the Railways were still under Government control as a wartime measure. There were five locomotives in each batch and they travelled 'dead' to Derby hauled behind a freight engine of an earlier design. We were routed via Carlisle and Leeds in order to join the Midland line as soon as possible at Carlisle. It was mid-winter, and a very cold job too. For my part I travelled mainly on the hauling locomotive with the driver and fireman, whereas my two worthy assistants, who were locomotive erectors normally employed in the Erecting Shop at Derby, travelled on different locomotives as exigency demanded, to keep in close touch with possible mechanical troubles, such as the failure of the mechanical lubricators supplying oil to the axleboxes. We had our fair share of hot axleboxes owing largely to the fact that Armstrong Whitworth had no facilities in their vast works compound other than a very short straight road in which to run the locomotives. Although we were scheduled to run at restricted speeds with fairly frequent stops to enable us to examine the locomotives in transit, it was always a problem as to whether we should be able to adhere to our time-table and in so doing keep out of the way of the Anglo-Scottish expresses between Carlisle and Leeds. Sometimes we were held up for two or three hours and on one occasion we spent most of the night at Hellifield in Yorkshire. The running shed foreman was very good to us and he shared his sandwiches with us and lit a fire in a snow plough and made us as comfortable as possible. On another occasion we were held up at Skipton, which is near to Leeds, and I took the opportunity of having a quick bath in the Company's hostel which was the lodging house for drivers and firemen. In those days there was a good deal of 'lodging away' for drivers and firemen, especially on freight trains, to enable the crews to return to their home stations with their own engine on the following day, and the railway company provided free accommodation.

During my first series of locomotive tests, involving differently designed mechanical lubricators, I also had to stay occasionally at Cricklewood on the outskirts of London, and at Wellingborough in Northamptonshire, half-way between London and the Midlands coalfields centred around Toton in Nottinghamshire. At Wellingborough the motive power superintendent arranged for me to stay at the home of a former driver who had been forced to retire early because he had unfortunately become blind. I was certainly well fed and looked after by his devoted wife on those occasions. Even if the money had been available to me hotels or boarding houses were out of the question because of the irregular hours I had to work.

These coal trains from the Midlands to London were running every hour or so, day and night. If we were single-headed we took sixty wagons, each of 10 or 12 tons capacity, and if we were double-headed (with two locomotives) we hauled over a hundred wagons. These were loose-coupled wagons and the driver's biggest job always was to apply his brake in a way that avoided the train parting. In those days, and, indeed, until after nationalisation in 1948, the railways were moving a million tons of coal every working day, of which 50 per cent was being carried by the Midland Division of the LMS Railway.

I remember another assignment, in which I had to test and report on the use of cylinder air relief valves. These were being tried out to keep down the temperature and reduce carbonization in the cylinders when coasting and they proved highly effective. To record the temperatures the metallurgist had designed a thermo-couple fitted to the back steam port of the left-hand cylinder and a pyrometer was fitted in the cab. The locomotive fitted up for the tests was a No. 4 Class Standard 0–6–0 Freight Engine, No. 3866, and the tests took place in 1923. Most of the readings were recorded when the engine was coasting along down gradients between Sharnbrook and Oakley, where the prevailing gradient was 1 in 119, between Elstree and Hendon, 1 in 160, between St Albans and Radlett, and between Ampthill and Bedford, both 1 in 200.

The steam chest temperature prior to the regulator being closed usually recorded around 430° F. Without air valves the temperature rose within thirty seconds to around 500° F, and continued to rise steadily to as much as 620° F by the time the regulator had to be re-opened, following some ten or twelve minutes of coasting. With air valves fitted and the regulator shut off the temperature rose quickly by about 40° F, and then gradually fell below the original steam chest temperature. It was a very conclusive test and was important as there were ultimately to be no less than 800 engines built of the same class.

On one occasion we were travelling towards London at a high speed when suddenly, miles from anywhere, the thermo-couple fractured and the pressure of steam was such that the broken experimental fitting went off like a gun and hit a cow grazing in a field. The startled cow and the rest of the herd went tearing away from the railway line. With a steam jet shooting out there was no alternative but for the driver to stop and allow me to examine the extent of the damage. We were on the main line and despite our having a clear signal to proceed, I thought that if I could fit a halfpenny it would enable me to blank off the steam jet which, apart from the loss of steam, could be dangerous to any passing train. Alas, the halfpenny was too big, but the driver came to my aid with a farthing which fitted perfectly, and within ten minutes the driver was able to signal that we could proceed. As I anticipated, the Control Office was appraised of what had happened and in due course I had to give a written explanation for having delayed the train.

There was one short period during this series of tests when my engine was re-rostered and I had to join it at Wigston Motive Power Depot, some three miles south of Leicester. To avoid missing my evening classes at Derby I remember on three occasions getting a very early morning train to Leicester and then walking along the main line to Wigston. One had to keep a very sharp eye in order to cope with passing trains. It involved a long day each time but it was worth the effort.

The amalgamation of the railways took effect, by Act of Parliament (the Railways Act, 1921), on 1 January, 1923. Instead of 120 companies there were only four, namely the London Midland and Scottish Railway (LMS), the London and North Eastern Railway (LNER), the Great Western Railway (GWR) and the Southern Railway. The LMS absorbed the Midland Railway and was the largest of the four new companies.

The area covered by the LMS extended from Goole on the east coast of England to Donegal Bay on the west coast of Ireland, and from Bournemouth on the English Channel to Thurso in the far north of Scotland; the whole route covered nearly 40 per cent of the total route mileage of the railways of the United Kingdom.

The LMS had 19 000 track miles and a staff of approximately 240 000. There were 7800 steam locomotives and over 300 000 units of passenger and freight rolling stock. In 1939 it carried 434 million passengers, representing 7500 million passenger miles of travel, and 125 million tons of freight, representing 6750 million ton/miles. Additionally, the LMS owned 25 docks, harbours and piers, several hundred acres of workshops, 66 steamships, 4000 road motor vehicles and 3000 trailers, 8000 horses, 28 hotels, 25 000 dwelling houses and 535 miles of canals. The pre-war replacement cost of the Company's property was conservatively extimated to exceed

£750 million – that was well over fifty years ago and long before the nation was suffering from present-day rates of inflation. It is a commentary on the contraction of the railways that the former LMS railway employed about 240 000 staff compared with a total staff on the modern British Railways network of about 200 000.

I well remember the Chief Mechanical Engineer receiving a telegram on Investing Day in 1923 from a constituent company called the Stratford-upon-Avon and Midland Joint Railway Company requesting certain spare parts for some of their locomotives. The Chief Draughtsman sent an older colleague of mine, William Bramley, to Stratford to see exactly what was required. They had few drawings and he came back with a bundle of hand sketches, beautifully executed by himself, giving precise details of a large number of parts required. It would seem their locomotives were in relatively poor shape judged by Midland Railway standards and the local Superintendent had been anxiously awaiting the opportunity to request the components he needed.

Just prior to the amalgamation of the railways, joint brake trials between Peterborough and Spalding were carried out by the Great Northern and the Midland Railway Companies. The trials lasted six weeks and throughout each week we stayed at the Great Northern Station Hotel, Peterborough. The object was to ascertain the performance of newly designed rapid acting valves on the carriage stock. The arrangement was made between two eminent locomotive engineers, Sir Henry Fowler, Chief Mechanical Engineer of the Midland Railway, and Sir Nigel Gresley, Chief Mechanical Engineer of the Great Northern Railway. The Great Northern Railway provided the facilities and stock and the Midland Railway provided the test team. The experimental train consisted of covered, close-coupled goods stock, with the front, middle and rear vehicles equipped with instruments. Those immediately in charge were Oliver V. Bulleid, Sir Nigel's principal Carriage and Wagon Assistant (later CME of the Southern Railway) and my chief, Herbert Chambers, who was acting for Sandham J. Symes, the Chief Draughtsman at Derby, who became Principal Assistant to Sir William Stanier, and finally Chief Stores Superintendent of the LMS railway.

I was the footplate observer and I received telephonic instructions, which I had to pass on to the driver, from Herbert Chambers, who was travelling in the dynamometer car next to the engine, of the speeds to be attained and when to apply a partial or full braking. Naturally I knew precisely when the driver would be operating the brake system and I held on firmly to the cab handrail at the precise moment. It was not at all uncommon for the empty train to be broken into two or three sections and the artisan staff who had fitted up the train and who were travelling with us would get to work and make good the damage, including the telephone system throughout the train.

When in due course I undertook some of the preliminary work in analysing the results I came across the following words in the report book of one of my senior colleagues, 'Regret was unable to take any readings of instruments – was on floor!' I well remembered the occasion; my instructions, to give to the driver, were 'Make an emergency application at milepost X.' This was done most effectively, at a speed of precisely 60 miles an hour, and the damage caused in breakages of couplings and instrument wiring was quite extensive. (It took an hour or so to marshall the train again and during this time I espied a young rabbit running alongside the line. I chased it and tried to catch it but without success! My Chief told me that Mr Bulleid wanted to know whether this was the best Larkin could do! In later years we got to know each other much better.)

Many years later when Oliver Bulleid had moved from the LNE at Doncaster to hold the important position of Chief Mechanical Engineer (CME) of the Southern Railway he arranged to visit me at Derby and asked whether I would accept his son, Anthony, as a graduate pupil (he had graduated in Engineering at Cambridge) because he wanted him to be trained as a locomotive engineer under me. We couldn't have been such bad friends after all. Anthony did a two years pupillage at Derby and had a distinguished career in the engineering industry.

After two years as an Improver Draughtsman, I was re-designated as Draughtsman and given a slight increase in pay. Even more important I was placed on the salaried staff, but before the latter was confirmed I had to see the Railway Medical Officer and get a clear certificate from him. For a technical man who had been an apprentice to be placed on the salaried staff at the comparatively early age of 23, and be admitted to the super-annuation scheme, was the exception rather than the rule. Clerical staff, on the other hand,

normally became eligible for salaried status at 16 years of age. This meant that by the time the latter were 60 years of age, the minimum retiring age, they had qualified for full pension, whereas a technical officer often had difficulty in qualifying for a full pension at 65 years of age.

I could never see the logic in this arrangement, and so when some twenty years later I was holding a key position at Departmental Headquarters I raised the question in the right quarters and was successful in pursuing the matter through all the four main line companies. This finally resulted in technical grades who had served an apprentice-ship being given the option of pre-dating their salaried status to 21 years of age, irrespective of their age when first becoming a member of the salaried staff. Many young railway engineers have benefited since, and I believe the current arrange-ment has gone one better and given pension rights to all staff from the commencement of their railway employment.

When in 1925 Sir Henry Fowler became CME of the LMS Railway with his headquarters at Derby, the dynamometer car of the former Lancashire and Yorkshire Railway, now the Central Division of the LMS, was transferred to Derby. It was my pleasure to take over this car at Derby from none other than E. S. Cox, who had travelled with the car from Horwich works, where at that time he was employed. Like myself Stewart Cox was an experimental draughtsman, and he subsequently rose to the highest position in his own field, that of Mechanical Engineer (Design) at British Railways Headquarters, Marylebone. Under Robert A. Riddles, CBE, he was closely identified with all the standard steam locomotives following nationalization. Of all my railway colleagues, Stewart Cox became the most travelled, because his work took him to India, to Russia and to the United States, in addition to his making countless visits to all the countries of Europe, in the quest for the latest technical developments in locomotive and rolling stock practice.

His six books on railway locomotive practice are read in many countries and they cover the whole field with the advantage of being written from 'within' rather than from 'without'. Most of his illustrations are reproductions of his own photographs. He is a Past President of the former Institution of Locomotive Engineers, now in essence the Railway Division of the Institution of Mechanical Engineers, and over the years he has presented an unrivalled set of papers to the Institution. He has the delightful facility of being able to talk in the same manner as he writes, indicating that his writings require little or no alteration from his original drafting.

I have spoken of the former Lancashire and Yorkshire Railway dynamometer car. In those days the instrumentation was accepted as the best and most accurate of its kind on any railway in the country. It is, however, worth recording that the original lighting was by gas, similar to the normal train lighting of the day.

It was considered that a more powerful locomotive was required on the former Somerset and Dorset Joint Line which ran from Bath to Bournemouth. The line, now closed, was 72 miles long and was single track. It could scarcely boast one straight mile. It twisted and turned and there were gradients, some quite severe, throughout its entire length.

The test team was in the capable hands of D. W. Sanford, a first class engineering honours graduate of Gonville and Caius College, Cambridge, and a brilliant mathematician. As usual I was the footplate observer. We had an empty train of passenger coaches and it was planned to try out a 4–4–0 Midland Compound. We started off from Bath station not far from which was a tunnel a quarter of a mile long with a rising gradient of 1 in 70. The tunnel had no ventilation and it was only single line and the top of the locomotive chimney was just a few inches below the roof of the tunnel. We had attained to a speed of about 15 miles an hour when we entered the tunnel and the locomotive wheels began to slip. The rails were wet and greasy. We lost speed and the smoke, charged with sulphur fumes, soon filled the locomotive cab. The driver called out to me 'Give me your handkerchief. I'll dip it in water and you can put it wet over your nose.' The driver and fireman did similarly, the former continually adjusting the opening of the regulator valve and the latter opening the sand ejector to keep the train moving. What an experience! The tunnel was called Devonshire Tunnel, but there was nothing like Devonshire about it. Thanks to an experienced locomotive crew we managed to keep moving at 3 to 4 miles an hour, and having eventually got through the tunnel we asked for a siding. All three of us felt ill. We were choking and near enough to suffocation. Nor was this surprising. Dudley Sanford came up to us from the dynamometer car and said he realized we must have been having a rough time because although they had managed to close all the windows the lack of oxygen in the tunnel had resulted in the gas lights in the car being extinguished. Needless to say we managed to recover and proceed with our train to Bournemouth. We were more prepared with our subsequent trips in the week. The tests, however, proved quite conclusively that the type of locomotive we were trying out was not suitable for the Somerset and Dorset Line and alternative plans were made. It is interesting to record that nearly forty years later the last steam locomotive to be built by British Railways, a standard Class 9F, 2–10–0 No. 92220 *Evening Star*, worked the Pines Express from Bath to Bournemouth. It proved eminently suitable for this up and down, twisting line.

The only decapod banking engine 0–10–0 to be built in this country was No. 2290, affectionately known as *Big Bertha*. It was designed at Derby in 1912, but because of the war was not built until 1920. Its purpose was to push both passenger and freight trains up the Lickey Incline from Bromsgrove to Blackwell, a section of the main line between Bristol and Birmingham. It is the stiffest main line gradient in England, being 1 in 37·7, and is a straight stretch of track 2 miles in length.

I was a member of the test team which carried out the trials at Bromsgrove to ascertain both the horsepower and the braking power of this unique locomotive. Dudley Sanford was in charge and one summer's evening the four of us called at a local pub for a drink. In my innocence I asked for an *Iron Brew*, a product of Derby and non-alcoholic. The barman looked puzzled and Sanford said, 'I don't think they have any "Iron Brew" here, Edgar – I should ask for a "Brass Brew".' He was a great character, respected by everyone who had the privilege of knowing him. Just before the Second World War when he was Chief Draughtsman at Derby I asked him whether he would oblige by giving a talk to the senior boys at the Bemrose School, Derby, a grammar school named after Alderman Bemrose, founder and Chairman of the world-famous Bemrose and Sons Printing Company in Derby. Sanford was an outstanding lecturer and his subject was Locomotive Design. In his customary roguish way he said he would give it if I would come too! I was pleased to accompany him,

Fig. 5.1 A unique locomotive. Midland Railway 0–10–0 banking engine built at Derby in 1920 for pushing trains up the Lickey Incline, Bromsgrove, on the main line between Bristol and Derby

particularly because I knew I should be in for a first class entertainment. I was not disappointed and when it came to discussion time a sixth former asked, 'Would you tell me, sir, what are the advantages of streamlining a locomotive?'

Sanford asked, 'Do you want the official railway opinion or do you want my own personal opinion?'

The boy said, 'I would like your own opinion, please.'

In a flash Sanford replied, 'I should take a lot of convincing that it pays to carry a two-ton load of tin cans around.'

It was proved some time later in the wind tunnel experiments carried out at the Railway Research Centre, Derby, that streamlining was only advantageous at speeds of over 70 mph, and for it to be of any practical value the entire train would have to be streamlined. As the average speed for most trains was less than this it was not a worthwhile investment, especially when one had to consider the additional time involved in removing the sheet steel for accessibility during maintenance operations. Streamlining looked good but it cost money all the time. Dudley Sanford's last position on the railway was that of Superintendent of the Locomotive Testing Station at Rugby, jointly provided by the LMS and the LNE.

I have spoken about some of my work in the Experimental Section. Design work in the drawing office was allocated to six leading draughtsmen each of whom was regarded as a specialist in the design of one or more major units of a locomotive. Working under each leading draughtsman were senior draughtsmen, and draughtsmen as well as one or two improver draughtsmen like myself. We each did our own calculations for any part which was under stress and where these calculations were important the full details were entered in calculation books for future reference. The speed at which some of my senior colleagues produced a new design of a major component often amazed me, and the standard of all finished drawings was high. The quality of some of those which had been prepared by Herbert Chambers before he became Chief Draughtsman were quite outstanding and although, over the years, I saw the work of scores of draughtsmen, I do not think I ever saw drawings of higher quality than some of his. I regret to record that he died at the early age of 53.

A Leading Draughtsman to whom I was responsible for long periods was James Doleman, a very fatherly figure despite his being a bachelor. He lived with his sister and she was a spinster. He was Edwardian in both dress and manner and he

was always dignified in appearance and gentlemanly in whatever subject he talked about.

At the office he was an authority on boiler
design and in that capacity he gave me the task of
designing a new firebox using high tensile steel
stays of $^{11}/_{16}$ in diameter, instead of the customary
copper stays of 1 in diameter, for use on the well
established 4–4–0 Midland Compound locomotives. It was an interesting enough task but like
so much which is produced in drawing offices
throughout the engineering industry, the new
design never came to fruition. The 4–6–0 Royal
Scot locomotives were introduced and for a time
everything else was subordinated to them. Away
from the office James Doleman was also an
authority on two diverse interests. He was most
knowledgeable on the cathedrals of England – he
was an accomplished organist too – and he was
well informed on countless pubs in many parts of
the country. It was an odd combination to be
sure, but I had the greatest respect and esteem for
him because he never failed to give encouragement. He had served his apprenticeship with
Fletcher and Stewart of Derby, the manufacturers
of sugar refining machinery, and he once told me
that the craftsman with whom he worked said the
same thing every night when he left the works. He
would say, 'Well, Jim, I haven't done much today,
but I'll give it sock tomorrow.' Of course, in these
circumstances, tomorrow never came and Jim
Doleman realized that although he was only the
apprentice he was doing most of the work.

There was one senior draughtsman in the office
who had a quite exceptional and unique ability in
producing, of his own volition, complete sections
of locomotives in true perspective; they were most
impressive and several of them were published in
the technical press. Although loudly acclaimed
they had no real commercial value because the
preparation of each one took upwards of two or
three months.

On the footplate I did innumerable test trips on
passenger trains in service between Derby and
St Pancras and Derby and Bristol. On one
occasion we were about to leave Derby for
London when the platform inspector handed a
note to the driver. He showed it to me and it was
an instruction to say that the driver had to make a
special stop at Melton Mowbray to pick up HRH
The Prince of Wales, later King Edward VIII,
and subsequently the Duke of Windsor. A first
class compartment in the front coach had been
reserved for the Prince, who was carrying a small

dog, and was accompanied by the Honourable
Mrs Dudley-Ward; on arrival at St Pancras a car
was waiting to take them off immediately.

These were the days when the regular express
driver had his name-plate on the side of the cab
and when the driver looked upon the locomotive
as his own. In the ordinary way no one else drove
the engine; nowadays such luxuries are out of the
question, especially with diesel-electric and
electric locomotives which are manned almost
continuously to justify the high capital cost
involved.

The Derby to Bristol line was used for our tests
with 4–4–0 express passenger locomotives,
Classes 2 and 3, fitted to burn oil instead of coal
during the 1926 coal strike, which developed into
the General Strike.

I did many footplate trips using different
designs of oil burners and differently designed
brick arches. A single burner was fitted just inside
the firehole door and they were not over-difficult
to control. We started them off by using a wood
fire and on the whole the improvisations worked
well. Only on one occasion did the engine I
happened to be testing have to come off the train,
at Birmingham New Street Station on our return
trip – the special brick arch had collapsed! These
temporary conversions certainly enabled the
railway to carry on without the normal quantity of
coal being available. For me it was a case of
ascertaining the steaming qualities of the engine
and the coal and water consumption with varying
train loads.

I well recall another series of locomotive tests
carried out between Derby and Manchester,
through the lovely Derbyshire Peak District, a
distance of 61 miles. This stretch of line had its
full share of heavy gradients up to Peak Forest
and was an exacting test for any locomotive in the
country. I was the footplate observer and we were
hauling normal express passenger trains to
ascertain the indicated horse power (IHP) of three
4–4–0 passenger tender engines. One was No.
1011, a super heated three-cylinder compound
locomotive, the second was No. 1017, a saturated
compound locomotive, and the third was a
superheated, non-compound locomotive of the
900 class, No. 997.

The customary 'indicating' cab was fitted on
the running platform near to the smokebox –
never a very comfortable contraption – and Frank
Sutherland ably assisted by Roland Bond were
jointly operating the instruments and obtaining

the necessary Crosby-type indicator diagrams. They would ring my electric bell in the locomotive cab and I would record the position of the regulator handle, the cut-off position of the reversing gear, the boiler pressure and temperature, the speed of the train and the exact location of the train at that precise moment. We had to be as quick as lightning to avoid confusion later. Of course the task of interpreting all the data obtained and producing a report with calculations, conclusions and recommendations was generally a much longer job than the tests themselves.

In 1924 I was the footplate observer in another decisive series of tests carried out in each direction on the steeply graded line between Carlisle and Leeds. It was the year following the grouping of the railways and the object was to compare and contrast the performance of express passenger locomotives drawn from three of the main constituent companies which had been absorbed into the LMS. I had the privilege of being the footplate observer throughout the tests and the dynamometer car, immediately behind the locomotive, contained its full share of 'top level brass' representing various interests, as well as the experimental team.

We tried out, in turn, on normal Anglo-Scottish express passenger trains, a Midland 4–4–0 Compound with 6 ft 9 in diameter wheels, another Midland 4–4–0 Compound with 7 ft diameter wheels, a London and North Western 4–6–0 Claughton and a 4–4–0 Caledonian. All the engines developed much the same drawbar horse power (DHP), as recorded in the dynamometer car, but the coal consumption of the two Compounds was appreciably less than the other two locomotives. There were several features in favour of the Compounds, and their overall superiority, especially following minor improvements to the valve gear, left none of us in doubt that they should be selected for future building programmes.

During the tests there was one occasion when I felt it prudent that the Caledonian engine should be taken off the train when we stopped at Hellifield because of a hot leading coupled wheel axlebox. I had long since learned when it was sensible to do so. The former Caledonian Railway officers, including D. C. Urie, riding in the dynamometer car with my senior colleague F. L. Sutherland, who was in charge of the tests, took a dim view of this (understandably so because it was

only a year following amalgamation), but after further discussion with other officers they grudgingly agreed and the engine was taken off to be put right for another day. It was a blow to their prestige, but we had a train full of passengers who no doubt were keen to complete their journey on time.

As I look back now I must have covered many thousands of miles on the footplate and far more than any of my contemporaries. In addition to all the experimental tests in which I took part I was required to do countless trips on new engines which had just left the works and which had been fitted with some new feature or features and some 'on the spot' reports were required. They were relatively short round trips from the Derby Motive Power Depot to Trent Junction and back, a distance of twenty-odd miles.

In 1928 whilst I was still in the drawing office – always reverently referred to as the 'holy of holies' – the Derby works were turning out a batch of newly-designed 2–6–4 tank engines. The leading draughtsman involved was the quietly spoken Thomas Hall. I recall the visit of HRH The Prince of Wales to the works on Shrove Tuesday at the time when Engine No. 2313 was ready to leave the Erecting Shop. The engine was carried down the shop by two overhead travelling cranes and in honour of the distinguished visitor was called *The Prince*.

A very informative part of my drawing office experience was my being required to carry out functional tests of specialized locomotive components at various manufacturers' works. They included pressure and vacuum gauges, live steam and exhaust steam injectors, mechanical lubricators, brake valves, safety valves, superheater headers, pyrometers and similar fitments, most of which we had designed in the drawing office and which were being manufactured in quantity by well-known contractors. This work took me to various parts of the country and, I suppose, occupied an average of one day a fortnight over a period of about three years. These responsibilities were taken over by a colleague a year or so before I left the drawing office.

Up to the age of 29 I continued to be employed as a Draughtsman. We worked a normal 5½ day week, but for those of us on outside work the hours were irregular and often long. I was sometimes engaged on the drawing board, designing castings and other fittings, sometimes testing on the footplate or with the dynamometer car, or

Fig. 5.2   LMS 4–6–0 express passenger tender engine, Royal Scot Class. (Original lettering by the author when employed in the Locomotive Drawing Office in 1928.)

Fig. 5.3   Travelling exhibition of the LMS Royal Scot locomotive in 1928

sometimes visiting contractors' works and carrying out inspections of specialized locomotive parts. Collectively it was all a very rewarding experience.

Towards the end of my service in the drawing office I was given an extremely interesting outside assignment. A total of seventy Royal Scot class 4–6–0 passenger locomotives had recently been built, fifty in the North British Locomotive Works at Glasgow and twenty in the Locomotive Works at Derby. It was decided that one of these should go on exhibition at various large cities and towns and I was appointed as Engineer–Demonstrator. A colleague was appointed to assist. It proved to be a worthwhile venture and I cannot do better than repeat the write-up which I produced for the LMS Magazine in 1928 under the title of 'Exhibiting the Royal Scot'. The ardent steam locomotive engineer will derive his own special enjoyment from it.

'The Chance of a lifetime! A wonderful example of engineering skill! An opportunity not to be missed! Magnificent!

Such are a few of the remarks which were poured on me daily during my tour as the Engineer–Demonstrator in charge of the *Royal Scot*, during the whole of the exhibition.

Wherever the town visited, whoever came along, the praise meted out was always the same. Everyone agreed that the *Royal Scot* was a triumph of British craftsmanship.

Some notable people who inspected the engine were the Prince of Wales, Princess Mary and Viscount Lascelles, Miss Ellen Wilkinson, MP for Middlesbrough, Sir Ernest Craig, MP for the Cheshire Division of Crewe, 'Dixie' Dean, England's renowned centre-forward, the Lord Mayor or Mayor of each town visited, and a host of eminent engineers. All were impressed.

At Leeds, the Lord Mayor asked whether the *Royal Scot* was of British manufacture. I informed him, with no little pride, that every cubic inch was British and, further, that the LMS was on the National Roll.

Fig. 5.4 *The author explains some of the driver's controls in the cab of the* Royal Scot *to a young visitor*

That the Exhibition was worthwhile is proved by the following figures:

Town Visited	Attendance
Manchester	23 066
Birmingham	16 284
Bradford	14 806
Sheffield	13 048
Liverpool	10 962
Derby	7670
London	7493
Leeds	7311
Preston	5700
Crewe	4184
Total	110 524

If we add to this the number who saw the engine during the equally successful Scottish tour, the grand total is 172 484 visitors. The amount raised was nearly £5000 which has been distributed to various local charities.

Manchester's effort was truly remarkable. The Birmingham result, too, was exceedingly fine. Bradford and Sheffield also did wonderfully well for a three days' exhibition. At the former the intention was to make a slight addition to the money raised and to dedicate a cot to be called the 'Royal Scot' Cot.

The highest attendance on any one day was made at Sheffield, when 7259 people paid for admission.

Perhaps to the majority of those who inspected the engine it appeared as one great mass of metal and intricate mechanism. If I were asked which of the statistics quoted many times impressed these visitors most, I should have no hesitation in saying that it was the water consumption of 9600 gallons (or 45 tons) for the non-stop run of 401¼ miles from Euston to Glasgow. In quoting this figure, I sometimes added that it would keep a large family in baths for at least twelve months.

There were, of course, technical visitors to be satisfied. One of these, a retired boiler inspector, enquired as to the efficiency of the riveted joints of the boiler; another engineer asked whether I could give him the shrinkage allowance for the tyres; some-one else wanted to know the piston speed at 80 miles per hour, and so on. It was a case of being ready for anything.

Even so, in an Exhibition of this kind, it was hardly to be expected that everyone would prove to be 'a wise old bird', and I will enumerate a few 'howlers'.

There was the 'pupil' (so I was informed), who asked his middle-aged friend, in all seriousness, to operate a simple catch which fastens the gangway doors between engine and tender. The expectation was that it would lower the scoop for the water pick-up, and as I climbed into the cab I found the friend vigorously moving this catch to and fro. At the same moment the 'pupil' called to his friend from the side of the tender, and said, 'Hurry up, I've been waiting for it for about five minutes.' On the other hand, we had to answer ladies who asked such questions as, 'What is the coal consumption per ton-mile?' or 'How does the Royal Scot compare with Gresley's Pacific?'

To return to the 'howlers'. A certain local publication reported that, 'By means of the "notching-up" gear the stroke of the piston is shortened, thus obtaining more compression for the steam in the cylinders'. It proved quite a 'draw', as a number of people came along to find out exactly how we did it.

Quite amusing, too, was the lady who, in describing her visit to some friends, said, 'Yes, it was really splendid. We climbed into the cab and came out through the smoke-box!' Some flue tubes to be sure! No less funny was the Scotsman who, having obtained his 6d admission ticket of the booking clerk, asked the ticket collector, 'How far does it go, and how long will the trip take?' But, perhaps, best of all, was the individual who, taking hold of the 6 in diameter handle which operates the soot blower for the boiler tubes, and which is fixed under the regulator handle, said, 'I suppose this is the steering-wheel.'

An incident which does not directly concern the engine is, I think, worthy of mention. Although it was not my business to take money for admission to the Exhibition, all of which went to charities, I sometimes accepted sixpences just before the opening. One evening a shilling was handed to me by a gentleman who hadn't time to make the inspection, but wished to make his contribution. With the money I obtained four 3d tickets and sallied forth to the front of the station. Here I espied three small boys whom I approached, and said, 'Have any of you seen the Royal Scot?' Simultaneously, they piped, 'No, sir.' I said, 'Would you like to see it?'; 'Yes, sir', came the unanimous reply. 'Well', said I, 'have you another pal?' 'Jack' was hailed forthwith, and I duly presented the four tickets. After an enthusiastic inspection, the boys scampered off, whilst I proceeded on my way, thinking, of course, the episode was over. But I hadn't gone 50 yards before I had 8, 10, 12, nay 20 more surrounding me. 'Have you any more tickets, please, sir?' they cried, to which I reluctantly had to reply, 'I'm afraid they've all gone this time'.

In summing up, I consider the Royal Scot Exhibition was a great success, and will, without doubt, long be remembered by the tens of thousands who took advantage of it.

Throughout my period in the drawing office at Derby there was an amusing ever-recurring experience. Someone at some time had provided a

Fig. 5.5 The Royal Scot *on exhibition at Preston, Lancashire, with the station master and the author – standing inside the smokebox!*

Fig. 5.6 2–10–0 No 92220 Evening Star, *built at Swindon Works in 1960, was the last steam locomotive built by British Railways, and it now has a place of honour in the National Railway Museum, York*

cycle chain sprocket wheel, polished it up and fitted it into an attractive felt-covered case complete with ribbon. Those draughtsmen who were presented with it for temporary retention were awarded it for meritorious performance, such as reporting to the office that their wife had given birth to twins (in my time this only happened on two occasions), that they had climbed a mountain, had been chosen for an out-of-the-ordinary assignment in the office or had achieved some distinction in their hobby or pastime. It was retained by the recipient until a new 'challenger' was recognized, and normally the medallion with the caption 'For services rendered' only changed ownership about twice a year. It was an occasion for a very jolly, if short, ceremony whenever the popular vote arose. Despite their exacting work I found that most draughtsmen were always ready for a laugh.

Shortly before my 30th birthday it was announced that George W. Woolliscroft, the Superintendent of Apprentices in the Derby locomotive works, and the engineer who interviewed me as an apprentice applicant, was to retire. Within a few days I was orally informed that I had been appointed to succeed him. It was an occasion for considerable satisfaction and I felt greatly honoured in this new appointment which operated from 18 January, 1930, and I left the drawing office with the best wishes of all my colleagues.

In the engineering industry there are many young engineers who are transferred into a drawing office on completion of their pupillage or apprenticeship and remain there for the rest of their working lives. These are the draughtsmen – not by any means all, of course – who usually blossom into the top strata of designers, and have job satisfaction in full measure. There are other engineers who, unfortunately, never have the privilege and opportunity of gaining experience in the drawing office. Every engineer is undoubtedly likely to be a better engineer for having had some such experience. We are left with those who are employed in a drawing office for varying periods, ranging from a few months to several years. Those who leave the drawing office after several years are relatively few but it is this category into which I fall. I have always regarded my drawing office work, both inside and outside, as a vital part of my career.

CHAPTER 6

THE TRAINING OF APPRENTICES AND ENGINEERS

I was appointed Superintendent of Apprentices in the Derby locomotive works on 18 January, 1930. I was to be responsible to Henry George Ivatt, the Works Superintendent and the worthy son of H. A. Ivatt of Doncaster fame. Like my predecessor I was also required to carry out certain special duties directly for Sir Henry Fowler, the Chief Mechanical Engineer of the LMS.

This distinctive and rather individualistic promotion from the drawing office gave me considerable satisfaction. I felt, nevertheless, that there were other colleagues and more senior candidates around, not necessarily in the drawing office, who might well have been preferred. But encouragingly for me was the fact that on the eve of my 30th birthday I was to take the place of a man of 65 who had distinguished himself in several fields. Firstly George Woolliscroft, a Whitworth Scholar, was recognized as an academic of no mean standard. Secondly, he was an engineer of considerable experience and one who had become a specialist in the selection of apprentices and pupils over many years. Thirdly he was a man of stature as a public figure. Surprisingly I was not asked to attend an interview before being selected. I was informed by my Chief Draughtsman, Herbert Chambers, that Sir Henry Fowler had told him that he wished me to succeed George Woolliscroft and that I was to take up my duties immediately.

These were the days long before annual appraisals and selection panels had been introduced. The 'boss' did the picking and the one who was picked was expected to accept the higher appointment with fervour and appreciation. I was no exception, particularly as I looked upon the new job as a welcome challenge in an extremely vital sphere of the railway administration.

I shared a large private office on the ground floor of the Works Superintendent's offices with Robert Kirkland, the Works Assistant, who was responsible for locomotive repairs which were the mainstay of the works. We became staunch friends, but after three years he accepted a senior post on the Kenya and Uganda State Railways in Nairobi. Just prior to his leaving England I became godfather to his first son, David. Regretfully I have only seen David, who became a successful farmer in Wiltshire, on two occasions since his christening – first when he was confirmed in the chapel of St John's School, Leatherhead, and then again when he was married some years later. Fortunately I have managed to keep in closer touch with my only other godson, Roger Larkam. His mother Peggy, who is the only daughter of my old railway colleague Dudley Sanford, and his father Patrick Larkam, a railway engineer who trained in Crewe locomotive works, have one other son, David.

In my new capacity I soon realized that I was now in the position of having to take the initiative in the training arrangements of nearly 600 young men and these arrangements had to be in the best interests of both the works and the young men concerned. In a drawing office as in many other spheres one frequently looks for a precedent, but in my new job I had the opportunity to create precedents which were novel and which were always much more to my liking.

The boys who became trade apprentices normally left school at 14 years of age and started at regular intervals throughout the year. The annual intake averaged seventy-five, although the number of applicants interviewed was more than twice this number, which ensured a fairly high standard of intake. Apprenticeships terminated at 21 years of age and this provided a seven year training for those who started at 14, with the first year as an office boy.

In making appointments and keeping the necessary records of training I had the able assistance of Thomas Lowe, a clerk who was previously at Crewe locomotive works and who finally became the Industrial Relations Officer at British Railways Workshops Headquarters at Derby.

My first goal was to review the training schedules applicable to privileged apprentices, forty in total, and graduate pupils, of whom there were normally four, following which I systematically effected an appreciable number of improvements. My second goal was to prepare a number of training charts showing the sections and types of work on which an individual would be employed and the length of time he would spend on the different classes of work, which were framed and posted for all to see and constituted a guarantee that the training schedules would be followed.

The year 1930 was the first and last in which I had the privilege of setting the questions and marking the candidates' papers for what had for a long time been described as the Directors' Annual Mechanical Examination. The customary subjects taken were Machine Design and Drawing, Heat Engines, Mathematics and Applied Mechanics. This annual examination was open to any member of the staff employed in mechanical or electrical engineering, and it was a pre-requisite for all privileged apprentices. The examination always evoked considerable interest. The first prize was the very considerable sum of £10. The outstanding entrant throughout the years prior to 1930 was Roland C. Bond who finished first in three consecutive years. For this unique success he was exceptionally promoted to pupil, and for him this was the forerunner of a distinguished railway career. He rose to the eminent position of Chief Mechanical Engineer of British Railways, then Technical Adviser, and finally General Manager of British Railways Workshops Division. He also had the honour of being President of both the Institution of Locomotive Engineers in 1953–54 and of the Institution of Mechanical Engineers in 1963. My recommendation that we should not continue with the Directors' Examination, as an alternative to extending it to all the LMS works, was accepted.

Soon after my appointment in 1930 I had a visit from Dr Alfred W. Richardson, Principal of the Derby and District College of Technology. He asked me whether I would consider the possibility of a full day each week at the college for privileged apprentices instead of the two mornings a week to which I had always been accustomed. In a nutshell it was his view that it would give better theoretical results. I asked him whether he would be able to stagger the days and he said this would not present him with any difficulty. In these circumstances, and following a careful review, I was able to agree to his proposal, especially as the 6.00 am start at the works had ceased towards the end of the war and the introduction of a 47-hour week with a later start had partially diminished the social advantage of the privileged apprenticeship – but not, of course, the wide training – on two mornings a week. We arranged for the alteration to come into effect with the new session commencing in September 1930.

By coincidence September 1930 was the same month as the centenary of the Liverpool and Manchester Railway, which is described in more detail in the next chapter, and soon after my appointment as Superintendent of Apprentices I was requested by Sir Henry Fowler, who was planning to visit the United States, to represent him and the Chief Mechanical Engineer's Department on the Organizing Committee. It was a tough assignment and I was kept extremely busy. The correspondence was voluminous and with Sir Henry in America I was loaned the additional

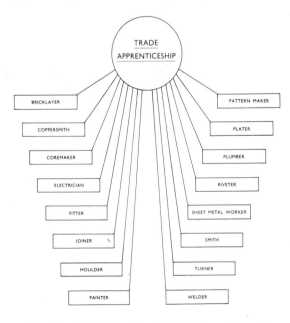

Fig. 6.1   Principal trades taught in BR locomotive works

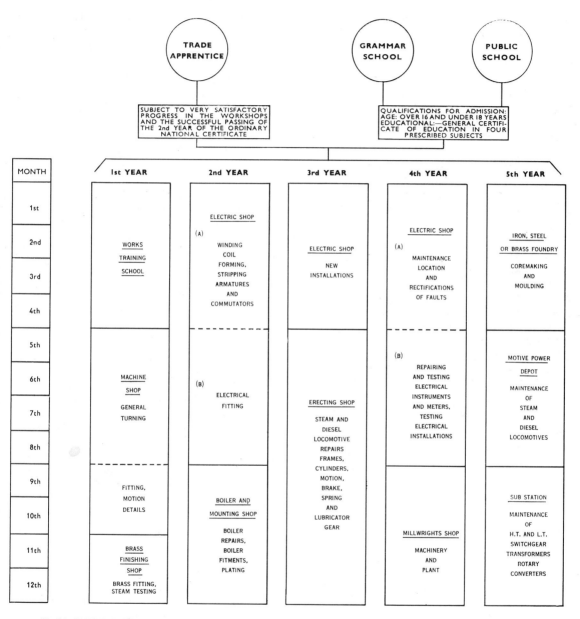

Fig. 6.2 *Typical planned training course for engineering apprentices in mechanical and electrical engineering*

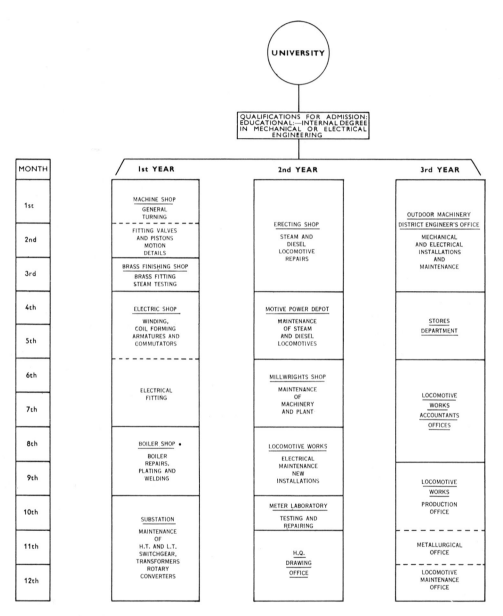

VACATIONAL WORK UNDERTAKEN DURING THE UNIVERSITY COURSE WILL BE REGARDED AS COMPLEMENTARY TO THE
PLANNED SCHEDULE OF TRAINING.

Fig. 6.3 Typical planned training course for mechanical and electrical engineering graduates

assistance of his very competent secretary, Eva Miller.

By the beginning of 1931 Sir Henry Fowler had become Assistant to Sir Harold Hartley, Vice President of the LMS Railway, and for me this was the end of a close relationship with Sir Henry and of his requesting my services from time to time.

I found that my predecessor had concentrated his attentions mainly on the privileged apprentices and the graduate pupils. In my new capacity, I realized there was a need for every trade apprentice also to be given adequate training and I was particularly anxious to eliminate its largely unplanned nature. Some were lucky, but I found that many others were decidedly unlucky in their lack of mobility and failed to obtain a balanced training.

Pioneering schemes are not developed overnight. After a great deal of thought and planning – a good deal of it at home – over a period of about six months I devised the Progressive System of Workshop Training in 1932. I called it progressive because the scheme was largely self-organizing and the apprentices automatically progressed from section to section. The system was based on logical and arithmetical principles and was put into operation throughout Derby locomotive works. It provided for:

(1) a regular intake of apprentices at predetermined intervals of time,
(2) a balanced course of training arranged in ascending order of training value,
(3) every apprentice being given the same opportunities in following a particular trade,
(4) the complete avoidance of any apprentice receiving training at the expense of another,
(5) the maintenance of an established quota of apprentices on each section and in each shop, thus simplifying the work of the supervisory staff and ensuring regular production for which purposes the works existed,
(6) a definite period of training on each class of work, based on the total volume of useful work normally available,
(7) a reasonable portion of the apprenticeship being spent on different classes of advanced work, to ensure a properly integrated and complete schedule of training,
(8) an independent report from each supervisor at the end of each period of training, based

on a standard code to facilitate comparisons being made,
(9) the maintenance of a comprehensive record of the training received and the ability and attention to duties of each apprentice,
(10) a 'master' schedule board controlling shop-to-shop transfers,
(11) shop schedule boards controlling section-to-section transfers within individual shops,
(12) the issue of a certificate of apprenticeship at 21 years of age signed by the Works Superintendent.

The system took into account three basic factors, namely:

(1) the number of apprentices for whom there was useful work to be done on each section of the shop,
(2) the relationship of this number to the total number of apprentices in the shop,
(3) the total time to be spent in the shop.

To ensure continuity of work from the points of view of both the employer and the apprentice, the period of training which was provided on each section of the shop needed to be made directly proportional to the number of apprentices employed on the section compared with the total number of apprentices in the shop. When these principles were put into practice the kind of situation which arose, say, in a small shop of three sections, all of which were suitable for apprentices, would probably be as shown below:

Section	Level of skill required	Number of apprentices required	Period on section (months)
A	Elementary	5	$5/10 \times 60 = 30$
B	Intermediate	3	$3/10 \times 60 = 18$
C	Advanced	2	$2/10 \times 60 = 12$
Total		10	60 months apprenticeship

If it was considered that two-and-a-half years was too long on elementary work – which of course had to be done – the volume of which work involved a normal complement of five apprentices, then this period could be shortened if additional work could be made available for them on sections B or C. Assume now that a greater volume of advanced work could be diverted to the senior apprentices in this shop and that four apprentices could be accommodated instead of

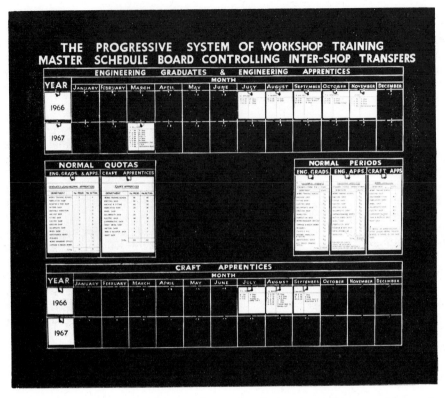

Fig. 6.4   Master training schedule board controlling inter-shop transfers. Each works would have one of these, and each workshop had a shop schedule board

two apprentices in section C, then we had the following revised situation:

Section	Level of skill required	Number of apprentices required	Period on section (months)
A	Elementary	5	5/12 × 60 = 25
B	Intermediate	3	3/12 × 60 = 15
C	Advanced	4	4/12 × 60 = 20
Total		12	60

In other words the elementary training could be reduced by five months and the advanced training extended from twelve to twenty months, equal to a third of the total apprenticeship of five years – a very satisfactory arrangement, with the training periods well balanced and the flow of work ensured. It was a scheme which readily appealed to the shop supervisory staff and so far as the apprentice was concerned he knew from the outset what had been planned for him.

With the introduction of the Progressive System of Workshop Training I had eliminated a considerable amount of repetitive administrative work and this gave me further opportunity to consider what other innovations I could introduce. I was well satisfied, assuming that continuity of production was to be ensured, that apprentices were being given the best 'on the job' training the works could offer. If the incidence of elementary work was too high it was necessary to inject a bigger volume of intermediate and advanced work into the training schedule and thus reduce the time spent on elementary work.

It is significant that, because the staff in railway workshops are largely engaged on highly specialized repair work rather than on new repetitive work, a high proportion of skilled labour is required compared with the general position in the outside engineering industry. It is of course highly desirable for an industry to train its own skilled craftsmen, and in 1950 this involved the employment of no fewer than 11 000 apprentices on British Railways at any one time, which placed British Railways as the largest employers of apprentice labour in the country. Most of these apprentices were employed at the sixteen main locomotive works and twenty main carriage and wagon works. The remainder were employed in power stations, electric car repair shops and outdoor machinery, civil engineering, motive power, signal engineering and road motor depots.

Over the years I formed the opinion that some initial theoretical and practical training would be advantageous to a new entrant prior to his starting in the workshop – the jump from school was too great. (I had not forgotten my own experience twenty years previously.) I also felt that it was wrong to allocate a boy to a trade based merely on a relatively short interview and possibly influenced by a request for a particular trade without the boy himself having any knowledge whatever of whether it was the most suitable trade for him. I recall the apprentice in my day who wrongly tapped a hole at the request of his chargehand.

I discussed the matter with Charles E. Fairburn, at that time Deputy Chief Mechanical and Electrical Engineer of the LMS and an engineering graduate of both Cambridge and Oxford, and it was agreed that I should experiment with a small group of about twenty boys just starting from school. Co-operation was forthcoming from the Derby and District College of Technology, with the Principal loaning one of his senior staff on a part-time basis to carry out classroom work whilst two well-chosen workshop instructors covered the practical work. I found a suitable building within the works and we decided on a three month course. The experiment was highly successful and we carried out another similar course. At the end we were all convinced that the tuition had proved extremely beneficial even though incomplete owing to our limited resources at that time. Pioneering work is never easy but on this occasion I had set the seal for further development.

Following a conversation late in 1940 between Sir Harold Hartley, FRS, Vice-President of the

Fig. 6.5   Relationship between theoretical and practical training in BR Works Training Schools

LMS, and Sir William Stanier, FRS, Chief Mechanical Engineer of the LMS, the latter invited me, at that time Assistant Works Superintendent of the Derby locomotive works, to investigate the possibility of initiating a training scheme. The scheme was to be devised to cover all apprentices, whether of the trade or engineering type, and to combine both practical and theoretical work as a full time course prior to the placing of the apprentices on productive work in the workshops. Provision was to be made in the training scheme to include such lecturing in workshop practices and associated subjects as might be considered consistent with a practical course. The underlying idea was for a scheme to be developed with a view to its introduction after the war.

Early in 1941 I submitted my report, a copy of which was sent by the Company to the Right Honourable Herwald Ramsbotham, MP, President of the Board of Education (the equivalent today of the Secretary of State for Education and Science). The proposals covered all the main works of the LMS and provided for the establishment of seven Works Training Schools and the inclusion in the schools of several novel features. Not the least noteworthy was the recommendation that the Board of Education should be invited to co-operate and allow full time lecturers under the local education authorities to visit the schools and lecture in a limited number of specified subjects, leaving other classroom subjects, such as Workshop Theory, to be covered by railway-appointed staff. The object of this proposal was to foster a closer link between the LMS and the Directors of Education of the local authorities concerned, and in no way reflected on the ability of the railway-appointed staff. Another interesting proposal was that all skilled trades should be covered in the school – an arrangement not to be found elsewhere. It was planned that the workshop equipment and classroom accommodation would be such that they were in use at all times, thus helping to ensure animation and a true busy workshop atmosphere. On 19 June, 1941, I was presented to the President of the Board of Education, when the latter said he was impressed with my proposals and would give them his full support. I was subsequently invited to meet the LMS directors at dinner and afterwards explain to them how the scheme would operate.

Authority was obtained in 1946 for the establishment of a Works Training School at Derby locomotive works. It was officially opened by Sir Robert Burrows, Chairman of the LMS, on 4 December 1947, and, subject to satisfactory results being achieved, consideration was to be given to the provision of similar facilities at each of the other six main works of the LMS.

Shortly after nationalization of the Transport Industry in January, 1948, members of the British Transport Commission, together with the labour and establishment members of the five executives set up by the Commission, visited Derby to inspect the Works Training School in operation. Following this visit, the British Transport Commission, in a report entitled 'Staff Training and Education', recommended that the general pattern of practical and theoretical training at the school at Derby should be developed and extended to the larger workshop centres of all five executives wherever practicable.

There are times when writing letters is predictably quite ineffective. The ideal way is to go and see people, especially if they do not know you, and so I made a point of meeting each Director of Education to explain what I had in mind. Mostly they could see that the local boys who came to the LMS would be getting a year's schooling, mainly vocational training, and the ratepayers would only be paying a fraction of what it would cost to run the Training School. There were one or two who, I surmised, had the feeling that we might be trying to do their job, but after seeing the new training school in operation at Derby and the high standard achieved, they went back to their committees and recommended that the scheme should be supported by the County or Local Education Committee.

Within a period of eleven years from 1948 to 1959, a training school had been officially opened and was in full operation at each of the main works of the London Midland Region. Crewe, as the largest locomotive works on British Railways, provided a unique and outstanding example of what was envisaged. The other Regions of BR followed on and collectively and individually the Works Training Schools have come to enjoy a reputation generally accepted as second to none in the engineering industry. Without doubt they have proved to be a first class investment.

The principal aims of the Works Training Schools were sixfold, and were as follows:

(1) to introduce the boy to new conditions,

(2) to acquaint him with the necessity for adapting himself to a new environment,

(3) to give definite and systematic training in manual skill,

(4) to ascertain the boy's natural aptitude and thus to try to place him in a trade in which he was considered likely to be successful,

(5) to give class instruction in allied subjects and so widen the field of knowledge and general outlook on life,

(6) to give the boy every encouragement to develop into a useful citizen.

The school training scheme provided preliminary practical and theoretical instruction to all trade apprentices upon engagement for one whole year. Engineering apprentices who started a year or so later, up to 18, entered the school for a period of four months. Approximately two-thirds of the time in the school was spent on practical work and the remainder on theoretical work.

The school hours for apprentice trainees were 8.15 am to 12.25 pm and 1.25 pm to 5.00 pm, Mondays to Fridays, giving a total of 38¾ hours per week. The shorter hours in the Works Training School as compared with the works provided a gradual transition between school and works. The midday break of the school conformed to the midday break of the rest of the works. This enabled the boys to use the works canteen and thus have some preliminary contact with the men with whom they would ultimately be working.

During the first four months' probationary period in the school, the apprentice trainee spent equal periods in each section of the workshop, after which the chief instructor was generally in a position to decide the trade for which the trainee was most suited. The number of apprentice trainees placed on each section of work after the first four months was determined by the annual intake of apprentices in the various trades. For the remaining eight months, the trainee was attached to the section which included the trade to

Fig. 6.6   General view of the first works training school, LMS Derby Locomotive Works, 1947

Fig. 6.7   Sheet metal section of the Works Training School, 1947

Fig. 6.8   Scale model of LMS 4–4–0 3-cylinder compound locomotive used in the fitting and assembly section of the Works Training School, Derby Locomotive Works

Fig. 6.9   Group instruction on a centre lathe in the machine section of the training school

which he would be apprenticed on leaving the school.

I always held the view that it was important that even in a training school, the apprentices should be trained in a truly productive atmosphere. To do so had considerable psychological value and tended to develop a higher level of productivity when the apprentice became a craftsman. With the greatly shortened apprenticeship of today as a result of the school leaving age having gone up in recent years from 14 to 16 years and the apprenticeship terminating at 20 years of age instead of 21, giving at the best only four years' apprenticeship, this aspect is, in my view, more important than ever.

The practical training of the relatively small percentage of the higher grade of apprentice or pupil who were destined to become professional engineers rather than skilled craftsmen was designed to give the best training possible by arranging certain selected periods of time in such

key places as the drawing office, the production planning office or the plant engineer's office, at the conclusion of their practical training in the workshops and motive power sheds. We only engaged pupils on merit and never by the payment of a premium. We required an Honours degree in Engineering and the planned training courses of two years minimum were quite outstanding in the quality of experience to be gained.

Some of those who trained under me, either as privileged apprentices, pupils or engineer-pupils, such as Ronald Jarvis and his younger brother Jim (both gained a London University External BSc. Honours Degree), Noel Hendricks, John le Cren Smith, Reginald Meads, Charles Loach, Dennis Peacock, A. J. Powell and K. W. Everett, and many, many more, including our first engineer-

Fig. 6.11   Apprentice trainee in electric arc welding section

pupil George Alan Hutcheson, who gained an M.Sc. before embarking on his three year training course, which I devised for him and those who followed, each made headway in a specialized sphere.

One scheme in which I was pleased to take the initiative when I had moved on to CM and EE headquarters in Derby concerned the temporary interchange of graduates between British Railways and certain prominent engineering firms. Agreements were legally drawn up in 1945 and a most wholesome arrangement made. It was good for industry as well as for British Railways, because the specially selected trainees had the benefit of experience with the manufacturer as well as the user.

Fig. 6.10   Woodworking section of the training school

My appointment as Superintendent of Apprentices in the Derby locomotive works at the beginning of 1930 fired my enthusiasm in the training of apprentices and embryo professional mechanical and electrical engineers throughout my working life. I held the position for four years and at the end of this time I was given the opportunity to take the initiative, first with the LMS Railway, and later with BR, in regard to further developments in this field. My contribution gave me a great deal of satisfaction because I realized the supreme importance of systematic training in producing craftsmen and mechanical and electrical engineers of the high calibre demanded by the railway industry.

In the early sixties BR introduced a scholarship training scheme for engineering graduates. The selection panel, comprising Roland Bond as chairman and three other senior engineers at board headquarters, included myself as the representative of the Workshops Division. It was an excellent scheme – which I am pleased to say still continues – popularly known as the 'thick sandwich' scheme for the reason that it involved a five year training period commencing with the

Fig. 6.12 Lecture in progress in science instruction room, Crewe Locomotive Works Training School

first year on BR followed by three years at university to obtain an Honours degree, and the graduate returning to BR for the final year. Some ten or twelve young men who had gained a place at university were tentatively selected for a year's initial practical work subject to their obtaining permission (and this was usually forthcoming) for admission to the university to be delayed for a year.

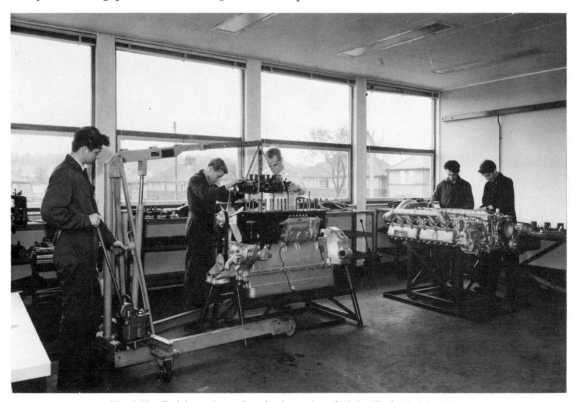

Fig. 6.13 Training on internal combustion engines, Swindon Works Training School

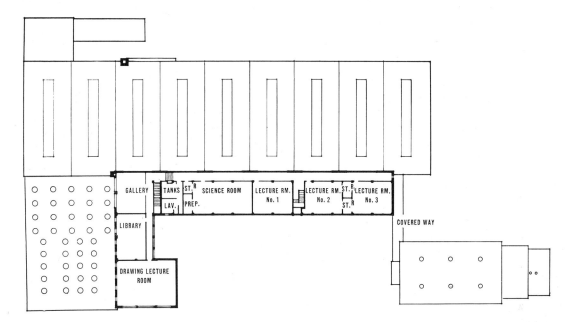

FIRST FLOOR

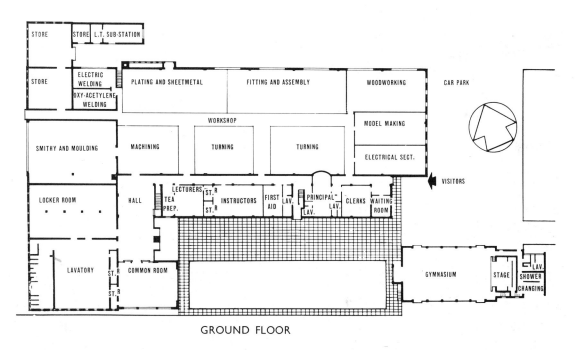

GROUND FLOOR

Fig. 6.14 Plan of Crewe Works Training School, with accommodation for 300 apprentice trainees. (The largest of the BR works training schools)

Fig. 6.15   Front view of Crewe Works Training School, excluding gymnasium and assembly hall

Fig. 6.16   Crewe Works Training School from the lake side

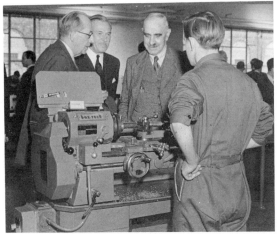

Fig. 6.17 *A memorable occasion at the opening of Crewe Works Training School in 1955 by Lord Robertson, Chairman of the British Transport Commission. (Left to right: H G Ivatt, formerly CM and EE of the LMS; R A Riddles, CBE, member of the Railway Executive for Mechanical and Electrical Engineering, who trained at Crewe and who laid the school foundation stone; and Sir William A Stanier, FRS, formerly CME of the LMS)*

In a span extending over thirty-five years, I held eight administrative jobs each markedly different in character. Four of these were in the Derby locomotive works, under the works superintendent, two were in the LMS CM and EE headquarters office at Derby, and two were at Marylebone in the headquarters offices of the British Transport Commission (from 1962, the British Railways Board). In all of these posts,

though not necessarily directly concerned with apprentice and graduate training, I always received encouragement and co-operation from senior officers and colleagues in every aspect of training which I wished to develop.

When the Crowther Committee was sitting in the 1960s, I was invited by the British Transport Commission to represent them and give evidence on behalf of British Railways.

Let me conclude by saying that no individual can ever achieve much on his own and any success which came my way, whether it was training or anything else, was due to the development of a good team spirit among those directly concerned. One colleague who immediately comes to mind is Harold A. J. Thomas. He was a planning engineer in the production planning office when we launched the first Works Training School at Derby in 1947 and we decided to appoint him as the chief instructor at the school. It proved to be an ideal appointment; he went from strength to strength and at the time of my retirement from British Railways he was the training officer for the whole of the workshops organization. He was an outstanding success and a real tower of strength to me in the field of training for many years. His successor was Robert E. Frank, another engineer who trained under my jurisdiction and who, I am pleased to know, has firmly established himself as a training officer of outstanding ability.

It has always been my considered view that the training for every apprentice should be the best the factory can offer, providing that the quota of apprentices attached to each section is maintained in order to ensure continuity of productive work.

I have formed the impression that the Engineering Industry Training Board, one of the many industrial training boards set up by the Government during the 1960s, have put too much emphasis on their module system of training for apprentices at the expense of production. I believe it is of paramount importance that both factors, training and production, should be kept in balance, otherwise skilled craftsmen will have to carry out elementary work which in the past has been properly regarded as that of apprentices, and in view of the difference in the rates of pay of the skilled craftsman and the apprentice, the customer will have to pay much more than is really necessary. Over-pricing of this kind is clearly uncompetitive and can only be detrimental to British industry and our vitally important export trade.

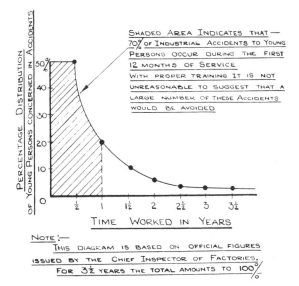

Fig. 6.18 *Graph showing accidents to juveniles*

It is not generally appreciated that there are fifteen Corporate Institutions associated with the profession of engineering, Corporate Membership of any one of them – and no others – entitling an engineer to append the letters CEng after his name.* Collectively they represent some 200 000 professional engineers. Appropriately enough the first President of the Institution of Mechanical Engineers in 1847 was none other than the father of railways, George Stephenson.

To be accepted as a professional mechanical or electrical engineer one had to qualify for corporate membership of the Institution of Mechanical Engineers or the Institution of Electrical Engineers. In my own case I became a student of the former when I was a teenager. It was necessary for the applicant to give proof that he was undergoing an approved apprenticeship or pupillage to mechanical engineering, and that he was also taking a recognized theoretical course in mechanical engineering. At a much later date I first qualified as an Associate Member, then as a Member, and for many years now it has been my pleasure to be a Fellow of the Institution.

*The Royal Aeronautical Society
The Institution of Chemical Engineers
The Institution of Civil Engineers
The Institution of Electrical Engineers
The Institution of Electronic & Radio Engineers
The Institute of Fuel
The Institution of Gas Engineers
The Institute of Marine Engineers
The Institution of Mechanical Engineers
The Institution of Mining and Metallurgy
The Institution of Mining Engineers
The Institution of Municipal Engineers
The Royal Institution of Naval Architects
The Institution of Production Engineers
The Institution of Structural Engineers

CHAPTER 7

CENTENARY OF THE LIVERPOOL AND MANCHESTER RAILWAY

The Liverpool and Manchester Railway was the first purpose-built passenger railway in the world and was opened by the Duke of Wellington on 15 September, 1830. It had been preceded by the opening of the Stockton and Darlington Railway some five years previously, when Stephenson's *Locomotion*, now at York Station, hauled the first coal train. The Stockton and Darlington Railway was built for coal-carrying but some of the trains provided limited passenger accommodation.

The significance of the Liverpool and Manchester Railway cannot be over-estimated, whether in relationship to the development of the railways, the growth of the cities of Liverpool and Manchester, or the speedy consummation of a process that has been aptly described as 'the greatest change in the habits of mankind that has ever come about otherwise than by a process of slow and gradual evolution'. It was the first successful commercial railway in the world, and the genesis of the LMS railway system, yet, in going ahead with the undertaking in the teeth of all manner of opposition, even its promoters had not determined what means of locomotion they were to utilize, and a majority of them favoured fixed engines until, in October 1829, after the project was well advanced, the Rainhill Trials vindicated the claims of Stephenson's *Rocket*. Of no group of men in human history can it be more truly said that 'they built better than they knew'.

The survey of the route for the Liverpool and Manchester Railway was carried out with great difficulty, as shown in the following extract from a letter written by George Stephenson:

We have had sad work with Lord Derby, Lord Sefton and Bradshaw, the great canal proprietor, whose grounds we go through with the projected railway. Their ground is blockaded on every side

to prevent us getting on with the survey. Bradshaw fired guns through his grounds in the course of the night to prevent the survey going on in the dark.

Eventually, the work went ahead and the following passage records how the official opening of the Liverpool and Manchester Railway on 15 September, 1830, was announced.

Town Criers: 'Oyez! Oyez! Oyez! By order of Charles Lawrence, Esquire, Mayor of Liverpool and Chairman of the Liverpool and Manchester Railway. It is hereby announced that the railway line running between the towns of Liverpool and Manchester will be opened this 15th day of September in the present year of our Lord, 1830, by his Grace, the Duke of Wellington, Prime Minister of England. There will also be present Sir Robert Peel, His Majesty's Secretary of State, the Marquis of Salisbury, Prince Esterhazy, the Earl of Cassilis, the Earl of Stanley, the Earl of Skelmersdale, Mr. Huskisson, Member of Parliament, the borough reeve of Manchester, the borough reeve of Salford and an assembly of the principal citizens of this borough. Other persons having business at the said opening ceremony are requested to be in their places 30 minutes of the clock before the appointed hour. All thieves, vagabonds, vagrants, beggars and other idle and worthless persons; all those afflicted with the smallpox and kindred distempers and all contumacious and disaffected persons, both men and women, are hereby warned to absent themselves on penalty of detention in the town gaol.

By order of the Board of Directors
Charles Lawrence, Chairman
John Moss
Robert Gladstone   } Deputy Chairmen
Joseph Sandars
Lister Ellis
Henry Booth, Secretary
George Stephenson, Engineer

God Save the King.

Fig. 7.1   Liverpool and Manchester Railway, 1831

TABLE 7.1   BRIEF HISTORY OF THE LIVERPOOL AND MANCHESTER RAILWAY, THE FIRST PASSENGER
RAILWAY IN THE WORLD

LIVERPOOL AND MANCHESTER RAILWAY

1822   Projected.
1824   Prospectus dated 25th November, 1824.
1826   Parliament passed "an Act for making and
       maintaining a Railway or Tram-road from the
       Town of Liverpool to the Town of Man-
       chester, with certain Branches therefrom, all
       in the County of Lancaster."
1829   Rainhill Contest.
1830   Opened 15th September.
1845   Amalgamated with Grand Junction Railway.
1846   Grand Junction Railway amalgamated with
       London & North Western Railway.
1923   L & NW amalgamated with LMS.
1948   LMS nationalized.

For the centenary celebrations, which lasted from 13 to 20 September, 1930, I was not directly involved in the exhibition of rolling stock, but, acting for Sir Henry Fowler, who was visiting the United States, I arranged with the Chief Mechanical Engineers of the other three main line companies the choice of the locomotives to be exhibited in Wavertree Park, Liverpool. I drew up the following notes at the time, giving the details of each locomotive exhibited:

Exhibit No. 1: The 'Rocket'.
The full-size model exhibited was built at the Crewe Works of the London and North Western Railway in 1911. The original *Rocket*, the recognised forerunner of the present-day locomotive, was built by Messrs Robert Stephenson and Company in 1829, and scarcely needs any note of introduction. It will be sufficient to say that it was successful in winning the £500 premium offered by the Directors of the Liverpool and Manchester Railway 'for the most improved Locomotive Engine', at the epoch-making trials held at Rainhill in October, 1829. Its top speed was fifteen miles an hour and along the route there were tens of thousands of spectators present whose eyes were unaccustomed to such a high rate of travel. Hitherto they had only seen horses running!

The original working drawings of the *Rocket* must have long ago disappeared. They were possibly little more than sketches, barely keeping pace with a construction, which in the case of the boiler and firebox was entirely experimental. It is, however, due to the excellent research carried out in recent years, chiefly by J. G. H. Warren, an authority on early locomotive design, on behalf of Messrs Robert Stephenson and Company that several doubtful points have been cleared up, and there is reason to believe that the model shown and recently altered is a fairly true reproduction of the *Rocket* as it appeared at the trials. The *Rocket*, of course, is a familiar exhibit at the South Kensington Science Museum.

Leading particulars
Cylinders (2): 8 in diameter, 17 in stroke. Motion: loose eccentric with hand valve lever. Diameter of driving wheels: 4 ft 8 in. Total heating surface: 137·8 ft^2. Grate area: 6 ft^2. Working pressure: 50 lb/in^2. Tractive effort: 825 lb. Weight in working order: 4 tons 5 cwts. Length over buffers: 20 ft 8¼ in.

Fig. 7.2   Full-size model of Stephenson's Rocket, *powered by an internal combustion engine*

CH. 7.

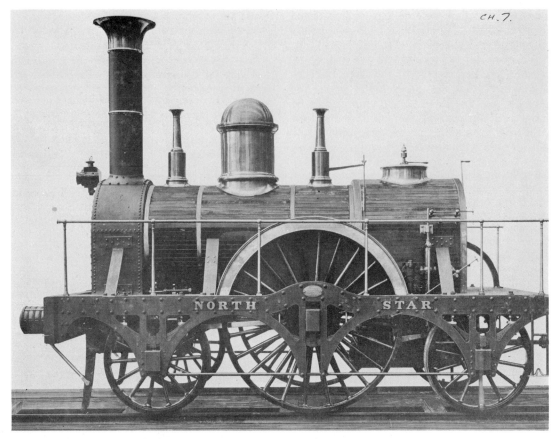

Fig. 7.3 North Star, *built for the Great Western Railway broad gauge*

Exhibit No. 2: Great Western 'North Star' engine.
The *North Star*, one of the earliest types of locomotive used on the Great Western Railway, was built by Messrs Robert Stephenson and Company in 1837. Steam was supplied at 50 lbs per square inch to two cylinders placed between the frames and the engine carried a single pair of driving wheels 7 ft diameter arranged for the old 7 ft broad gauge track. The slide valves were operated by Gab Motion. The *North Star* made its first run from Bishop's Road to Maidenhead on June 1st, 1838, when it conveyed 200 passengers and attained to a speed of 36 mph. It was in regular use between the years 1838 and 1870 and ran some 430 000 miles before being withdrawn from traffic. The engine now shown is a copy of the original and contains several portions of the old engine.

Leading particulars
Cylinders (2): 16 in diameter, 16 in stroke. Motion: Gab. Diameter of driving wheels: 7 ft. Total heating surface: $694 \cdot 7$ ft^2. Grate area: $13 \cdot 62$ ft^2. Working pressure: 50 lb/in^2. Tractive effort: 2070 lb. Weight in working order: 18 tons 10 cwts. Length over buffers: 20 ft 3 in.

Exhibit No. 3 Liverpool and Manchester Railway 0–4–2 engine 'Lion'.
During the Centenary celebrations this interesting old engine will work the 'Train of 1830' and carry passengers on the Ring Railway. After the celebrations, arrangements have been made for the *Lion* complete with tender, to be given a place of honour at Lime Street Station, Liverpool, as a permanent exhibit.

This locomotive was built for the Liverpool and Manchester Railway in 1838 by Messrs Todd, Kitson and Laird of Leeds, and in all probability was the first engine made by that firm. It was No. 57 of the Liverpool and Manchester Railway, and was taken over with other stock by the Grand Junction Railway in August, 1845. Upon further amalgamation, it became No. 116 of the London and North Western Railway, which, by the Railways Act of 1923, became a constituent Company of the London Midland and Scottish Railway.

The *Lion* was sold for the sum of £400 by the London and North Western Railway Company to the Mersey Docks and Harbour Board on the 26th May, 1859, and worked as a pumping engine at Princes

Graving Dock from that date until August, 1928, when it was presented to the Liverpool Engineering Society, whose property it remains in order that it might be preserved for the city of Liverpool. It has been restored during the present year, in the Crewe Shops of the London Midland and Scottish Railway Company, with the assistance of J. G. H. Warren, an authority on early locomotive design. The frames, cylinders, valve and driving gear, wheels and axles are original, and the *Lion* is probably the only locomotive now in working order having the original gab valve motion. The present boiler is of later date, with raised firebox crown not on the original. It has, however, been clothed on period lines and the restored engine as a whole represents a type in use on British Railways (as for example the North Midland), 1838–1848. The tender is not original but has been adapted from an early tender from the Furness Railway.

Leading particulars

Cylinders (2): 12 in diameter, 18 in stroke. Motion: Gab. Diameter of coupled wheels: 5 ft. Working pressure: 50 lb/in². Tractive effort: 2160 lb. Weight in working order (with modern boiler): 26 tons 11 cwt. Length over buffers: 31 ft 8 in.

Exhibit No. 4 LMS 2–2–2 passenger tender engine 'Columbine'.

The *Columbine* is particularly noteworthy as being the first engine to be built at Crewe in 1845, when Francis Trevithick, the son of Richard Trevithick (one of the earliest pioneers in locomotive construction) was the Chief Mechanical Engineer, and Mr Alexander Allan, the Locomotive Superintendent of the London and North Western Railway Company. Its original number was 49. The engine belonged to a class known as the 'Crewe Pattern', a name which was afterwards changed to 'Crewe Class' and later still to 'Old Crewe Class'.

In the year 1846 when the Grand Junction, London and Birmingham, and the Manchester and Birmingham Railways amalgamated and became the London and North Western Railway, this class of locomotive was built as a Standard Passenger Engine for the Northern Division of that Railway. The *Columbine* was on main line service from 1845 to 1877, and for many years worked the fast expresses between Crewe and London, Crewe and Carlisle, and Crewe and Holyhead, but towards the end of its main line service it was on local traffic work. In November, 1877, it was transferred to the engineer's department and attached

Fig. 7.4 The Lion *locomotive coupled to a train consisting of three replica first class carriages and three replica second class carriages. The carriages were built at Derby Carriage and Wagon Works specially for the Centenary*

Fig. 7.5 LMS 2–2–2 passenger tender locomotive Columbine – *the first locomotive to be built at Crewe*
(Crown copyright, National Railway Museum, York)

Fig. 7.6 LMS 2–2–2 passenger tender locomotive Cornwall
(Courtesy of the National Railway Museum, York)

to the engineer's private coach at Bangor, North Wales, and named *Engineer Bangor*. In January, 1902, it was taken out of service and placed in the paint shop, Crewe Works, as an exhibition engine of an early type locomotive.

Leading particulars
Cylinders (2): 15¾ in diameter, 20 in stroke. Motion: Stephenson link. Diameter of driving wheels: 6 ft 3 in. Total heating surface: 709 ft². Grate area: 10·5 ft². Working pressure: 120 lb/in². Tractive effort: 6325 lb. Weight in working order: 26 tons 6 cwt. Length over buffers: 38 ft 1¼ in.

Exhibit No. 5 LMS 2–2–2 passenger tender engine 'Cornwall'.

The *Cornwall* was built in 1847 to the designs of the late Francis Trevithick, Locomotive Superintendent to the London and North Western Railway, at Crewe. Its chief feature, as originally built, was the position of the driving axle which was placed above the barrel of the boiler. This was done to keep the centre of gravity as low as possible, thus getting a large boiler area and heating surface, and at the same time ensuring safety in running at high speed. It was thought at the time by most locomotive engineers, that a large boiler fixed in the ordinary way made the engine top heavy and was not compatible with safety in narrow-gauge engines running at high speed. As originally constructed, the *Cornwall* was not a success, and was subsequently re-built at Crewe in 1858 and fitted with an ordinary type boiler above the axle. Later a cab, vacuum brake pipes, carriage heating apparatus and other fitments were added. The cylinders are still of the original size, and its single driving wheels, 8 ft 6 in in diameter, are

amongst the largest of any locomotive ever built.

Leading particulars
Cylinders (2): 17½ in diameter, 24 in stroke. Motion: Stephenson link. Diameter of driving wheels 8 ft 6 in. Total heating surface: 1068·3 ft². Grate area: 15 ft². Working pressure: 140 lb/in². Tractive effort: 8575 lb. Weight in working order: 31 tons 1 cwt. Length over buffers: 45 ft 2¼ in.

Exhibit No. 6 LMS 4–2–2 express passenger tender engine No. 118.

Engine No. 118 was built at the Derby Works of the Midland Railway, in March 1897, and represents a distinctive class of 95 express passenger engines, built between 1897 and 1899, to the designs of the late Samuel W. Johnson, Locomotive Superintendent of the Midland Railway. These locomotives have single driving wheels and one, the *Princess of Wales*, was awarded the Grand Prix at the Paris Exhibition of 1900. With an average train the class proved highly satisfactory and was remarkable for the high speed performances. On one notable occasion a speed of no less than 90 miles per hour was attained, and for 13 consecutive miles a speed of 80 miles was maintained. The engine exhibited is the only example retained, and was withdrawn from active service in 1928, having run 774 359 miles.

Leading particulars
Cylinders (2): 19½ in diameter, 26 in stroke. Motion: Stephenson Link. Total heating surface: 1235 ft². Grate area: 21·3 ft². Working pressure: 170 lb/in². Tractive effort: 15 279 lb. Weight in working order: 88 tons 10 cwt 2 qr. Length over buffers: 53 ft 7½ in.

Fig. 7.7   4–2–2 Express passenger tender locomotive No. 118

Fig. 7.8   LMS 0–8–0 freight tender locomotive

Fig. 7.9   LMS 2–6–0–0–6–2 Beyer-Garratt freight locomotive No. 4990, fitted with rotary coal bunker

Exhibit No. 7 LMS 0–8–0 superheater freight tender engine No. 9599.

Engine No. 9599 represents the LMS Company's standard freight tender engine for the heaviest mineral traffic, which is a development of the London and North Western engine of this type. The cylinders are 19 in diameter by 26 in stroke, instead of 20½ in diameter by 26 in stroke, and the valve gear, Walschaert's with long travel, instead of Joy's with short travel. The original boiler design has been largely retained, but the steam pressure has been raised from 175 to 200 lb/in² and the wheels made slightly larger. A hundred were built at Crewe in 1929, and 20 more are following this year, the numbers being 9500–9619.

Leading particulars

Cylinders (2) 19 in diameter, 26 in stroke. Motion: Walschaert (between frames). Diameter of coupled wheels 4 ft 8½ in. Total heating surface (including superheater) 1936·375 ft². Grate area: 23·6 ft². Working pressure: 200 lb/in². Tractive effort: 28 250 lb. Weight in working order: 101 tons 18 cwt 3½ qr. Length over buffers: 56 ft 1 in.

Exhibit No. 8 LMS 2–6–0–0–6–2 'Beyer–Garratt' locomotive No. 4990.

Engine No. 4990 represents the 'Beyer–Garratt' articulated locomotives, three of which were built in 1927, and of which 30 more are now under construction by Messrs Beyer, Peacock and Co. Ltd, Manchester, to the designs of Sir Henry Fowler, the Chief Mechanical Engineer of the LMS. These engines are the first of their type to be introduced for ordinary traffic working in Great Britain, although the LNE Railway have an engine of a similar type, but heavier and more powerful, which was designed exclusively for banking purposes on the Wath incline. The introduction of these articulated locomotives provides a means of hauling the heaviest mineral traffic and dispenses with double heading, the engine being designed with a tractive effort of 45 620 lb, which gives sufficient power for hauling the mineral trains which hitherto had necessitated the use of two freight locomotives. The overall wheel base of this engine is 79 feet, so it will be appreciated that the engine cannot be turned except at triangles, and, therefore, every attention has been given to the design to ensure satisfactory operation in whichever direction the engine is running.

Leading particulars

Cylinders (4): 18½ in diameter, 26 in stroke. Motion: Walschaert. Diameter of coupled wheels: 5 ft 3 in. Total heating surface (including superheater): 2637 ft². Grate area: 44·5 ft². Working pressure: 190 lb/in². Tractive effort: 45 620 lb. Weight in working order 148 tons 15 cwt. Length over buffers: 87 ft 10½ in.

Exhibit No. 9 LMS 4–6–0 passenger tender engine Royal Scot Class, No. 6161, 'The King's Own'.

The *King's Own* represents the celebrated 'Royal Scot' class of engines, which deals with the very heavy and fast passenger traffic between London and Scotland. The first 50 of these engines were built by the North British Locomotive Company to the designs of Sir Henry Fowler, the Chief Mechanical Engineer of the LMS Railway, and another 20 are now in course of completion at the Company's Works at Derby. On April 17th, 1928, when the northbound traffic was so heavy that the 'Royal Scot' train had to leave London in two portions, for Glasgow and Edinburgh, each portion ran through to its destination without a halt. The distance from Euston to Central Station, Glasgow, is 401¼ miles, and to Prince's Street Station, Edinburgh, 400 miles. This was, and still is, a world's record in long-distance railway travel without intermediate stop. They are the first of their type to be introduced for passenger service in Great Britain, with three simple cylinders, each of which is provided with independent Walschaert valve gear. Standard locomotive fittings have been provided, where possible, to facilitate interchangeability, and in addition, every attention has been given to the provision of a comfortable, roomy and well ventilated cab, and easy control of all fittings.

Leading particulars

Cylinders (3): 18 in diameter, 26 in stroke. Motion: Walschaert. Diameter of coupled wheels 6 ft 9 in. Total heating surface (including superheater): 2526 ft². Grate area: 31·2 ft². Working pressure: 250 lb/in². Tractive effort: 33 150 lb. Weight in working order: 127 tons 12 cwt. Length over buffers: 63 ft 2¾ in.

Exhibit No. 10 LNER 4–6–4 high pressure compound engine No. 10000.

This locomotive represents an entire departure from orthodox design, in that it is fitted with a Yarrow–Gresley water-tube boiler in place of the usual smoke-tube type. The working pressure of the steam is 450 lb/in², and this steam is utilised in two high-pressure cylinders placed between the frames and which exhaust into a receiver supplying two low pressure cylinders located outside the frames. The front end of the engine is of novel design. Owing to the fact that the boiler is built to the maximum permissible dimensions it is not possible to fit an ordinary chimney, and the contour of the front is so arranged that the smoke is thrown upwards clear of the driver's line of sight. The three openings in the front allow air to pass alongside the flues keeping the outer casing cool and at the same time supplying pre-heated air to the ashpan. The trailing end is also of unusual design, being carried on a radial axle and a pony truck. The tender is of the standard corridor type.

Fig. 7.10   LMS 4–6–0 Royal Scot Class express passenger tender locomotive The King's Own

Fig. 7.11   LNER 4–6–4 high pressure express passenger compound locomotive No. 10000

Leading particulars

Cylinders (4): 2 h.p., 12 in diameter, 2 l.p. 20 in diameter, 26 in stroke. Motion: Walschaert. Diameter of coupled wheels: 6 ft 8 in. Total heating surface: 2136 ft^2 (including superheater). Grate area: 34·95 ft^2. Working pressure: 450 lb/in^2. Tractive effort: 32 000 lb. Weight of engine and tender in working order: 166 tons. Length over buffers: 75 ft 3 in.

Exhibit No. 11 GWR 4–6–0 King Class engine No. 6029, 'King Stephen'.

This engine represents a new 4-cylinder 4–6–0 type express passenger class, built to the designs of C. B. Collett, the Chief Mechanical Engineer. They are named after the Kings of England, and rank as the most powerful express passenger locomotives in the country. Superheated steam is supplied at 250 lb/in^2 to the inside cylinders by 9 in piston valves operated direct from Walschaert gear placed between the frames, the valves for the outside cylinders being operated by rocking levers from the inside gear. The inside cylinders are set well forward and drive on to the leading coupled axle whilst the outside cylinders drive on to the middle pair of coupled wheels, which are 6 ft 6 in diameter. The cab is spacious and well protected with its extended roof and side windows, and tip-up seats are provided for the driver and fireman. 'King' class engines are used on the celebrated *Cornish Riviera*

express (Paddington to Plymouth), a non-stop run of 226 miles in 240 minutes.

Leading particulars

Cylinders (4): 16¼ in diameter, 28 in stroke. Motion: Walschaert. Diameter of coupled wheels: 6 ft 6 in. Total heating surface: 2514 ft^2. Grate area: 34·3 ft^2. Working pressure: 250 lb/in^2. Tractive effort: 40 300 lb. Weight in working order (engine and tender): 135 tons 14 cwt. Length over buffers: 68 ft 2 in.

Exhibit No. 12 Southern Railway 4–6–0 Lord Nelson Class, 4-cylinder express passenger locomotive, engine No. E. 850, 'Lord Nelson'.

In order to meet the increasing weight of fast passenger traffic on the Southern Railway, a new and heavier type of locomotive, built at the Company's Works at Eastleigh to the designs of R. E. L. Maunsell, the Chief Mechanical Engineer, has been introduced. This engine is a 4–6–0 four-cylinder simple superheater engine with double bogie tender, slightly heavier and more powerful than the well-known 'King Arthur' type. The first of the class is named *Lord Nelson* and the engines are known as the 'Nelson' class. A glance at the ample proportions of both boiler and running gear will show that the moderate weight of this powerful machine has been secured by close attention to design of details. The bogie tender is similar to that used on

Fig. 7.12   GWR 4–6–0 King Class express passenger locomotive No. 6029, King Stephen

Fig. 7.13 Southern Railway 4–6–0 Lord Nelson Class express passenger locomotive, Lord Nelson

the 'King Arthur' class, and the overall dimensions of the engines will permit of their working on the main lines of any section of the Company's system.

Leading particulars
Cylinders (4): 16½ in diameter, 26 in stroke. Motion: Walschaert. Diameter of coupled wheels: 6 ft 7 in. Total heating surface (including superheater): 2365 ft². Grate area: 33·50 ft². Working pressure: 220 lb/in². Tractive effort: 33 500 lb. Weight of engine and tender in working order: 140 tons 4 cwt. Length over buffers: 69 ft 9¾ in.

Former colleagues of mine in the locomotive drawing office at Derby acted as demonstrators for the LMS locomotives and technical staff from the other three main line companies acted similarly for their own locomotives.

The Pageant of Transport was the crowning event of the celebrations each day. It took place in Wavertree Park on a stage 100 yd long and was enacted by 4000 performers. The evolution of transport from the earliest times to the present day was dramatized in a manner never before attempted.

The Railway Exhibition in St George's Hall,

Liverpool, consisted primarily of models, miniature railways and historical and pictorial matter relating to the Liverpool and Manchester Railway. It was designed to present a complete conspectus of the evolution of railways from the beginning to the present day. The material brought together was, I imagine, the finest collection of its kind ever assembled. Among the best of the many models in the Exhibition were the following:

Model of the *Lord of the Isles* (Lady of the Lake type) North Western engine made by G. G. Poston, Moreton, Wirral. The making of this model, which was one of the finest in the Exhibition in finish and measured 4 ft 6 in in length, had occupied Mr Poston's leisure time for over twenty years.

North British 'Atlantic' engine made by W. T. Hardwick of Sheffield and measuring 5 ft 5 in in length.

Caledonian engine made by W. Ballantyne, Annan, Dumfriesshire. The making of this engine, which was of the Dunalastair type, had occupied Mr Ballantyne for twelve years and, together with Mr Poston's, it represented the finest workmanship in the Exhibition.

A very interesting model and the largest in the collection was that of an articulated engine from the Aitchison Topeka Santa Fé Railway, which was one of four models lent by Messrs Thomas Parsons and Sons, Oxford Street, London. Complete with bogie and cow-catcher, it was 6 ft 8 in long.

Of what may be called the 'primitives' or original models the following were perhaps the most notable in the collection:

Cugnot's road engine, the forerunner of them all, of which the finest model in the country had been lent by the Royal Automobile Club of London.

The original model made by William Murdoch himself in 1785 of his engine and lent by Sir Lincoln Tangye and family.

Model of one of Richard Trevithick's original engines lent by E. D. Lowry, London.

Original model of Blenkinsop–Murray engine made by Matthew Murray of Leeds in 1812 and lent by its owner, P. H. Rosenbach, the famous American bibliophile.

Model of one of William Hedley's original engines made in 1813–14; *Wylam Dilly*, lent by the Royal Scottish Museum.

There was an official opener at St George's Hall each day and I remember that one of them was Major C. R. Attlee, who became the Labour Prime Minister from 1945 to 1951. Three others were the Lord Mayors of Liverpool and Manchester, and General Dawes, the American Ambassador in London.

Although the locomotive and rolling stock display in Wavertree Park was unique and very impressive I feel that the *pièce de résistance* was the old engine *Lion*, which had been reconditioned at Crewe locomotive works, and which drew a specially constructed replica of a train of 1830 around a circular track. The railway staff were dressed in the uniform of the period. There was always a queue of would-be passengers waiting to pay for a ride throughout the week's celebrations. For me the most interesting visitor to this engine was Colonel E. Kitson-Clark, TD, MA, grandson of the builder and President of the Institution of Locomotive Engineers from 1921 to 1922. It gave him great pleasure when I invited him to ride on the footplate and, with the driver at his side, take over the controls for one trip. The passengers were informed who their special guest was and they gave him some very sincere and hearty applause at the end of their ride.

CHAPTER 8

LOCOMOTIVE BUILDING AND MAINTENANCE

Up to 1948 the LMS had nine main works and a number of outstation depots, in which were employed a total of approximately 40 000 staff. The workshop staff, the supervisory staff, the clerical staff, the professional and technical staff and the management staff which constituted this large total were all under the jurisdiction of the Chief Mechanical Engineer – certainly one of the most responsible posts in the engineering industry.

At the main works and the outstation shops the maintenance of locomotives and rolling stock was the principal activity, whilst new construction in the works represented about a quarter of the total wages bill.

In 1932, with the support of H. G. Ivatt, the Works Superintendent, I had introduced the Progressive System of Workshop Training in the Derby locomotive works, for apprentices and junior technical staff. It was largely self-organizing and had been running smoothly for many months when my colleague Robert Kirkland, the Works Locomotive Assistant, resigned to take up a senior appointment in Nairobi on the Kenya and Uganda Railways. Sir Henry Fowler had become assistant to Sir Harold Hartley, FRS, Vice President of the LMS, and I was no longer carrying out the special duties for Sir Henry which I had hitherto been doing. Sir William Stanier was the CME at Euston HQ. It was in these circumstances that H. G. Ivatt asked me whether I could undertake the control of the locomotive repairs office and take charge of the locomotive repairs at Derby and the eight outstation shops at Belle Vue, Bow, Bristol, Carlisle, Kentish Town, Leeds, Saltley and Sheffield. I gladly agreed, and broadly my new responsibilities in this field covered the following activities.

(1) Maintaining liaison with the HQ shopping bureau and the motive power department in connection with the shopping of locomotives.
(2) Allocating and classifying locomotives and tenders agreed for repairs.
(3) Determining, through the initial examiners, the extent of repairs necessary and authorizing the replacement or reconditioning of worn parts.
(4) Supervising the operation of progressive repair schemes.
(5) Co-ordinating the initiation of stocks of replacement components for locomotive maintenance, including the preparation of advance programmes for the renewal of major components such as boilers, cylinders, tyres and axles.
(6) Making advance arrangements for the breaking up of locomotives and boilers and arranging for the disposal of recovered components.
(7) Co-ordinating the supply of repaired and replacement components required by the motive power department.

It was the practice for Derby locomotive works and Bow locomotive works to carry out all the heavy repairs whilst the other outstation shops catered for the light service repairs. On the Midland division of the LMS we had 3000 engines to maintain and employed nearly 5000 staff, most of whom were engaged on locomotive repair work.

Initial examination had as its aim two main objectives: firstly to detect all items which required attention if a locomotive to be repaired was afterwards to function safely and efficiently, and secondly to ensure that only essential work was authorized. The second objective was of great

74

benefit to the economical running of the works because initial examination procedure, if properly related to the desired limits of wear, constituted a major check on unnecessary repair expenditure in the shops. Moreover, by having the initial examiners answerable to an independent authority and not to the shop foremen, there could be no opportunity of using their services as a means of 'finding' work if the volume had temporarily fallen off.

The initial examination was only concerned with the repair of locomotives. It was clearly unnecessary to provide initial examiners in the manufacturing shops, e.g. foundries and forge. Most of the work was centred around the erecting shop, but there were other shops such as the boiler shop and the wheel shop, which were involved in the rectification or replacement of components.

A preliminary general examination of locomotives for repair took place to confirm the information already received from the depot and to amplify this, if necessary, with particulars of any points requiring special attention. Initial examination in detail commenced as soon as the engine was brought into the erecting shop and proceeded concurrently with the stripping of the engine. This involved a complete inspection prior to repairs of specific parts either in position on the engine or dismantled, according to the item and the class of repair the engine was undergoing.

Where accepted standards for limits of wear had been laid down, the precise amount of work which was necessary could be determined. The initial examiners authorized this work by filling in the appropriate quantities on pre-printed forms which embodied not only full details of all possible operations for each section of the repair work, but also the registered piecework prices for carrying out this work. These documents were the authority for the artisan staff to proceed with the work and ultimately served as the wages documents upon which the work was finally charged. Only the initial examiners had the authority to make entries on these forms regarding the work to be done.

Staff designated as finished work inspectors, responsible to the inspection assistant, verified that the work had been satisfactorily carried out by the artisan staff and the former endorsed the initial examiners' forms accordingly. The repair of every unit was executed in sequence for re-assembly, and kept to a minimum the amount

of time a locomotive was out of service. Our target was to ensure that the number of locomotives out of service and not earning revenue never exceeded 5 per cent of the total stock. It was a never-ending battle which called for the utmost vigilance, and it can truly be said that no firm engaged solely in manufacturing has ever had the same problem as was to be found in the railway workshops, with their emphasis on assessing what repair should be carried out and what limits of wear should be prescribed. Day-to-day repairs, reported by the engine driver when signing off each day, were carried out by the artisan staff in the local running sheds. It was during my time as the locomotive maintenance assistant at the Derby works that our turn-round time improved so much – let me say at once that it was a management team effort led by H. G. Ivatt – that we realized that it would be much more economic to close the outstation shops and concentrate the work at Derby, for a relatively modest investment in new plant and equipment which would result in an appreciable overall saving. It was my very first unpleasant task to undertake a major transfer of work and certain grades of men to Derby. It was done gradually over a period of some two or three years, in order to cushion the displacement of the men involved. The overall plan went smoothly and I cannot recall any major problem arising. From an economic standpoint, it was a most logical and sensible step. So far as the apprentices at the outstation shops were concerned, all of them were offered places at Derby with financial assistance for accommodation in order to complete their apprenticeship. I am happy to say that an appreciable number of the total number involved took advantage of these special facilities. I recall some of the apprentices making such good progress that ultimately they obtained worthwhile promotions.

The normal procedure for calling a locomotive into the main works at Derby for repairs started with the district locomotive running superintendent at the depot to which the locomotive was allocated. Using a well drawn up works shopping proposal form the district running superintendent would send to the Works Superintendent at Derby locomotive works a recommendation for major repairs to be carried out based on mileage and general condition of the particular locomotive. The condition of the locomotive was certified by the separate reports of the district locomotive superintendent of the locomotive running shed where the engine was stationed, and of an independent boiler inspector attached to the staff of the Chief Mechanical Engineer. The reports on the prescribed forms would come to me as the locomotive maintenance assistant to the works superintendent. I would carefully study the report, and it was then my responsibility to decide on the type of repair to be carried out. This would be the normal case but if when the engine came into the works the initial examination system indicated that something extra was needed to be done, my authority, on behalf of the works superintendent, would first be sought.

There were normally three alternative types of classified comprehensive repair.

(1) A Heavy General Repair, in which there was an overhaul involving a complete strip-down of every sub-assembly and component. On leaving the works the locomotive was regarded as being in new condition.
(2) Heavy Service Repair, involving a change of boiler and/or cylinders.
(3) Light Service Repair in which certain specified work, other than the above, was carried out.

A Heavy Service Repair was scheduled to be completed in 6 working days and a General Repair in 8 working days, plus 1½ days initial stripping and then finally the paint shop. Overall, the time out of service was in the region of 16 working days or, say, 20 calendar days.

Where a locomotive had been involved in a mishap, it would be regarded in the works as a casual repair and the repair work carried out would normally be confined to the damaged components. In the case of (1) and (2) above a systematic progressive repair system was in full operation. This was such that the engines were moved stage by stage to the specialized groups of men. By this system all-round efficiency was ensured because neither specialized equipment nor men had to be moved about the shop and the men achieved greater proficiency by being regularly employed on the same type of operation or operations.

The essential requirement of such a system was a definite time-table, which had to be prepared for each of the individual stages of repair, and which had to be strictly adhered to in operation.

The use of graphs is an essential ingredient in the life of an engineer in control of production. In the progress office at Derby we called for engines to be sent into the works for repairs and we controlled everything concerning them whilst they were under repair. To enable them to be returned to revenue-earning traffic as quickly as possible we maintained a series of graphs and these graphs were under constant inspection.

The undermentioned list of graphs posted in the office will give a good general impression of the various facets which had to be considered and action which had to be taken where necessary:

1. Number of engines on works.
2. Output of engines with four graphs indicating (a) heavy repairs, (b) light repairs (no boiler change), (c) total repairs, (d) cumulative weekly average.
3. Average number of days on works with two graphs: (a) weekly number of engines turned out and (b) cumulative weekly average.
4. Cumulative output with six graphs: (a) and (b) new engines, target for the year and actual, (c) and (d) repaired engines, target for the year and actual, (e) and (f) new boilers, target for the year and actual.
5. Number of engines agreed for repairs with two graphs: (a) engines agreed and (b) engines stopped (included in engines agreed).
6. Engines under and waiting repair, with two graphs: (a) number of engines and (b) percentage of maintained stock.
7. Manufacturing stock order position, with five graphs: (a) stock orders outstanding, (b) stock orders overdue, (c) stock orders issued, (d) stock orders completed, (e) stock orders waiting material (orders returned to stores).
8. Actual stock position, with five graphs: (a) total number of stores stock items, (b) percentage of empty bins, (c) total number of empty bins, (d) empty bins (stores responsibility), (e) empty bins (works responsibility).

In the case of the stores stock position there was an economic manufacturing ordering quantity laid down to avoid unnecessary expenditure, and for all units there was a maximum stock to avoid unnecessary capital lying idle.

Each locomotive works of the LMS was responsible for the maintenance of specific classes

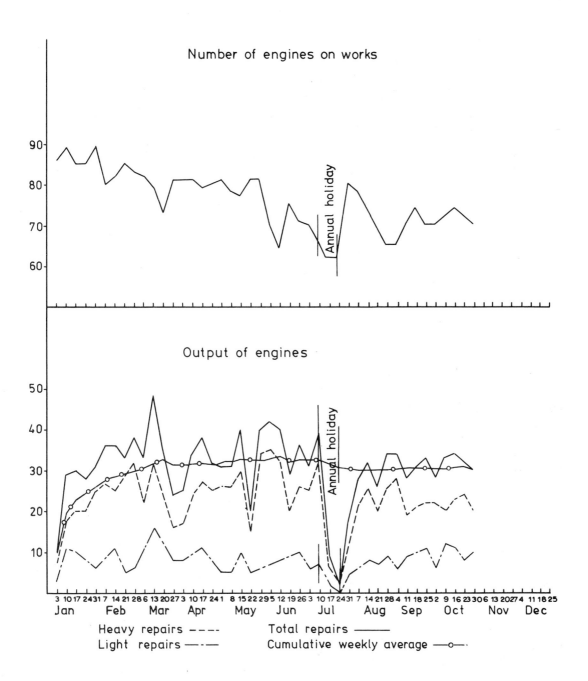

Fig. 8.1   Graphs used in the locomotive repairs office for controlling output of locomotives

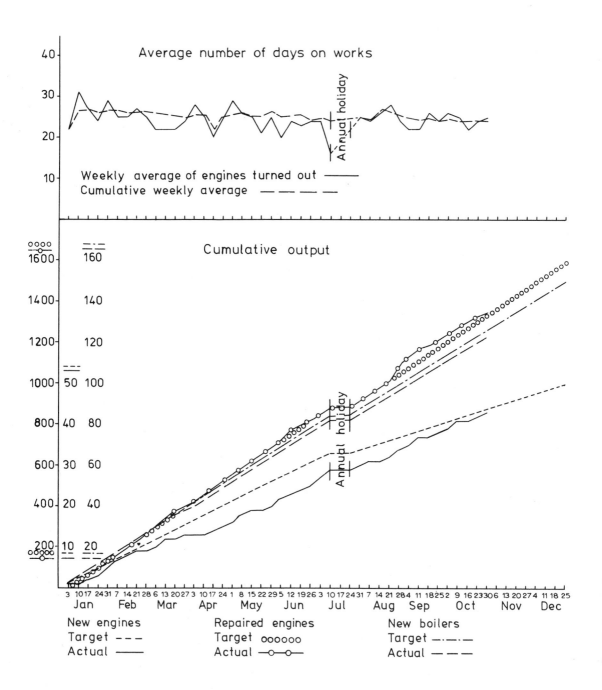

Fig. 8.1 (contd)

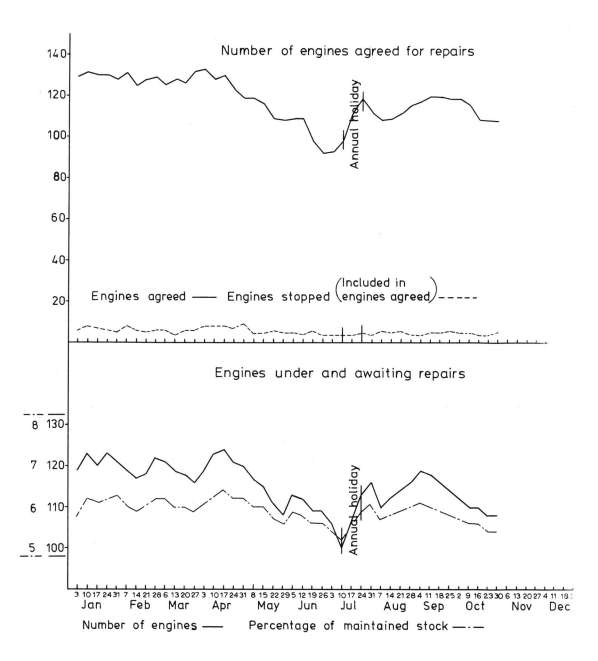

Fig. 8.1 (contd)

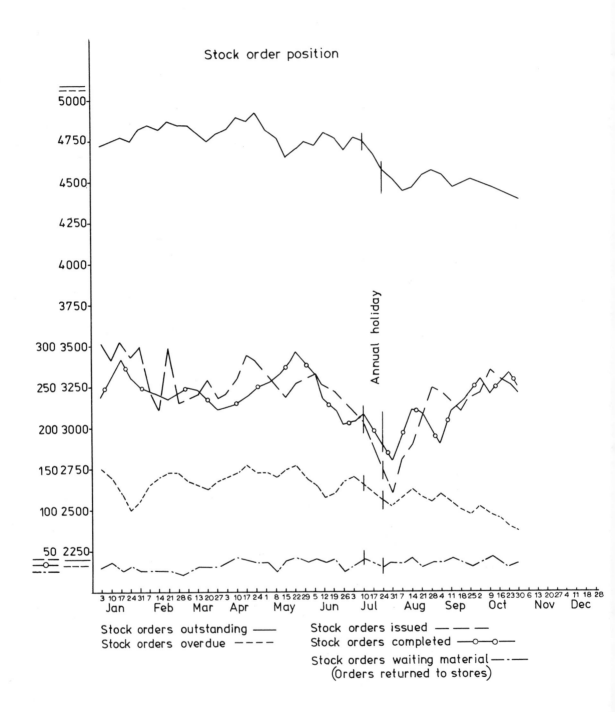

Fig. 8.1 (contd)

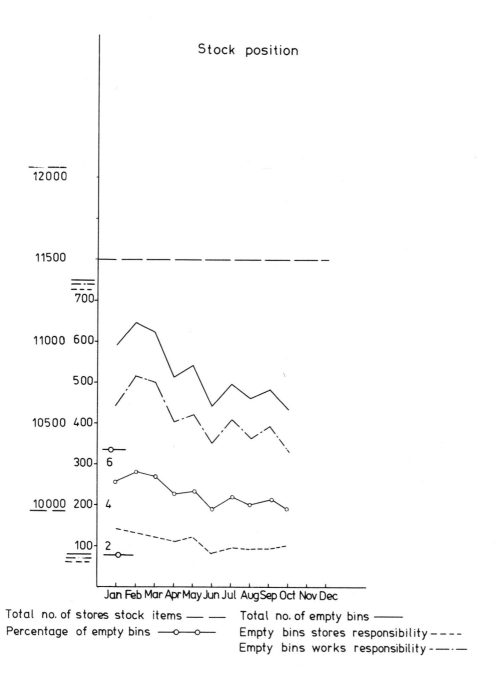

Stock position

Total no. of stores stock items — —   Total no. of empty bins ——

Percentage of empty bins —o—o—   Empty bins stores responsibility ----

Empty bins works responsibility -—·—

Fig. 8.1 (contd)

of locomotives. To assist in overcoming diffi-culties there was a daily conference, at 10.00 am, on the telephone, between the Shopping Bureau at Departmental HQ and the various locomotive works.

Railway workshop standards are very high indeed, the need for utmost safety and avoidance of a mechanical breakdown being ever in the minds of all railway engineers. When a locomotive had received a classified general repair, it left the works as good as new. Except for the occasional write-off due to a major mishap, it was only obsolescence which caused an engine to be withdrawn from service. The average life of a steam locomotive was 33 years, during which time it would normally receive one new replacement boiler. The total mileage before scrapping varied between classes, but not infrequently exceeded a million miles.

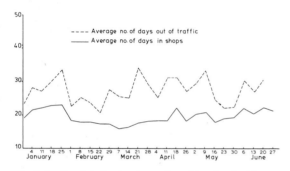

Fig. 8.2 Graph indicating the number of days involved in repairing locomotives during the first six months of 1936

The Derby system had been gradually developed over a period of years and, under the direction of Sir Henry Fowler, the LMS Chief Mechanical Engineer, the system had been advantageously extended to all the main loco-motive works of the LMS Company and covered nearly 8000 steam locomotives, of which 3000 were maintained at Derby. In my time we were constantly receiving official visitors and delega-tions from railway companies from various countries around the world, and there is no doubt that they went away greatly impressed.

One important feature in the repair system which had emerged was the fact that the repairs to the locomotive boiler took longer than any other unit, and this controlled the overall time during which the locomotive was in the works and therefore out of service. This difficulty was overcome by the setting up of an economic stock

of spare boilers for each main class of locomotive. This enabled a locomotive coming in for a general repair or a change of boiler to be fitted with another boiler which had already been repaired. The scheme normally worked like a charm and substantially reduced the days the locomotive was out of service.

The Works Superintendent was H. G. Ivatt, a great engineer by intuition rather than of academic brilliance, a gentleman at all times and a chief for whom I and all those who had the privilege of knowing him had the greatest respect and affection. He was of an extremely practical nature and in the early 1930s he completely reorganized the boiler and boiler mounting shops at Derby and introduced a systematic stage by stage repair system with new electric and pneumatic tooling. Instead of the various groups of men moving to the boiler in turn, the boiler was moved to the men. This, in itself, reduced the time needed to repair a boiler, and a reduction from eighty to forty boilers in the shop gave added savings in minimizing the capital lying idle.

An interesting occurrence took place at a time when the technical Press were interested in the layout of the newly arranged boiler and boiler mounting department, and H. G. Ivatt asked me whether I would do a write-up covering the new development. This I was pleased to do, and when the article duly appeared in print, with several diagrams and stage by stage photographs in-. cluded, the editor had a footnote in which he extended his thanks to Mr Ivatt for furnishing him with some 'notes'. On reading this article in the magazine H. G. Ivatt was extremely indignant and of his own volition wrote to the editor and pointed out that the 'notes' to which reference had been made were a very full and complete technical article, not one word of which had been altered by the editorial staff of the particular magazine. He said his assistant who had written it should be recognized for his contribution. As a result H. G. Ivatt received an apology and I received a complimentary letter from the editor, together with a cheque for £5 5s 0d – an amount which meant considerably more in those days than £5.25 does now. My chief was delighted.

Since the steam locomotive days there has been further progress in the reduction of shopping time by the use of modern management techniques such as network analyses which come under the umbrella of Work Study. With electric and diesel electric motive power units having taken the place

Fig. 8.3 Boiler shop jig for stay drilling and tapping

Fig. 8.4 Boiler shop jig for running in stays

of steam locomotives on BR since 1955, this has become more important than ever. The cost of these modern locomotives is several times greater than the beloved steam locomotives, but overall they win in performance, availability and lower maintenance costs per mile.

At the beginning of 1932 William Arthur Stanier FRS, of Great Western Railway fame, startled us all when it was announced that he had been appointed to the post of Chief Mechanical Engineer of the LMS, succeeding Sir Ernest Lemon, who had only held the position for twelve months and who had become one of the three Vice-Presidents of the LMS Company. It was an appointment which the rest of the railway world never contemplated if only because of the traditional insular practice of the Great Western Railway. After all, even the grouping of the railways in 1923 had not affected them in the least. W. A. Stanier soon established himself on the LMS as a locomotive designer of outstanding merit. Indeed he had an immediate impact on the drawing office and revolutionized LMS locomotive design. It was clear that design was his forte and apart from his considerable interest in modern machine tools he left organizational matters largely in the hands of his competent principal assistant, R. A. Riddles. W. A. Stanier was a very likeable and much respected engineer and many writers have recorded his work. He will probably be best remembered for his renowned Pacifics. When he retired he called me into his office at Derby and said I could have any of his books from his large bookcase. I subsequently took the handsome bound volumes of the LMS magazine and when I myself retired, some 22 years later, I sent them to the railway Archivist.

H. G. Ivatt went to Scotland as Mechanical and Electrical Engineer, Scottish Divison, in 1934 and his place at Derby was taken by George Sydney Bellamy. I continued to have control of the locomotive repairs office for a year or so until the organization at all the LMS main works was altered and I was given a complete change of responsibility and designated second assistant to the Works Superintendent. Instead of locomotive repairs, my new responsibilities put me in charge of new locomotive building, drawing up the manufacturing specifications, ordering the materials and preparing the necessary documentation including requisitions and wages tickets. The work also included all rate fixing for the works, control of the manufacturing costs office and workshop expenses. There was a sizeable number of staff to control. It proved a fascinating change and called for a good deal of initiative. I was still doing this job when war was declared on 3 September, 1939, by which time I had developed and introduced a completely new system of production planning for building new locomotives.

In setting up the production planning organization, which was the first of its kind on the LMS, I had the full support of my Works Superintendent George Bellamy. I realized that the key to success would be in the choice of staff, who would be required to take the initiative in defining the manufacture, operation by operation, of every single unit. It was no use my thinking in terms of choosing the up and coming graduate, or any of the intelligent young men who had served an apprenticeship, and had obtained the Higher National Certificate before being transferred to any one of the technical offices. It needed the best type of workshop supervisor the works could offer – men who were not only in charge of skilled artisan staff on the shop floor, but who knew the capacity of the works equipment available to them for the group of trades they would cover. On transfer to the newly created Production Planning Office I re-graded the chosen supervisors, each of whom I knew extremely well, as planning engineers. It was their function to prepare material specifications and operation layout sheets. If they were dealing with a new locomotive, it was first necessary for them to prepare a chart indicating when each class of material would need to be ordered and delivered to set the foundation for economic production. Locomotive building is not a job for a simpleton, and these hand-picked planning engineers ensured that an orderly economic manufacturing procedure was provided. An added advantage was that the workshop supervisors as a whole were relieved of a lot of office work and could devote much more time with their staff on the shop floor.

In the new organization there were five distinct sections.

1. Process planning of manufacture, complete with manufacturing specifications.
2. Jig and tool design.
3. Rate fixing and wages tickets.
4. Technical costs control, including workshop expenses.
5. Materials control and documentation.

Fig. 8.5(a)   Stage one: main frames placed in position on supporting jacks in erecting shop

Fig. 8.5(b)   Stage two: cylinders and other main components fitted to frames

Fig. 8.5(c)   Stage three: boiler fitted to frames

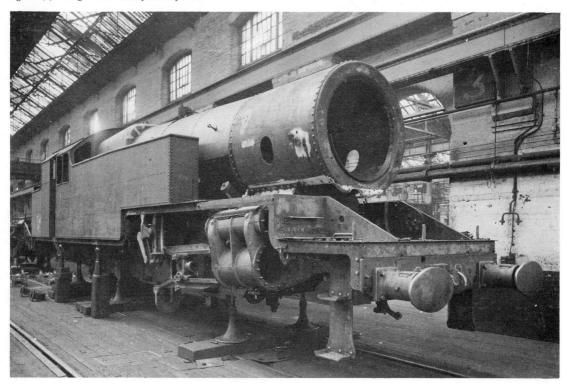

Fig. 8.5(d)   Stage four: driver's cab and side tanks fitted

Fig. 8.5(e)   Stage five: locomotive lifted by two overhead travelling cranes and wheels fitted

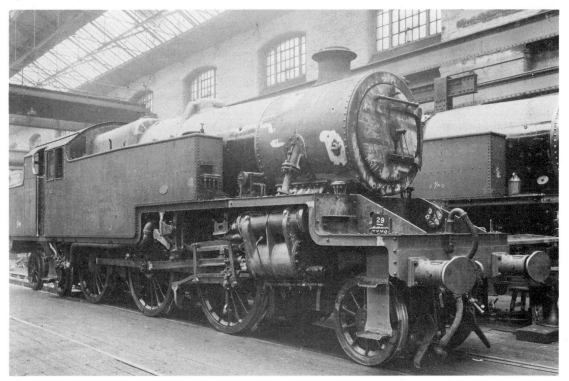

Fig. 8.5(f)   Stage six: motion, coupling rods and all remaining components fitted

Fig. 8.5(g)   Stage seven: two 50-ton capacity overhead travelling cranes carry complete locomotive to the end of the erecting shop from where it will be shunted to the test pit and paint shop

Fig. 8.5   Construction of one of 37 Stanier 3-cylinder 2–6–4 passenger tank locomotives at Derby Works in 1934 for the London, Tilbury and Southend line of the LMS

With regard to item three, I always felt it was an unsatisfactory situation for the railway negotiators to give considerable attention to the relative value of the various grades of workshop staff, to differences of as close as a shilling, when at a much lower level of management, piecework prices could be fixed in an unscientific manner. This completely upset the wages structure and could for the same speed of working result in a man on a lower base rate getting higher earnings than a man on a higher base rate. Since those early days there has been a thorough review of the arrangements.

In due course the planning organization came to the notice of Charles E. Fairburn, at that time Deputy CM and EE of the LMS Railway – a most able administrator who was the first engineer to graduate at Oxford University and was also a graduate of Cambridge University. He had previously been General Manager of the English Electric Company under Sir George Nelson, Chairman of the company. He asked me to review the situation at Crewe Locomotive Works, the largest locomotive works in the country, following

an approach to him by R. C. Bond, the Crewe Works Superintendent. I made certain recommendations in line with the Derby set-up and in due course these proposals were implemented and proved equally successful.

What could fairly be described as the beginning of the changeover to diesel-electric traction started at the Derby works in 1939, at a time when I had the responsibility for drawing up the manufacturing specifications for the first batch of 0–6–0 diesel-electric shunting locomotives of 350 bhp. By 1967, the works had built no less than a thousand diesel locomotives – a splendid and unrivalled achievement.

In 1941 there was a change of Works Superintendent at Derby and the assistant, James Rankin, replaced G. S. Bellamy. In turn I was promoted to the position of Assistant Works Superintendent and I was told of this promotion by Sir Harold Hartley, FRS, Vice-President of the LMS and certainly the most eminent scientist I ever had the privilege of getting to know well. The meeting took place in the CME's office, and Charles Fairburn, who was present, was clearly behind the promotion.

We were still building our first batch of 0–6–0 diesel-electric shunting locomotives, the last locomotives to be built until after the war, and we had begun to take on an increasing volume of Government work. One of my first sizeable war-work jobs was to convert most of the extensive locomotive paint shop to a repair shop for Hampden bombers. We had an excellent team – William Good, the talented Plant and Machinery Assistant, and Frank Hunt, the pattern and joiners' shop Chief Foreman, together with Ray Hitchings, a production planning enthusiast, and Ellis Brown, the Works Inspection Assistant. There were others too, some of whom I recruited from outside the railway service. At this time, with a high proportion of the works staff working long hours and with strict food rationing, there was a real need for adequate canteen facilities. Accordingly, I took the initiative to convert three large messrooms into a large modern canteen to accommodate over 1000 men at one sitting. The conversion resulted in a very presentable and well-equipped building with a good stage; over the years it has proved an excellent venue for both local and national events.

In 1941 I had to pay a visit with a colleague to the Air Ministry which was temporarily evacuated to Balliol College, Oxford. We had to stay overnight to be in time for an early morning meeting to discuss our aircraft contracts. My colleague was booked in at The Cock Hotel in Watling Street, Stony Stratford, Buckinghamshire, and I was booked in at The Bull Hotel, which was next door. Both are famous old coaching inns and were used for changing horses. We learned that in those earlier days some of the travellers would prefer to stay at The Cock and others at The Bull. They would each pick up hair-raising stories from the local inhabitants and when the travellers got together again to resume their journey they found that their versions were usually widely different, hence the origin of the well-known expression 'It's a cock and bull story'.

The last steam locomotive to be built in the Derby Locomotive Works was No. 73154, the last

Fig. 8.6   The dining hall, Derby Locomotive Works, created by the author from three nineteenth-century mess rooms and providing seating for 1000 employees, the largest canteen on British Railways. It also combined a stage and dressing rooms. It is shown during a lunch hour in the early 1940s

of an order of thirty BR Standard Class 5 4–6–0 locomotives. It left the works in June 1957 and like the rest of this batch was fitted with the relatively expensive Caprotti valve gear. I had left Derby the year before and was no longer directly involved in the LMS locomotive works. It is an interesting fact that, since the first new steam locomotive was built in Derby in 1851, the total number built fell just short of 3000. When new locomotives were to be constructed we normally planned for the completion of one a week and, in some circumstances, three a fortnight, to be completed. In the two World Wars this particular activity was re-directed to Government work of many types and represented about 30 per cent of the total workload.

As well as new locomotives the Derby works supplied boilers and cylinders to the NCC at Belfast, to the S and DJR at Highbridge and to the M and G NJR at Melton Constable.

In June 1942 I left the works which had occupied such a prominent place in my life to become Staff Assistant to the LMS CM and EE at his headquarters in Derby. With my transfer to the headquarters' office my total service of twenty-eight years in the Derby Locomotive Works came to an end. It was true that I would continue to have a considerable interest in the works, but direct control of any of the staff and activities undertaken would in future be the responsibility of others. I was very conscious of the fact that I was leaving a splendid management team and hundreds of friends and colleagues, from the humblest labourer to the senior assistants and workshop supervisors, who had given me their full support. There was Herbert W. Mear, always reliable and one who never failed to make a worthwhile contribution, especially when I set up the new production planning organization. It was fitting that on his retirement in 1972 he occupied the key position of Works Manager at Swindon Works. There were Gilbert F. Parker, Special Investigator, Reginald M. Meads, Estimating Assistant, Walter F. Pope, Planning Engineer, J. H. Kelk, another Planning Engineer, and Walter Orme, Jig and Tool Drawing Office Assistant, and their supporting staffs. I remember them and many more with affection. Although we were in the throes of the Second World War, it did not prevent these colleagues putting their heads together and kindly presenting me with useful parting gifts. I still retain them all, including an oak aneroid barometer, suitably engraved and dated June 1942, from the Foremen's Association.

CHAPTER 9

THE LMS RAILWAY CHIEF MECHANICAL AND ELECTRICAL ENGINEER'S HEADQUARTERS

In September 1939, at the beginning of the Second World War, the Headquarters organization of the CM and EE of the LMS Railway was transferred from its London offices at Euston, to Derby. Here the CM and EE and his principal assistants controlled the activities of nine main works and forty-two subsidiary works where the locomotives and rolling stock were built and maintained, as well as the design, erection and maintenance of cranes, turntables, water supplies, lifts, coaling plants, and the lighting of works, stations, goods depots and offices, and many other ancillaries, including the electrified lines of the Company and electricity generating stations.

Following nationalization in January 1948 the Derby headquarters became the CM and EE headquarters of the London Midland Region of British Railways. Until then the department had been the largest technical department of the four main line railway companies operating in the British Isles.

The following figures, showing the total number of locomotives, rolling stock and other major items of plant and equipment on the LMS in 1939, will give some idea of the large volume of work which was undertaken at that time by the CM and EE's department.

Locomotives	7800
Carriages	22 700
Wagons	306 700
Road vehicles	16 000
Containers	10 000
Cranes	7500
Hoists and lifts	600
Mechanical coaling plants	80
Stationary boilers	1700
Appliances for providing water for locomotives	3000
Electrified track	325 miles

Such a diversity of work, involving the employment of over 40 000 staff, called for a high proportion of skilled craftsmen to be employed in the workshops, and involved the employment of more than 700 apprentices each year in order to meet requirements.

In 1942 Charles E. Fairburn was the Acting CM and EE of the LMS in the absence of Sir William Stanier, FRS, who was on a Government assignment as an adviser to the Ministry of Production. Sir William retired in 1944 and Charles Fairburn succeeded him. He was a first-class administrator, a brilliant mathematician and a tireless worker. We had met several times during his fairly frequent visits to the Derby locomotive works and at his request I had been to his headquarters office in Derby in my capacity as Assistant Works Superintendent to discuss our proposed layout for the repair of Hampden bombers. Early in 1942, in the middle of the Second World War, he wanted to learn more about the system of production planning which I had introduced in the Derby locomotive works, and which was applied to the manufacture of all new products. He came to the works to discuss the organization with me and met the senior staff engaged in it. He was obviously impressed with the system, and a month or so later he sent for me and said he wanted me to introduce a similar system in each of the other large main works of the LMS. For this purpose he proposed to transfer me to Departmental Headquarters at Derby as a senior assistant reporting directly to him. I moved to Headquarters in 1942 and was designated Staff Assistant to the CM and EE and was given a fairly open remit to introduce any new organization which commended itself to me. I was also requested to take over the manufacturing costs organization at HQ, through which new work was allocated to the various locomotive and carriage and wagon works on a cost basis. I also became the first chairman of the newly formed CM and EE sub-committee to deal with policy making on a wide scale throughout each of the four main line railway companies. This committee soon became accepted as essential for dealing satisfactorily with national agreements covering professional and technical staff as well as all railway shopmen, for the entire railway system of the country. Apart from myself as chairman and A. E. Record, my assistant, there was a senior representative from each of the other three main line companies. Almost invariably the committee's recommendations were accepted by the top railway management and were presented to the staff representatives within the framework of the negotiating machinery. Quite regularly I attended the negotiations along with the chief Labour and Establishment officers of the four main line companies in order to give technical advice.

As Staff Assistant I was blessed with a completely loyal team, an essential ingredient for success in any sphere. A. E. Record had a lifetime's experience in this field and his capacity for work was enormous. Indeed, throughout all my years at Derby Headquarters I had a very

competent and willing staff. My secretary, Kathleen Gamble, was originally a typist who had become a member of my staff in the locomotive works directly from school and who had been transferred to HQ some two years before I had myself moved. She could take minutes at a meeting and produce them in next to no time. Small in stature, she was at all times extremely competent. When in 1954 I became Assistant M and EE of the LM Region she remained with me and continued as my secretary for a total of 14 years, until 1956, when I left Derby to go to the British Transport Commission Headquarters in London. She subsequently gave excellent service at the CM and EE Departmental headquarters in Derby as an administrative officer, and was one of the few women I know who qualified for first class travel. George Podmore (the perfect Podmore!) and George Dean, in turn my personal clerical officers, were attentive and loyal to an outstanding degree.

For the greater part of my first post at Derby Headquarters, my chief was H. G. Ivatt, who had succeeded C. E. Fairburn on the latter's untimely death in 1945. H. G. Ivatt was a most friendly man by nature and, unlike most senior executives, never in a hurry. He gave me unstinting support

Fig. 9.1   LMS 1600 hp diesel-electric locomotive built at Derby Locomotive Works. This was the first main line diesel locomotive to run in England, the inaugural run being from Derby to London on 16 December 1947. The photograph shows the locomotive heading the Bournemouth Belle out of Southampton

TABLE 9.1   TYPICAL CONSTRUCTION COSTS FOR LOCOMOTIVES BUILT IN LMR WORKSHOPS

Type	Programme	No. built	Works	Dates into traffic		Average construction cost per locomotive	Notes
				First loco	Last loco		
Ex LMS Railway designs						£	
4–6–2 'Coronation' – Roller bearing	1946	2	Crewe	Dec. 1947	May 1948	20 810	
4–6–0 Cl. 5 M.T.Tdr – Standard	1949	10	Crewe	May 1949	July 1949	11 363	£164 for electric light on one engine (extra)
Skefko bearings on driving coupled axle	1949	10	Horwich	Dec. 1949	Apr. 1950	13 792	
Timken bearings on driving coupled axle	1949	10	Horwich	Aug. 1950	Dec. 1950	14 054	£1328 extra on each of 2 locos for coal weighing ap.
Skefko bearings on all axles	1949	8	Horwich	May 1950	Aug. 1950	15 281	
Skefko bearings on all axles and Caprotti gear	1949	2	Horwich	Apr. 1951	May 1951	19 435	
2–6–0 Cl. 4 M.T.Tdr	1949	10	Horwich	July 1949	Nov. 1949	11 847	
2–6–0 Cl. 2 M.T.Tdr	1950	15	Crewe	Apr. 1950	June 1950	8930	
2–6–4 Cl. 4 M.T.Tk	1950	16	Derby	Sep. 1950	Dec. 1950	11 058	
2–6–2 Cl. 2 M.T.Tk	1950	20	Crewe	Sep. 1950	Dec. 1950	8415	
0–6–6–0 Main line diesel electric		2	Derby	Dec. 1947	July 1948	78 265	
0–6–0 Diesel electric shunter	1949	10	Derby	Nov. 1949	Mar. 1950	15 812	
0–6–0 Diesel electric shunter	1950	19	Derby	July 1950	Dec. 1950	16 425	
2–6–2 Cl. 2 M.T.Tk [Nos 41290–319]	1951	30	Crewe	Sep. 1951	June 1952	9570	
[Nos 41320–329]	1951	10	Derby	Jan. 1952	May 1952	11 450	Fitted V.C.R.
2–6–0 Cl. 4 M.T.Tdr [Nos 43112–26–28–36]	1951	24	Horwich	Mar. 1951	Jan. 1952	13 316	Monitor injectors
[Nos 43127]	1951	1	Horwich	Oct. 1951	—	13 805	Monitor injectors Poultney rev. gear
0–6–0 (350 hp) Diesel electric shunter [Nos 12088–93]	1951	6	Derby	June 1951	Aug. 1951	16 734	Power unit £11 858 Chassis £2051
0–6–0 (350 hp) Diesel electric shunter [Nos 12094–102]	1951	9	Derby	Sep. 1951	June 1952	18 927	Power unit £14 051 Chassis £2051
			Engines and power equipment by Fell Development Ltd			47 500	Four Davey Paxman engines 510 hp
4–8–4 Diesel mechanical [Fell]		1	Derby	Jan. 1952	—	32 697	Rly ex portion only. Also excludes final paint cost
BR Standard designs							
4–6–2 Cl. 7 M.T.Tdr [Nos 70000–14]	1951	15	Crewe	Jan. 1951	Oct. 1951	18 651	Timken bearing (E and Tdr)
[Nos 70015–24]	1951	10	Crewe	June 1951	Oct. 1951	18 774	Timken bearing (E and Tdr) Also A.T.C.
4–6–2 Cl. 6 M.T.Tdr [Nos 72000–9]	1951	10	Crewe	Dec. 1951	Mar. 1952	19 044	
4–6–0 Cl. 5 M.T.Tdr [Nos 73000–29]	1951	30	Derby	Apr. 1951	Jan. 1952	a) 16 618 b) 16 632	The cost given under (b) embraces the modified Lubrication arrgts on eng. nos 73018–29 inc.
4–6–2 Cl. 7 M.T.Tdr [Nos 70025–29]	1952	5	Crewe	Sep. 1952	Nov. 1952	21 363	Timken bearings (E and Tdr) also A.T.C.

Table 9.1 (contd.)

Type	Programme	No. built	Works	Dates in traffic		Average construction cost per locomotive	Notes
				First loco	Last loco		
[Nos 70030–34]	1952	5	Crewe	Nov. 1952	Dec. 1952	21 208	Timken bearings (E and Tdr)
[Nos 70035–39]	1952	5	Crewe	Dec. 1952	Feb. 1953	21 060	Timken bearings (bogie, Pony truck & driving wheels Tender: All wheels)
[Nos 70040–42]	1952	3	Crewe	Mar. 1953	Apr 1953	20 976	Timken bearings – bogie & tender only
[Nos 70043–44]	1952	2	Crewe	June 1953	June 1953	20 975	Timken bearings – bogie & tender only. Also Westinghouse brake equip.
2–6–4 Cl. 4 M.T.Tk [Nos 80000–9]	1951	10	Derby	Sep. 1952	Dec. 1952	14 643	
2–6–2 Cl. 2 M.T.Tk [Nos 84000–19]	1952	20	Crewe	July 1953	Oct. 1953	12 246	
4–6–0 Cl. 5 M.T.Tdr [Nos 73030–49]	1952	20	Derby	June 1953	Dec. 1953	18 966	Timken bearings throughout Mileage indicators
2–6–0 Cl. 4 M.T.Tdr [Nos 76000–5]	1952	6	Horwich	Dec. 1952	Dec. 1952	16 892	
[Nos 76006–19]	1952	14	Horwich	Jan. 1953	July 1953	16 984	Speedometer gear
4–6–2 Cl. 7 M.T.Tdr [Nos 70045–49]	1953	5	Crewe	June 1954	July 1954	23 192	Roller bearings on bogie and tdr; speed ind.
[Nos 70050–54]	1953	5	Crewe	Aug. 1954	Sep. 1954	23 733	Roller bearings throughout Speed indicators
4–6–2 Cl. 8 Pass. Tdr [No. 71000]	1953	1	Crewe	May 1954	—	33 919	Roller bearings throughout Double chimney Speed indicators
2–10–0 Cl. 9 F.Tdr [Nos 92000–7]	1953	8	Crewe	Jan. 1954	Feb. 1954	22 352	Roller bearings on tender
[Nos 92008–9]	1953	2	Crewe	Mar. 1954	Mar. 1954	22 263	Roller bearings on tender
[Nos 92010–14]	1953	5	Crewe	Apr. 1954	May 1954	22 213	Roller bearings on tender
[Nos 92015–19]	1953	5	Crewe	Sep. 1954	Oct. 1954	22 071	Roller bearings on tender
[Nos 92030–49]	1954	20	Crewe	Nov. 1954	Mar. 1955	21 671	Roller bearings on tender
[Nos 92020–29]	1953	10	Crewe	May 1955	July 1955	23 853	Roller bearings on tender and fitted with Franco Crosti boiler These costs do not include the amount authorised in respect of royalty
7–6–0 Cl. 5 M.T.Tdr [Nos 73050–52]	1953	3	Derby	April 1954	May 1954	19 508	Roller bearings throughout
[Nos 73053–54] [Nos 73065–74]	1953	12	Derby	June 1954	Dec. 1954	20 034	Roller bearings throughout
[Nos 73055–64]	1953	10	Derby	June 1954	Oct. 1954	19 840	Roller bearings throughout
2–6–4 Cl. 4 M.T.Tk [Nos 80054–58]	1952	5	Derby	Dec. 1954	Jan. 1955	16 761	

Type	Programme	No. built	Works	Dates in traffic		Average construction cost per locomotive	Power unit £	Chassis £
0–6–0 350 hp Diesel shunter [Nos 13000–24]	1952	25	Derby	Oct. 1952	Mar. 1953	21 330	15 339	2685
[Nos 13025–59]	1953	35	Derby	Oct. 1953	Aug. 1954	21 607	14 749	3473
[Nos 13092–101]	1954	10	Derby	Nov. 1954	Feb. 1955	21 544	15 213	2902
[Nos 13082–91] } [Nos 13102–116] }	1954	25	Derby	Oct. 1954	April 1955	21 744	15 213	3052

This information has been extracted from the author's personal records.

in any scheme I wished to develop. There was mutual respect between us and together we made many works visits, attended meetings together, and occasionally visited each other's homes. If we were both in London we sometimes managed to enjoy a social evening together. Our long association is something I shall always treasure. H. G. Ivatt, in conjunction with the English Electric Company, was the pioneer in introducing the first main line diesel-electric locomotive on British Rail. This was No. 10000, built at Derby in 1947, to be followed by her twin, No. 10001, in 1948. When the former made her first trip to London on 16 December, 1947, I had the pleasure of accompanying H. G. Ivatt who invited me to go with him on the footplate; this was quite an occasion. I remember saying to him that the locomotive cab was so comfortable that the biggest job for the driver would be staying awake.

When the time came for H. G. Ivatt to retire, he was invited to become a Director of the Brush Diesel Group which at that time was pioneering diesel-electric locomotives at Loughborough. The diesel engine units were built by Mirrlees Bickerton at Cheadle Hulme, the electrical control equipment was supplied by Brush, and the vehicle portions of the locomotives were built by Bagnalls of Stafford. H. G. Ivatt asked me to accompany him to each of the three companies to see jointly what we thought about the proposal, especially in the light of his having controlled one of the largest engineering concerns in the country. We went and I told him he could not go wrong in accepting the directorship. After all it was a relatively small commitment compared with his railway job, and with his home at Melbourne, near Derby, he was conveniently situated for Loughborough. H. G. Ivatt retired on 5 June, 1951. He was the last of the pre-nationalization CM and EEs in this country. My colleagues, Roland Bond and Stewart Cox, as well as other writers, have done no less than justice to his distinguished career. He was a Director of the Brush Group for several years and for a period agreed to serve as General Manager. There is no doubt that his vast experience proved invaluable to the Company.

J. F. (Freddie) Harrison succeeded H. G. Ivatt. He had previously held the equivalent position on the E and NE Regions of British Railways and before nationalization was a senior assistant to Sir Nigel Gresley, another distinguished name in the locomotive world. It was during J. F. Harrison's time at Derby as CM and EE that I

Fig. 9.2 The erecting shop, Crewe Locomotive Works

Fig. 9.3 Contrasting products of Crewe Locomotive Works: Britannia, *first of the BR Class 7 Pacifics, built in 1951, alongside* Cornwall, *built in 1847*

became Assistant M and EE of the LM Region. In this capacity I was his deputy and I took a lively interest in all activities of the department. We quickly developed a very satisfactory working relationship. The HQ Locomotive Office took up much of my time in dealing with the Locomotive Shopping Bureau as well as boiler inspection, and breaking-up programmes, and on behalf of the Chief I approved schemes for the installation of new plant and equipment in each of the main locomotive works of the LMR. These were strenuous but happy days and my work became intimately connected with the 1954 modernization and re-equipment plan of British Railways.

The British Railways' programme as it stood at that time provided for the introduction of multiple-unit diesel trains in six areas, namely:

West Riding of Yorkshire, North Eastern Region: eight two-car units
West Cumberland, London Midland Region: thirteen two-car units

Lincolnshire, Eastern Region: thirteen two-car units
East Anglia, Eastern Region: fourteen two-car units
Newcastle–Middlesbrough, North Eastern Region
Edinburgh–Glasgow, Scottish Region.

It was planned that lightweight diesel units would operate partly as substitutes for existing steam services, and partly in addition to them. Except in the case of the proposed Edinburgh–Glasgow route, where the design would conform to the requirements of a longer distance inter-city service and would include additional amenities such as a buffet, the basis of the new type of service would be a two-car unit, one vehicle powered by two road omnibus-type horizontal engines, of at least 125 hp, under the floor, and the other a trailer or another railcar as required.

Each two-car unit could be driven from either end and could be operated either as a self-contained unit or alternatively could be fitted into multiple-unit trains of four, six or eight vehicles according to traffic requirements.

Whilst I was serving in this post, a number of important policy-making committees, covering the whole of BR, were set up. The direction came from Robert A. Riddles, CBE, a former Vice-President of the LMS who, on nationalization, became the member of the Railway Executive for mechanical, electrical and road motor engineering at Headquarters in Marylebone.

Throughout my total of fourteen years in the Derby Headquarters office of the CM and EE of the former LMS Railway and, later, the LM Region of British Railways, I was chairman of many of the all-region policy committees affecting the whole of British Railways. Each committee was differently constituted according to the problem to be resolved. I don't know of any colleague who chaired so many policy committees. Fortunately the committee work never troubled me and I usually managed to retain close contact with my staff and everyday responsibilities.

I recall in particular the two important Locomotive Works and Carriage and Wagon Works Organization Committees, the All-Region Productive Efficiency Committee (a full-time Committee for over a year except for myself as chairman), the BR Foundry Re-organization Committee, the BR Piecework Committee, the BR Diesel Spare Parts Committee and the BR Special Joint Committee on the maintenance of diesel and electric locomotives in motive power depots and electric car repair depots, R. A. Riddles had appointed Roland C. Bond as his Principal Officer for locomotive engineering and Ernest Pugson as his Principal Officer for carriage and wagon engineering. A similar organization was carried through to each of the six newly-formed Regions of British Railways with the titles of CM and EE and Carriage and Wagon Engineer, respectively.

The Locomotive Works Organization Committee was formed almost immediately after nationalization and for this reason it was constituted on a main line group basis. The Carriage and Wagon Works Organization Committee was formed the following year. The terms of reference were the same for both Committees, each of which I chaired, with the competent Gilbert F. Parker as secretary. The Regions each nominated their own representatives and it is of interest to record who they were:

Locomotive Works
Organization Committee (1948)

W. A. Smyth, HQ Production Engineer, E and NE Regions.

P. H. J. Woolfrey, Assistant Works Manager, Swindon Works, Western Region.

W. Marsh, Assistant to O. V. Bulleid, Brighton HQ, Southern Region.

Carriage and Wagon Works
Organization Committee (1949)

A. E. Robson, OBE, Carriage and Wagon Engineer, E and NE Regions. (At retirement in 1973 he was Managing Director of British Rail Engineering Ltd.)

E. R. Parsons, Works Manager, Cowlairs Carriage and Wagon Works, Scottish Region.

F. B. Illston, Works Manager, Lancing Carriage Works, Southern Region. (At retirement Carriage and Wagon Engineer, Southern Region.)

H. G. Johnson, Works Manager, Swindon Carriage and Wagon Works, Western Region.

Besides being Chairman I served on each Organization Committee as the LM representative. Between us we produced two valuable reports which became the basis for considerable reorganization.

The informative pie diagrams in Figure 9.4 show at a glance, and by way of an example, the expenditure incurred in carrying out various activities in the works of the Southern Region. The areas of the circles and segments are proportional to the costs and in this example the large circle can be assumed to represent a total expenditure of about £10 million. This type of information was required before one could formulate plans for effecting changes, assuming it was thought desirable to do so. I was a great advocate of pie diagrams as they are extremely simple to understand and can be very revealing.

By 1951, only three years after nationalization, the dynamic R. A. Riddles, member of the Railway Executive for mechanical, electrical and road motor engineering, had his plans well advanced for the building of ten new designs of steam locomotives to cover all passenger and freight services of BR. In that same year the first of the new locomotives began to appear but as events will show the Modernization and Re-equipment Plan of BR overtook the building of the steam engines envisaged. But this was not until a total of 999 of the new design of locomotives had been turned out of the shops.

The Foundry Reorganization Committee was set up in 1953. The following Remit, dated 21 April 1953, was received from R. A. Riddles:

> Now that we have experience of the output and the cost of chairs, baseplates and brake blocks produced in the mechanised foundry at Horwich, it has been decided to reconstitute the Committee set up some time ago to consider the productive capacity existing in our Foundries in relation to requirements and to examine what possibilities for further economies exist.
>
> I should like Mr Larkin to represent mé on this Committee and to act as chairman thereof. Other members of this Committee will be as follows:
> Representing General Sir Daril G. Watson, Member of the Railway Executive for Stores and General Services –
> Mr A. W. Pitman, Assistant (Steel Section)
> Representing Mr J. C. L. Train, Member of the Railway Executive for Civil and Signal and Telecommunications engineering –
> Mr D. A. S. Conran, Assistant (Development)
> Representing Mr V. Radford, Chief Financial Officer to the Railway Executive –

> Mr J. H. Conway, Assistant to Accountant (M and E and C and W HQ Accounts), London Midland Region.
> Considerable importance is attached to the work this Committee is asked to undertake, and I shall be obliged if you will arrange for Mr Larkin to take the matter in hand as soon as possible.

The earlier Committee to which reference was made in the Remit was set up shortly after nationalization in 1948, but that Committee did not reach the stage of producing a report.

At the outset of this enquiry, R. C. Bond, Chief Officer for Locomotive Construction and Maintenance, requested the Chairman to give a liberal interpretation to the Remit: to regard it as an instrument to set the Committee in being and to include in the Report any feature which was considered relevant to meeting the requirements of iron castings for all Regions of British Railways in the most economical manner.

The enquiries carried out by the Committee made it possible, for the first time on British Railways, for the total requirements of iron castings as well as the internal iron foundry potential to be obtained. Briefly, the Report set out:

(1) the total requirements of all Regions of British Railways,
(2) the total output of the foundries of British Railways,
(3) the costs of manufacture in railway foundries,
(4) the foundry staff employed in railway foundries,
(5) the volume of orders placed on the foundry trade, and trade prices,
(6) the main features of the foundries of British Railways,

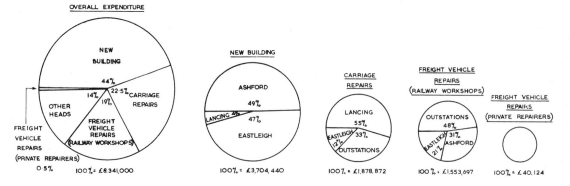

Fig. 9.4 Expenditure incurred on Southern Region of BR in the building and maintenance of rolling stock in 1954 (Report of the BR Carriage and Wagon Reorganization Committee)

(7) suitable layouts for continuous casting plants,

(8) the future policy recommended to give additional foundry capacity.

The difficulty in recruiting skilled foundry labour was a common problem for many years in the engineering industry, and there was a constant endeavour to change the method of manufacture so that it would be possible to use semi-skilled instead of skilled labour. An important feature of a mechanized foundry was that almost the entire productive staff could be recruited from men with no previous foundry experience. Admittedly the tempo of a mechanized foundry is high and calls for fairly laborious work but, as the positioning of the work is such that the operators can work in an upright position, it makes the work far more pleasant and much less strenuous than floor moulding as carried out in a general foundry. Of course quantities of repetitive castings have to be high in order to justify the cost of installing the equipment for a mechanized foundry.

Fig. 9.6 clearly illustrates the relative outputs of the various British Railways foundries in 1953. Since those days British Railways has carried out its fair share of foundry re-organization and mechanization and some impressive layouts for repetitive work have been introduced. Concurrently with this development and rationalization much foundry work was superseded by fabrication using various highly developed types of welding. As in British Railways, the foundry trade which continues to practise floor moulding and uses hand tools for relatively small quantities of castings, and where skilled moulders and coremakers are still needed, is now only a shadow of what it used to be. It is reasonable that, as in many other situations, the picture in 1978 provides a striking contrast.

The All-Region Productive Efficiency Committee to which I have referred was constituted as follows:

Chairman:

E. J. Larkin, Assistant Mechanical and Electrical

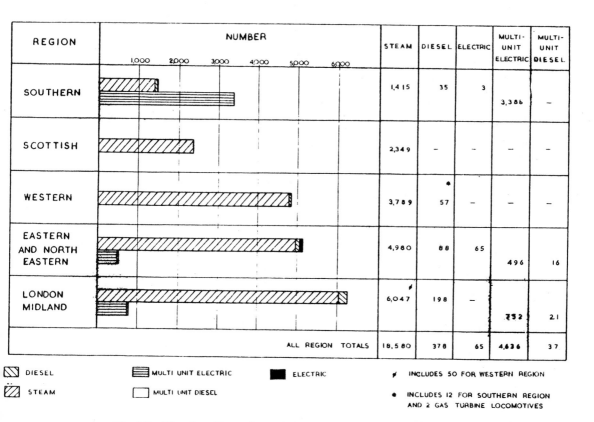

REGION	NUMBER	STEAM	DIESEL	ELECTRIC	MULTI-UNIT ELECTRIC	MULTI-UNIT DIESEL
SOUTHERN		1,415	35	3	3,386	–
SCOTTISH		2,349	–	–	–	–
WESTERN		3,789	57	–	–	–
EASTERN AND NORTH EASTERN		4,980	88	65	496	16
LONDON MIDLAND		6,047	198	–	752	21
ALL REGION TOTALS		18,580	378	65	4,636	37

DIESEL   MULTI UNIT ELECTRIC   ELECTRIC   ♪ INCLUDES 50 FOR WESTERN REGION

STEAM   MULTI UNIT DIESEL   ♣ INCLUDES 12 FOR SOUTHERN REGION AND 2 GAS TURBINE LOCOMOTIVES

Fig. 9.5   *Allocation of locomotives and other motive power stock to regions in 1954*

Engineer, London Midland Region, Derby

E and NE Regions:
C. F. Rose (Deputy Chairman), formerly Acting Works Manager, Locomotive Works, Doncaster

LM Region:
M. A. Henstock, Assistant Works Manager, Locomotive Works, Derby

Scottish Region:
G. Guthrie, Works Manager, Carriage and Wagon Works, St Rollox

Southern Region:
L. I. Sanders, Works Manager, Carriage and Wagon Works, Ashford

Western Region:
R. H. N. Bryant, Works Manager, Locomotive Works, Wolverhampton

Accountants' Representative:
(Part-time, with the approval of the General Managers, to co-ordinate and verify statistical information)
W. Beech, Locomotive and Carriage and Wagon Works Accountant, London Midland Region, Derby

Secretary:
D. W. Baker, Chief Mechanical and Electrical Engineer's Department, London Midland Region, Derby

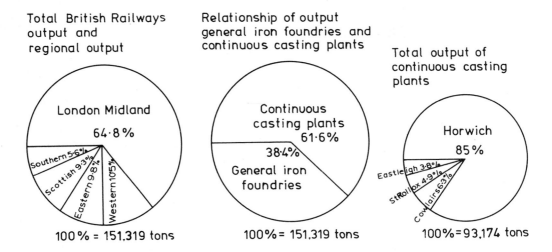

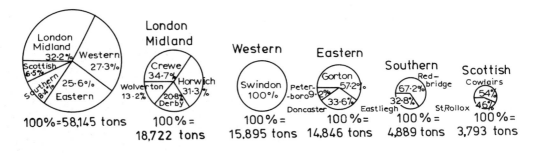

*Fig. 9.6   Pie diagram illustrating the output of BR iron foundries during 1953
(Report of the British Railways Foundry Reorganization Committee)*

The Committee's Remit, dated 27 July 1954, was an extremely wide one. It read as follows:

In pursuance of the general drive for increased productive efficiency, it has been decided to supplement the Regional departmental investigations so far as the Mechanical and Electrical and Carriage and Wagon Engineering Departments are concerned by the appointment of a special visiting Committee under the chairmanship of Mr E. J. Larkin, Assistant Mechanical and Electrical Engineer, London Midland Region, to:

'review, on broad lines, the existing departmental organisation, works and district organisation down to shop or outstation supervisory level, workshop practices and workshop processes and advise the Chief Regional Managers and Regional departmental officers on matters which might repay special investigation with a view to greater efficiency and economy.'

It is desired that the Committee should confine its activities to the steps which can be taken within the framework of the existing agreements on the matters referred to above. Action falling within the scope of domestic workshop management will be left to the Regions under their own special 'productivity' arrangements, and matters such as changes in allocation of work among the Regions will continue to be dealt with by the appropriate Departmental Committees, and should be regarded as outside the scope of the remit.

With the exception of the Chairman, the Committee will operate on a full-time basis and visit each of the Regions in turn in the following order:

Scottish Region
Southern Region
Western Region
Eastern and North Eastern Regions
London Midland Region

The Committee will comprise the Chairman, who will direct the policy of the Committee and make such visits and hold such meetings as he considers necessary, and one representative from each Region. One of these representatives will act as Deputy Chairman for the purpose of co-ordinating the detailed investigations to be carried out by the Committee. It is desired that the M and E and C and W Engineer of each Region should agree mutually as to who should represent their Region on the Committee. The Committee will address their reports, on matters affecting one Region only, to the Departmental Officers concerned, sending a copy at the same time to the Chief Regional Manager. Reports on matters affecting more than one Region, or of general application, will be sent to all Departmental Officers concerned, with copies to the appropriate Chief Regional Managers.

In my capacity as Chairman I was subsequently informed by J. W. Watkins, General Manager, London Midland Region, and R. C. Bond, Principal Officer for Locomotive Engineering, British Railways, that it was particularly desired that the Committee should interpret the Remit widely and should pursue in the two Departments concerned any line of enquiry which it was considered might ultimately lead to economy or increased efficiency. All the main works had to be investigated, and it took about eighteen months for this Committee to produce two reports for each Region, as well as two all-Region reports.

Another Policy Committee was first set up under the chairmanship of my colleague, M. S. Hatchell, my immediate predecessor at CM and EE HQ, Derby, to report on the manufacture, distribution and holding in stock of spare parts for BR Standard Locomotives, including diesel traction. In view of his appointment as Mechanical and Electrical Engineer, Scottish Region, in 1952, I was asked to take over as chairman of the Committee. The Railway Executive had already planned to build twelve types of BR Standard locomotives, including the diesel shunters, which would eventually bring the BR complement to some 19 000 locomotives. Design work for these new standard BR types of train had begun in 1949, the year following nationalization. Tangible progress was being made with the report when the British Railways Modernization and Re-equipment Plan, dated December 1954, appeared on the scene. The Commission proposed to build no new passenger or suburban steam locomotives after the completion of the 1956 programme and to terminate the building of all new steam locomotives within a few years. Accordingly we found it necessary to review the entire situation and virtually start our thinking all over again.

The work of the BR Special Joint Committee, one of my last major assignments before transferring to the British Transport Commission in London was of great importance. The Committee had to decide the allocation of repair work, as between the main works, the motive power depots, and the electrical car repair depots. The Committee was constituted as follows:

E. J. Larkin, Assistant Mechanical and Electrical Engineer, London Midland Region, Derby (Chairman).

A. H. Emerson, Assistant Electrical Engineer (Modernization), London Midland Region. (Later Chief Mechanical and Electrical Engineer, LM Region.)

B. Adkinson, Assistant Motive Power Superintendent, London Midland Region, Euston.

T. C. B. Miller, Assistant Motive Power Superintendent, Eastern Region, Liverpool Street. (Later Chief Mechanical and Electrical Engineer, British Railways Board, HQ.)

J. S. Scott, Locomotive Works Manager, Eastern and North Eastern Regions, Gorton, Manchester. (Later Chief Works Manager, Swindon Works.)

There was a considerable amount of effort involved in sorting out the lines of demarcation. It had its reward because the Committee was one whose recommendations were accepted in full.

The last Policy Committee of which I was Chairman was the BR Diesel Spare Parts Committee. In our terms of reference we were required to review the stock of spare parts needed for diesel locomotives and diesel railcar engines. A great deal of money was involved and it was essential to keep the stock at a minimum, consistent with avoiding unnecessary delay on units undergoing repairs in a main works or keeping a motive power unit out of service at a motive power depot. Almost every important item had to be considered and recommendations made as to how many major items should be purchased from the manufacturers and held at each main works and how many individual components should be kept at the running sheds. No one would describe it as a spectacular investigation, but the need for it in the early days of changing over from steam to diesel traction was paramount. I believe the committee produced a worthwhile document and one which could be modified periodically in the light of experience gained and the number of motive power units in service.

When R. A. Riddles, CBE, retired from British Railways in 1953, he wrote to me in the following terms:

> . . . I have read your reports from time to time and have appreciated, and do appreciate, the great work that you and your committee are doing.
>
> The system of Policy Committees which I set up in the very early days has been of inestimable value in getting things going and raising our department to the level which it has attained. The fact that you, an expert in the particular subjects which you are investigating, are enabled to draw on the experience of all Regions and make a recommendation as to the right policy to adopt, had short-circuited by many months, if not years, the policy of standardization and of using the best practice immediately, rather than adopting one of dictatorship through trial and error.

His biography by Colonel H. C. B. Rogers, entitled *The Last Steam Locomotive Engineer*, records a fascinating and notable career. I am happy to say that I have remained in touch with R. A. Riddles and whenever we meet we are never at a loss to find something interesting to talk about.

During this period, from 1948 to 1955, I served on only one Committee of which I was not chairman. This was the LM Region Diesel Railcar Committee chaired by the genial Edgar Hunt, Assistant Chief Regional Officer of the LM Region. As the representative of the CM and EE I was instrumental in submitting speed-power curves for any part of the LMR where the committee considered that a viable diesel railcar scheme might be introduced. For these I had the able assistance of Eric A. Langridge, a former colleague in the Locomotive Drawing Office who had become Development Assistant to the CM and EE.

This Committee was comprised of the following Assistant Departmental Officers:

E. S. Hunt, Assistant Chief Regional Manager (Chairman)

R. Varley, Assistant to Assistant Chief Regional Manager

B. Adkinson, Assistant Motive Power Superintendent

N. H. R. Dade, Assistant to Chief Accountant

T. Fiske, Assistant (Works and Equipment), Office of Chief Regional Manager

S. A. Fitch, Assistant Operating Superintendent

E. J. Larkin, Assistant Mechanical and Electrical Engineer

H. G. N. Read, Assistant Commercial Superintendent

E. Stanley, Assistant Carriage and Wagon Engineer

C. Lakin, Office of Chief Regional Manager (Secretary)

The first multiple-unit diesel lightweight passenger train to be built at Derby, in the carriage and wagon works, was demonstrated on a trial run from Marylebone to Beaconsfield and back on 29 April, 1954.

Our task was to examine different rail services and ascertain whether the introduction of a railcar service would be a viable investment. Our work as a Committee involved visits to a number of venues in England, Northern Ireland and to Holland. We went to Northern Ireland to see the working of the diesel railcars already running there, and to Holland because the use of railcars throughout the Netherlands was already well established.

In the Netherlands we visited Utrecht, Amsterdam, Arnhem, Nijmegen and Tilburg. The inspection saloon of the President, Ir. F. G. den Hollander, of the Netherlands Railways, was placed at our disposal and there was something to learn at each of our points of call. The railway works at Tilburg were especially interesting and included a thoroughly modern diesel engine test house. It was a rewarding visit lasting three days and we were all impressed with the competence of the Netherlands Railways.

The railways in the Netherlands were a limited liability company with all its shares state-owned. The headquarters were at Utrecht, and the Railways were run as an industrial enterprise on a profit-making basis. With the exception of the war year 1945, there had been no deficit from the operation of the Netherlands Railways since 1941. The year 1945 could not be considered as a normal year as the NR were instructed by the Dutch Government in London to go on strike on 19 September, 1944, and the strike lasted until 5 May, 1945, the year of liberation.

I was much impressed with, amongst other things, the automatic coupling in use in Holland. It was a great time saver whenever it was necessary to lengthen or shorten a train to meet the traffic available. We were being conducted around by Ir. F. G. den Hollander, and I asked him whether he would be prepared to loan us a set of couplings. He agreed at once, but it was six months before we received the set of couplings due to customs formalities. The couplings were fitted to vehicles in the carriage and wagon works at Derby as a mock-up, and after much experimentation, a modified form was designed for use on BR stock.

One of our visits in England took us to see the tramcar maintenance depot at Blackpool and it was here, following our inspection, that the Chairman of the Blackpool Transport Department invited me to drive a tram. I was game for this and with an inspector by my side and the Committee sitting inside the tram we did a journey of about a mile along the Blackpool sea-front. I found the tram very simple to operate compared with my experience of footplate requirements. It was, however, a novel and unexpected interlude. It brings to mind that over the years, I have known railway engineers take up a variety of appointments in diverse fields outside railway service, and I have always recognized that a well-trained railway engineer could turn his hand to any manner of jobs.

During my term of office in the position of Assistant Mechanical and Electrical Engineer of the LMR, I took the opportunity of completing the schemes I had developed for the provision of a Works Training School at each of the LM main works. It was very gratifying to see no fewer than seven of these schools eventually operating, each doing an excellent training job and adding considerable prestige to the LMR even beyond the various localities where the particular works were located. There was no shortage of apprentice applicants and this gave the opportunity for a relatively high level of selection of apprentice trainees.

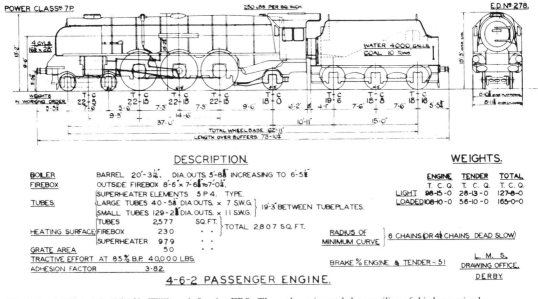

DESCRIPTION.

BOILER   BARREL 20'-3⅞". DIA. OUTS. 5'-8⅜" INCREASING TO 6'-5⅝"
FIREBOX   OUTSIDE FIREBOX 8'-6" × 7'-6⅜" TO 7'-0⅜".
     SUPERHEATER ELEMENTS   5 P 4. TYPE.
TUBES.   LARGE TUBES 40-5⅜ DIA. OUTS. × 7 S.W.G. } 19'-3" BETWEEN TUBE PLATES.
     SMALL TUBES 129-2⅜ DIA. OUTS. × 11 S.W.G. }

HEATING SURFACE		
TUBES	2,577	SQ. FT.
FIREBOX	230	" "
SUPERHEATER	979	" "

TOTAL 2,807 SQ. FT.

GRATE AREA   50
TRACTIVE EFFORT AT 85% B.P.   40,000 LBS.
ADHESION FACTOR   3·82.

RADIUS OF MINIMUM CURVE } 6 CHAINS (OR 4½ CHAINS DEAD SLOW)

BRAKE % ENGINE & TENDER = 51

WEIGHTS.

	ENGINE	TENDER	TOTAL
	T. C. Q.	T. C. Q.	T. C. Q.
LIGHT	98-15-0	28-13-0	127-8-0
LOADED	108-10-0	56-10-0	165-0-0

L. M. S.
DRAWING OFFICE.
DERBY.

4-6-2 PASSENGER ENGINE.

Fig. 9.7 *LMS 4–6–2 6256 Sir William A Stanier FRS. The author witnessed the unveiling of this locomotive by Sir William Stanier at Marylebone Station on 16 December, 1947, having travelled earlier the same day on the footplate of LMS diesel-electric locomotive No. 10000 on its inaugural run from Derby to Marylebone*

PHOTOGRAPHS AND LEADING PARTICULARS OF THE THIRTEEN CLASSES OF BRITISH RAILWAYS STANDARD STEAM LOCOMOTIVES

When the four main line railway companies were nationalized, on 1 January, 1948, the overall responsibility for the design of locomotives and rolling stock was given to R A Riddles, CBE, Member of the newly formed Railway Executive, for Mechanical, Electrical and Road Motor Engineering. Soon after nationalization he set up the Locomotive Standards Committee consisting of the Chief Draughtsmen from the constituent regions, with E S Cox as chairman. The following Standard Locomotive designs are the result of their combined efforts.

Class 9, 2–10–0 freight tender locomotive

Class 9, 2–10–0 Crosti freight tender locomotive

Class 8, 4–6–2 passenger tender locomotive, *Duke of Gloucester*

Class 7, 4–6–2 passenger tender locomotive, *Britannia*

Class 6, 4–6–2 mixed traffic tender locomotive

Class 5, 4–6–0 mixed traffic tender locomotive

Class 4, 4–6–0 mixed traffic tender locomotive

Class 4, 2–6–0 mixed traffic tender locomotive

Class 4, 2–6–4 mixed traffic tank locomotive

Class 3, 2–6–0 mixed traffic tender locomotive

Class 3, 2–6–2 mixed traffic tank locomotive

Class 2, 2–6–0 mixed traffic tender locomotive

Class 2, 2–6–2 mixed traffic tank locomotive

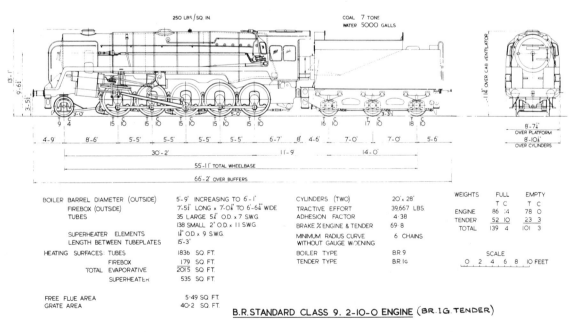

BOILER BARREL DIAMETER (OUTSIDE)   5'-9" INCREASING TO 6'-1"
FIREBOX (OUTSIDE)   7'-5¾" LONG x 7'-0⅛" TO 6'-6¼" WIDE
TUBES   35 LARGE 5¼" O.D. x 7 S.W.G.
   138 SMALL 2" O.D. x 11 S.W.G.
SUPERHEATER ELEMENTS   1¼" O.D. x 9 S.W.G.
LENGTH BETWEEN TUBEPLATES   15'-3"
HEATING SURFACES: TUBES   1836 SQ. FT.
   FIREBOX   179 SQ. FT.
   TOTAL EVAPORATIVE   2015 SQ. FT.
   SUPERHEATER   535 SQ. FT.

FREE FLUE AREA   5·49 SQ. FT.
GRATE AREA   40·2 SQ. FT.

CYLINDERS (TWO)   20" x 28"
TRACTIVE EFFORT   39,667 LBS.
ADHESION FACTOR   4·38
BRAKE % ENGINE & TENDER   69·8
MINIMUM RADIUS CURVE   6 CHAINS
WITHOUT GAUGE WIDENING
BOILER TYPE   B.R. 9
TENDER TYPE   B.R. 1G

WEIGHTS	FULL		EMPTY	
	T	C	T	C
ENGINE	86	14	78	0
TENDER	52	10	23	3
TOTAL	139	4	101	3

SCALE
0 2 4 6 8 10 FEET

B.R. STANDARD CLASS 9. 2-10-0 ENGINE (BR.1G. TENDER)

Fig. 9.8   Class 9, 2–10–0 freight tender locomotive

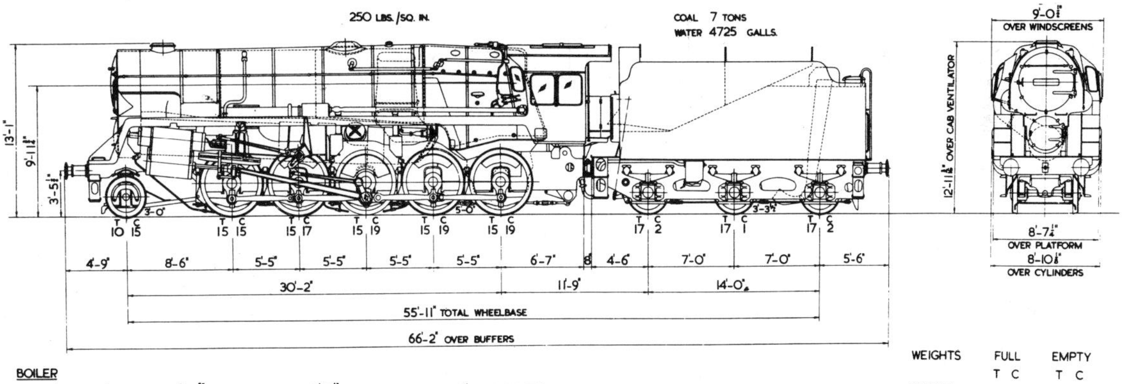

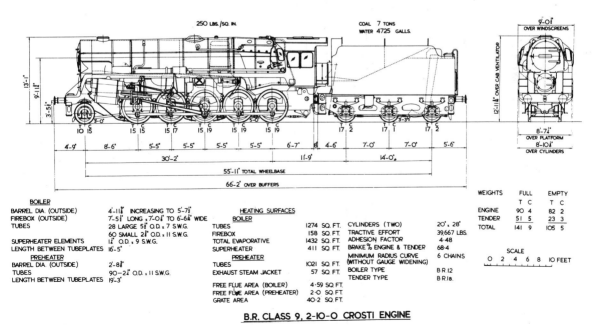

BOILER

BARREL DIA. (OUTSIDE)	4'-11$\frac{5}{8}$" INCREASING TO 5'-7$\frac{1}{2}$"
FIREBOX (OUTSIDE)	7'-5$\frac{1}{2}$" LONG x 7'-0$\frac{1}{8}$" TO 6'-6$\frac{7}{16}$" WIDE
TUBES	28 LARGE 5$\frac{1}{2}$" O.D. x 7 S.W.G.
	60 SMALL 2$\frac{1}{8}$" O.D. x 11 S.W.G.
SUPERHEATER ELEMENTS	1$\frac{1}{4}$" O.D. x 9 S.W.G.
LENGTH BETWEEN TUBEPLATES	16'-5"

PREHEATER

BARREL DIA. (OUTSIDE)	2'-8$\frac{3}{8}$"
TUBES	90–2$\frac{1}{4}$" O.D. x 11 S.W.G.
LENGTH BETWEEN TUBEPLATES	19'-3"

HEATING SURFACES

BOILER

TUBES	1274 SQ. FT.
FIREBOX	158 SQ. FT.
TOTAL EVAPORATIVE	1432 SQ. FT.
SUPERHEATER	411 SQ. FT.

PREHEATER

TUBES	1021 SQ. FT.
EXHAUST STEAM JACKET	57 SQ. FT.
FREE FLUE AREA (BOILER)	4·59 SQ. FT.
FREE FLUE AREA (PREHEATER)	2·0 SQ. FT.
GRATE AREA	40·2 SQ. FT.

CYLINDERS (TWO)	20" x 28"
TRACTIVE EFFORT	39,667 LBS.
ADHESION FACTOR	4·48
BRAKE % ENGINE & TENDER	68·4
MINIMUM RADIUS CURVE (WITHOUT GAUGE WIDENING)	6 CHAINS
BOILER TYPE	B.R.12
TENDER TYPE	B.R.1B.

WEIGHTS	FULL T	FULL C	EMPTY T	EMPTY C
ENGINE	90	4	82	2
TENDER	51	5	23	3
TOTAL	141	9	105	5

SCALE 0 2 4 6 8 10 FEET

B.R. CLASS 9, 2-10-0 CROSTI ENGINE

Fig. 9.9 Class 9, 2–10–0 Crosti freight tender locomotive

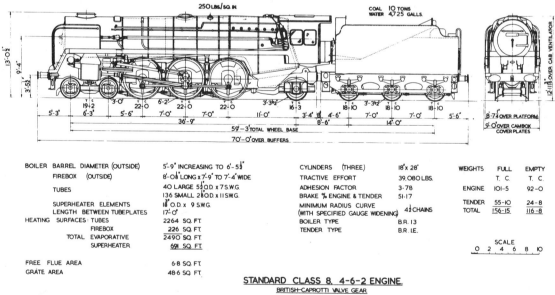

BOILER BARREL DIAMETER (OUTSIDE)	5'-9" INCREASING TO 6'-5½"	CYLINDERS (THREE)	18"x 28"	WEIGHTS	FULL	EMPTY
FIREBOX (OUTSIDE)	8'-0⅛" LONG x 7'-9" TO 7'-4" WIDE	TRACTIVE EFFORT	39,080 LBS.		T. C.	T. C.
TUBES	40 LARGE 5¼"O.D. x 7 S.W.G.	ADHESION FACTOR	3·78	ENGINE	101-5	92-0
	136 SMALL 2⅛"O.D. x 11 S.W.G.	BRAKE % ENGINE & TENDER	51·17			
SUPERHEATER ELEMENTS	1⅜" O.D. x 9 S.W.G.	MINIMUM RADIUS CURVE	4½ CHAINS	TENDER	55-10	24-8
LENGTH BETWEEN TUBEPLATES	17'-0"	(WITH SPECIFIED GAUGE WIDENING)		TOTAL	156-15	116-8
HEATING SURFACES: TUBES	2264 SQ. FT.	BOILER TYPE	B.R. 13			
FIREBOX	226 SQ. FT.	TENDER TYPE	B.R. 1E.			
TOTAL EVAPORATIVE	2490 SQ. FT.					
SUPERHEATER	691 SQ. FT.					
FREE FLUE AREA	6·8 SQ. FT.					
GRATE AREA	48·6 SQ. FT.					

STANDARD CLASS 8. 4-6-2 ENGINE.
BRITISH-CAPROTTI VALVE GEAR.

Fig. 9.10   Class 8, 4–6–2 passenger tender locomotive, Duke of Gloucester

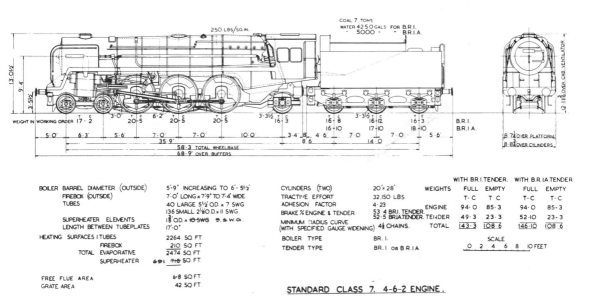

	5'-9" INCREASING TO 6'-5½"
BOILER BARREL DIAMETER (OUTSIDE)	5'-9" INCREASING TO 6'-5½"
FIREBOX (OUTSIDE)	7'-0" LONG x 7'-9" TO 7'-4" WIDE
TUBES	40 LARGE 5½" O.D. x 7 SWG
	136 SMALL 2⅛" O.D. x 11 SWG
SUPERHEATER ELEMENTS	1⅜" O.D. x 10 SWG 9 S.W.G.
LENGTH BETWEEN TUBEPLATES	17'-0"
HEATING SURFACES : TUBES	2264 SQ FT
FIREBOX	210 SQ FT
TOTAL EVAPORATIVE	2474 SQ FT
SUPERHEATER	691 718 SQ FT
FREE FLUE AREA	6·8 SQ FT
GRATE AREA	42 SQ FT

			WITH B.R.I. TENDER.		WITH B.R.I.A TENDER.	
		WEIGHTS	FULL	EMPTY	FULL	EMPTY
CYLINDERS (TWO)	20" x 28"		T·C	T·C	T·C	T·C
TRACTIVE EFFORT	32,150 LBS					
ADHESION FACTOR	4·23	ENGINE	94·0	85·3	94·0	85·3
BRAKE % ENGINE & TENDER	53·4 B.R.I. TENDER.	TENDER	49·3	23·3	52·10	23·3
	52·5 B.R.I.A TENDER.					
MINIMUM RADIUS CURVE (WITH SPECIFIED GAUGE WIDENING)	4¼ CHAINS.	TOTAL	143·3	108·6	146·10	108·6
BOILER TYPE	B.R.I.					
TENDER TYPE	B.R.I OR B.R.I.A					

SCALE
0 2 4 6 8 10 FEET

STANDARD CLASS 7, 4-6-2 ENGINE.

Fig. 9.11   Class 7, 4–6–2 mixed traffic tender locomotive, Britannia

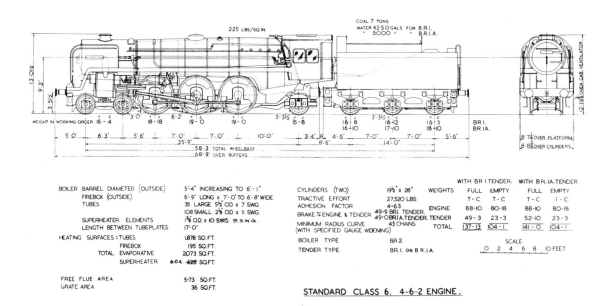

		WITH B.R.I.TENDER.		WITH B.R.I.A.TENDER.	
CYLINDERS (TWO)	19½" x 28"	WEIGHTS	FULL	EMPTY	FULL	EMPTY
TRACTIVE EFFORT	27,520 LBS		T-C	T-C	T-C	T-C
ADHESION FACTOR	4·63					
BRAKE % ENGINE & TENDER	49·9 BRI. TENDER.	ENGINE	88-10	80-18	88-10	80-18
	49·OBRJ.A.TENDER.	TENDER	49-3	23-3	52-10	23-3
MINIMUM RADIUS CURVE	4½ CHAINS	TOTAL	137-13	104-1	141-0	104-1
(WITH SPECIFIED GAUGE WIDENING)						
BOILER TYPE	BR.2.					
TENDER TYPE	B.R.I. OR B R.I.A.					

BOILER BARREL DIAMETER (OUTSIDE)   5'-4" INCREASING TO 6'-1"
FIREBOX (OUTSIDE)   6'-9" LONG x 7'-0" TO 6'-8" WIDE
TUBES   35 LARGE 5½" OD x 7 SWG.
   108 SMALL 2⅛" OD x 11 SWG.
SUPERHEATER ELEMENTS   1⅜" OD x 10 SWG. 9.S.W.G.
LENGTH BETWEEN TUBEPLATES   17'-0"
HEATING SURFACES : TUBES   1,878 SQ.FT.
   FIREBOX   195 SQ.FT.
   TOTAL EVAPORATIVE   2,073 SQ.FT.
   SUPERHEATER   604 625 SQ.FT.
FREE FLUE AREA   5·73 SQ.FT.
GRATE AREA   36 SQ.FT.

SCALE   0 2 4 6 8 10 FEET

STANDARD CLASS 6, 4-6-2 ENGINE.

Fig. 9.12 Class 6, 4–6–2 mixed traffic tender locomotive

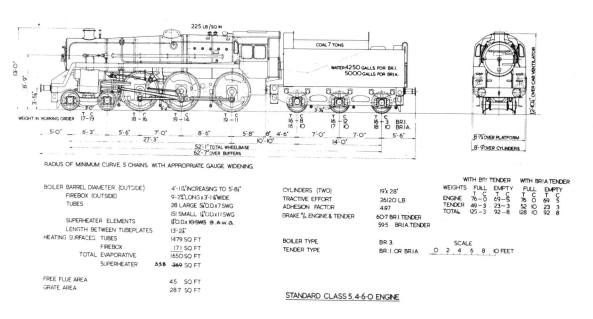

225 LB/SQ IN

COAL 7 TONS

WATER 4250 GALLS FOR BR.I.
5000 GALLS FOR BR.I.A.

13'-0"

8'-9"

3'-5½"

12'-10½" OVER CAB VENTILATOR

WEIGHT IN WORKING ORDER

	T	C		T	C		T	C		T	C		T	C		T	C		T	C		
	17	19		18	16		19	14		19	11		16	8		16	12		16	3	BR.I.
													16	10		17			18	10	BR.I.A.

5'-0"   6'-3"   5'-6"   7'-0"   8'-6"   5'-8" 4'-6"   7'-0"   7'-0"   5'-6"

27'-3"   10'-10"   14'-0"

52'-1" TOTAL WHEELBASE

62'-7" OVER BUFFERS

RADIUS OF MINIMUM CURVE. 5 CHAINS. WITH APPROPRIATE GAUGE WIDENING.

8'-7¼" OVER PLATFORM
8'-9" OVER CYLINDERS

BOILER BARREL DIAMETER (OUTSIDE)	4'-11¼" INCREASING TO 5'-8½"	
FIREBOX (OUTSIDE)	9'-2¼" LONG x 3'-11½" WIDE	
TUBES	28 LARGE 5¼"O.D x 7 SWG	
	151 SMALL 1¾"O.D x 11 SWG	
SUPERHEATER ELEMENTS	1⅛"O.D x 10 SWG 9 S.W.G.	
LENGTH BETWEEN TUBEPLATES	13'-2⅛"	
HEATING SURFACES TUBES	1479 SQ FT	
FIREBOX	171 SQ FT	
TOTAL EVAPORATIVE	1650 SQ FT	
SUPERHEATER	358 369 SQ FT	
FREE FLUE AREA	45 SQ FT	
GRATE AREA	28.7 SQ FT	

CYLINDERS (TWO)	19"x 28"	
TRACTIVE EFFORT	26120 LB	
ADHESION FACTOR	4.97	
BRAKE % ENGINE & TENDER	60.7 BR.I. TENDER	
	59.5 BR.I.A. TENDER	
BOILER TYPE	BR.3.	
TENDER TYPE	BR.I. OR BR.I.A.	

	WITH BR.I TENDER				WITH BR.I.A TENDER			
WEIGHTS	FULL		EMPTY		FULL		EMPTY	
	T	C	T	C	T	C	T	C
ENGINE	76	0	69	5	76	0	69	5
TENDER	49	3	23	3	52	10	23	3
TOTAL	125	3	92	8	128	10	92	8

SCALE
0 2 4 6 8 10 FEET

STANDARD CLASS 5. 4-6-0 ENGINE

Fig. 9.13 Class 5, 4–6–0 mixed traffic tender locomotive

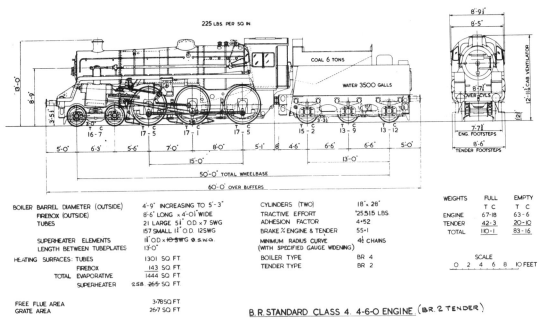

225 LBS. PER SQ. IN.

COAL 6 TONS

WATER 3500 GALLS

8'-9¼"
8'-5"

8'-7½"
OVER CYLS

12'-11¼" CAB VENTILATOR

7'-7½"
ENG. FOOTSTEPS

8'-6"
TENDER FOOTSTEPS

13'-0"

8'-9"

3'-5½"

T C   T C   T C   T C   T C   T C   T C
16-7   17-5   17-1   17-5   15-2   13-9   13-12

5'-0"   6'-3"   5'-6"   7'-0"   8'-0"   5'-1" 8 4'-6"   6'-6"   6'-6"   5'-0"

15'-0"

50'-0" TOTAL WHEELBASE

60'-0" OVER BUFFERS

BOILER BARREL DIAMETER (OUTSIDE)	4'-9" INCREASING TO 5'-3"		CYLINDERS (TWO)	18" x 28"
FIREBOX (OUTSIDE)	8'-6" LONG x 4'-0¾" WIDE		TRACTIVE EFFORT	˙25,515 LBS.
TUBES	21 LARGE 5⅛" O.D. x 7 SWG		ADHESION FACTOR	4·52
	157 SMALL 1⅝" O.D. 12SWG		BRAKE % ENGINE & TENDER	55·1
SUPERHEATER ELEMENTS	1⅛" O.D. x 10 SWG 9 S.W.G.		MINIMUM RADIUS CURVE	4½ CHAINS
LENGTH BETWEEN TUBEPLATES	13'-0"		(WITH SPECIFIED GAUGE WIDENING)	
HEATING SURFACES: TUBES	1301 SQ. FT.		BOILER TYPE	BR 4
FIREBOX	143 SQ. FT.		TENDER TYPE	BR 2
TOTAL EVAPORATIVE	1444 SQ. FT.			
SUPERHEATER	258 265 SQ. FT.			
FREE FLUE AREA	3·78 SQ. FT.			
GRATE AREA	26·7 SQ. FT.			

WEIGHTS	FULL	EMPTY
	T C	T C
ENGINE	67-18	63-6
TENDER	42-3	20-10
TOTAL	110-1	83-16

SCALE
0 2 4 6 8 10 FEET

B.R. STANDARD CLASS 4. 4-6-0 ENGINE. (BR.2 TENDER)

Fig. 9.14   Class 4, 4–6–0 mixed traffic tender locomotive

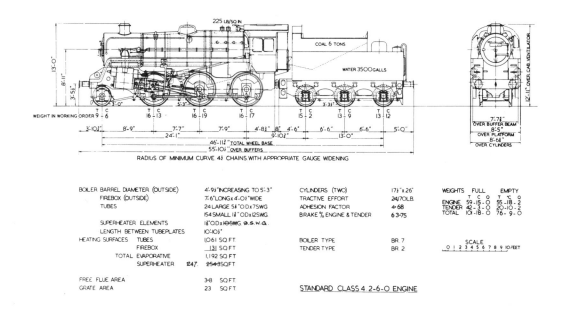

BOILER BARREL DIAMETER (OUTSIDE)		4'-9½"INCREASING TO 5'-3"	CYLINDERS (TWO)		17½"x26"	WEIGHTS	FULL	EMPTY
FIREBOX (OUTSIDE)		7'-6"LONG x 4'-0½"WIDE	TRACTIVE EFFORT		24170LB.		T C O	T C O
TUBES		24 LARGE 5⅛"OD x 7SWG	ADHESION FACTOR		4·68	ENGINE 59 -15 -0	55 -18 -2
		154 SMALL 1⅜"OD x 12SWG	BRAKE % ENGINE & TENDER		63·75	TENDER 42 -3 -0	20 -10 -2
SUPERHEATER ELEMENTS		1⅝"OD x 10SWG 9.S.W.G.				TOTAL 101 -18 -0	76 - 9 -0
LENGTH BETWEEN TUBEPLATES		10'-10⅜"					
HEATING SURFACES TUBES		1,061 SQ FT	BOILER TYPE		BR 7	SCALE	
FIREBOX		131 SQ FT	TENDER TYPE		BR 2	0 1 2 3 4 5 6 7 8 9 10 FEET	
TOTAL EVAPORATIVE		1,192 SQ FT					
SUPERHEATER	247	254·3 SQ FT					
FREE FLUE AREA		3·8 SQ FT					
GRATE AREA		23 SQ FT	STANDARD CLASS 4 2-6-0 ENGINE				

Fig. 9.15 Class 4, 2–6–0 mixed traffic tender locomotive

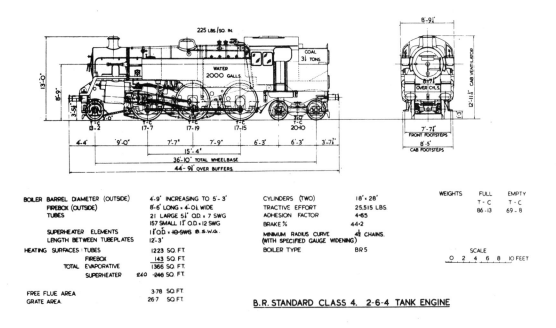

BOILER BARREL DIAMETER (OUTSIDE)	4'-9" INCREASING TO 5'-3"	CYLINDERS (TWO)	18" × 28"	WEIGHTS	FULL T-C	EMPTY T-C
FIREBOX (OUTSIDE)	8'-6" LONG × 4'-0½" WIDE	TRACTIVE EFFORT	25,515 LBS.		86-13	69-8
TUBES	21 LARGE 5¼" O.D × 7 SWG	ADHESION FACTOR	4·65			
	157 SMALL 1⅝" O.D × 12 SWG	BRAKE %	44·2			
SUPERHEATER ELEMENTS	1" O.D × 10 SWG B.S.W.G.	MINIMUM RADIUS CURVE	4½ CHAINS.			
LENGTH BETWEEN TUBEPLATES	12'-3"	(WITH SPECIFIED GAUGE WIDENING)				
HEATING SURFACES : TUBES	1223 SQ. FT.	BOILER TYPE	BR5			
FIREBOX	143 SQ. FT.					
TOTAL EVAPORATIVE	1366 SQ. FT.					
SUPERHEATER	240 246 SQ. FT.					
FREE FLUE AREA	3·78 SQ.FT.					
GRATE AREA	26·7 SQ.FT.					

SCALE
0 2 4 6 8 10 FEET

B.R. STANDARD CLASS 4. 2-6-4 TANK ENGINE

Fig. 9.16 *Class 4, 2–6–4 mixed traffic tank locomotive*

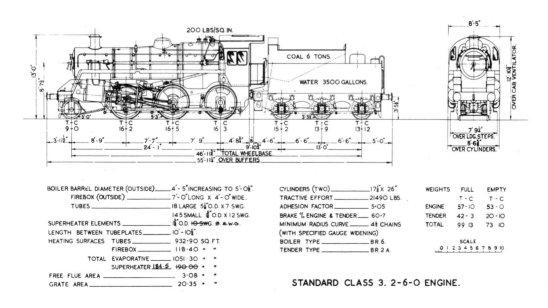

BOILER BARREL DIAMETER (OUTSIDE)	4'- 5" INCREASING TO 5'-0¾".
FIREBOX (OUTSIDE)	7'-0" LONG X 4'-0" WIDE.
TUBES	18 LARGE 5¼" O.D. X 7 S.W.G.
	145 SMALL 1⅝" O.D. X 12 S.W.G.
SUPERHEATER ELEMENTS	1⅛" O.D. 10 S.W.G. 9 S.W.G.
LENGTH BETWEEN TUBEPLATES	10'-10¼".
HEATING SURFACES TUBES	932·90 SQ. FT.
FIREBOX	118·40 " "
TOTAL EVAPORATIVE	1051·30 " "
SUPERHEATER	184·5 190·00 " "
FREE FLUE AREA	3·08 " "
GRATE AREA	20·35 " "

CYLINDERS (TWO)	17½" X 26".
TRACTIVE EFFORT	21490 LBS.
ADHESION FACTOR	5·05
BRAKE % ENGINE & TENDER	60·7
MINIMUM RADIUS CURVE	4½ CHAINS
(WITH SPECIFIED GAUGE WIDENING)	
BOILER TYPE	BR. 6.
TENDER TYPE	BR. 2 A.

WEIGHTS	FULL	EMPTY
	T - C	T - C
ENGINE	57 - 10	53 - 0
TENDER	42 - 3	20 - 10
TOTAL	99 13	73 10

SCALE
0 1 2 3 4 5 6 7 8 9 10

STANDARD CLASS 3. 2-6-0 ENGINE.

Fig. 9.17   Class 3, 2–6–0 mixed traffic tender locomotive

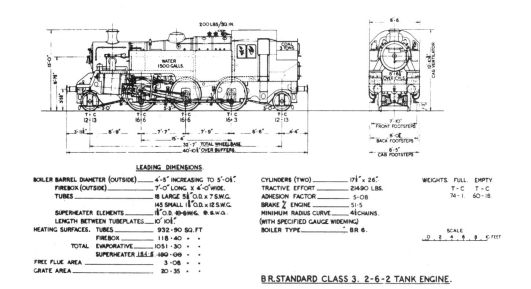

LEADING DIMENSIONS.

BOILER BARREL DIAMETER (OUTSIDE)	4'-5" INCREASING TO 5'-0½".	
FIREBOX (OUTSIDE)	7'-0" LONG X 4'-0" WIDE.	
TUBES	18 LARGE 5⅛" O.D. X 7 S.W.G.	
	145 SMALL 1⅝" O.D. X 12 S.W.G.	
SUPERHEATER ELEMENTS	1⅛" O.D. 10 S.W.G. ⊗ S.W.G.	
LENGTH BETWEEN TUBEPLATES	10' 10½".	
HEATING SURFACES. TUBES	932·90 SQ.FT	
FIREBOX	118·40 " "	
TOTAL EVAPORATIVE	1051·30 " "	
SUPERHEATER 184·5 190·00	" "	
FREE FLUE AREA	3·08 " "	
GRATE AREA	20·35 " "	

CYLINDERS (TWO)	17½" x 26".
TRACTIVE EFFORT	21490 LBS.
ADHESION FACTOR	5·08
BRAKE % ENGINE	51·5
MINIMUM RADIUS CURVE	4¼ CHAINS.
(WITH SPECIFIED GAUGE WIDENING)	
BOILER TYPE	BR 6.

WEIGHTS. FULL. EMPTY.
T-C   T-C
74-1.   60-18

SCALE
0 2 4 6 8 10 FEET

B R. STANDARD CLASS 3. 2-6-2 TANK ENGINE.

Fig. 9.18 Class 3, 2-6-2 mixed traffic tank locomotive

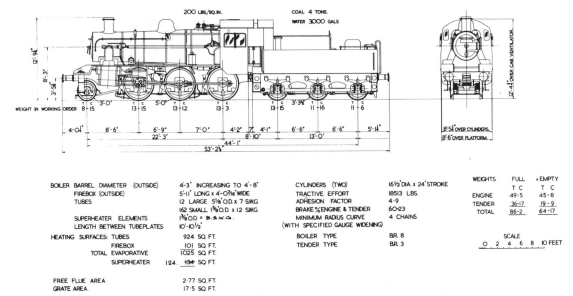

WEIGHTS	FULL		EMPTY	
	T C		T C	
ENGINE	49·5		45·8	
TENDER	36·17		19·9	
TOTAL	86·2		64·17	

BOILER BARREL DIAMETER (OUTSIDE)	4'-3" INCREASING TO 4'-8"	CYLINDERS (TWO)	16½" DIA x 24" STROKE
FIREBOX (OUTSIDE)	5'-11" LONG x 4'-0⁷⁄₁₆" WIDE	TRACTIVE EFFORT	18513 LBS.
TUBES	12 LARGE 5⅛" O.D. x 7 S.W.G	ADHESION FACTOR	4·9
	162 SMALL 1⅝" O.D. x 12 S.W.G	BRAKE % ENGINE & TENDER	60·23
SUPERHEATER ELEMENTS	1⅜" O.D x 9 S.W.G.	MINIMUM RADIUS CURVE	4 CHAINS
LENGTH BETWEEN TUBEPLATES	10'-10½"	(WITH SPECIFIED GAUGE WIDENING)	

BOILER BARREL DIAMETER (OUTSIDE) 4'-3" INCREASING TO 4'-8"
FIREBOX (OUTSIDE) 5'-11" LONG x 4'-0⁷⁄₁₆" WIDE
TUBES 12 LARGE 5⅛" O.D. x 7 S.W.G
  162 SMALL 1⅝" O.D. x 12 S.W.G
SUPERHEATER ELEMENTS 1⅜" O.D x 9 S.W.G.
LENGTH BETWEEN TUBEPLATES 10'-10½"

HEATING SURFACES: TUBES 924 SQ. FT.
  FIREBOX 101 SQ. FT.
  TOTAL EVAPORATIVE 1025 SQ. FT.
  SUPERHEATER 124 SQ. FT.

FREE FLUE AREA 2·77 SQ. FT.
GRATE AREA 17·5 SQ. FT.

CYLINDERS (TWO) 16½" DIA x 24" STROKE
TRACTIVE EFFORT 18513 LBS.
ADHESION FACTOR 4·9
BRAKE % ENGINE & TENDER 60·23
MINIMUM RADIUS CURVE 4 CHAINS
(WITH SPECIFIED GAUGE WIDENING)
BOILER TYPE BR. 8
TENDER TYPE BR. 3

SCALE
0 2 4 6 8 10 FEET

STANDARD CLASS 2. 2-6-0 ENGINE.

Fig. 9.19   Class 2, 2–6–0 mixed traffic tender locomotive

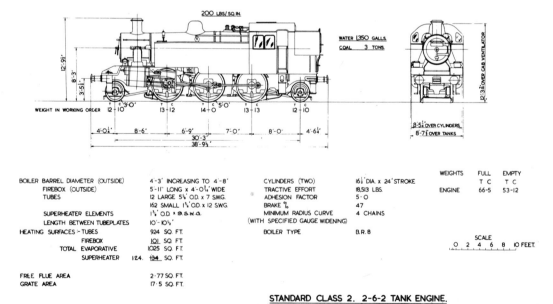

WEIGHTS	FULL	EMPTY
	T C	T C
ENGINE	66-5	53-12

BOILER BARREL DIAMETER (OUTSIDE)   4'-3" INCREASING TO 4'-8"
FIREBOX (OUTSIDE)   5'-11" LONG x 4'-0¾" WIDE
TUBES   12 LARGE 5⅛" O.D. x 7 S.W.G.
    162 SMALL 1⅝" O.D. x 12 S.W.G.
SUPERHEATER ELEMENTS   1¼" O.D. x 9 S.W.G.
LENGTH BETWEEN TUBEPLATES   10'-10½'
HEATING SURFACES :- TUBES   924 SQ. FT.
FIREBOX   101 SQ. FT.
TOTAL EVAPORATIVE   1025 SQ. FT.
SUPERHEATER   124. 134 SQ. FT.

FREE FLUE AREA   2·77 SQ. FT.
GRATE AREA   17·5 SQ. FT.

CYLINDERS (TWO)   16½" DIA. x 24" STROKE
TRACTIVE EFFORT   18,513 LBS.
ADHESION FACTOR   5·0
BRAKE %   47
MINIMUM RADIUS CURVE   4 CHAINS
(WITH SPECIFIED GAUGE WIDENING)
BOILER TYPE   B.R. 8

SCALE
0 2 4 6 8 10 FEET

STANDARD CLASS 2. 2-6-2 TANK ENGINE.

Fig. 9.20 Class 2, 2–6–2 mixed traffic tank locomotive

CHAPTER 10

BRITISH RAILWAYS MODERNISATION PLAN

Sir Brian Robertson, later Lord Robertson, was Chairman of the British Transport Commission – of which BR was the largest division – when the plan for the modernization and re-equipment of British Railways was authorized by the Government in 1955. The original authorization was for a mammoth £1250 million and this was subsequently increased to £1500 million, an unprecedented capital sum to be spent on the railways of this country. After the Second World War, British Railways had paid their way until 1952, after which they increasingly ran into the red.

Under the Modernization Plan, steam had to be replaced as a form of motive power, and electric or diesel traction introduced as might be most suitable in the light of the development of the plan over the years; this would involve the electrification of large mileages of track, and the introduction of some thousands of electric or diesel locomotives. It spelt the beginning of the end of the much loved steam locomotive. Tables 10.1 and 10.2 summarize the final years of the new building programmes.

The existing steam-drawn passenger rolling stock had to be replaced, largely by multiple-unit electric or diesel trains; the remaining passenger rolling stock, which would be drawn by locomotives (whether electric, diesel or steam) had to be modernized; the principal passenger stations and parcel depots would also require considerable expenditure. As mentioned in the previous chapter, the Commission proposed to build no new passenger or suburban steam locomotives after the 1956 programme, and to terminate the building of all new steam locomotives within a few years.

The plan stated that there was a wide and accepted field for electrification in suburban services, and proposals for substantial schemes were to be considered. There was also a wide range of main-line services upon which the density of traffic indicated that there was a good economic case for electrification. But the key factor was the volume of civil and signal engineering work that was involved; and there was therefore a limit to the amount of main-line electrification that appeared practicable within the

TABLE 10.1 NUMBER OF STEAM LOCOMOTIVES OF COMPANY DESIGN BUILT FOLLOWING NATIONALIZATION IN 1948

Former Railway Company	Steam locomotives built
GWR	452
LMSR	640
LNER	396
SR	50
Total	1538

TABLE 10.2 NUMBER OF BR STEAM LOCOMOTIVES OF NEW STANDARD DESIGNS BUILT BETWEEN 1951 AND 1960

Wheel classification	Power classification	Number built
4–6–2	8	1
4–6–2	7	55
4–6–2	6	10
4–6–0	5	172
4–6–0	4	80
2–6–0	4	115
2–6–0	3	20
2–6–0	2	65
2–6–4	4	155
2–6–2	3	45
2–6–2	2	30
2–10–0	9	251
Total		999

fifteen year period covered by the plan. As regards the remainder of the principal main-line services, it was intended to introduce diesel traction as quickly as possible. Conversion to diesel traction would be carried out through annual building programmes, and the rate of investment could thus be speeded up or slowed down according to circumstances. If it were subsequently decided that it was practicable to electrify a section upon which diesel traction had already been introduced, the diesel units could be used elsewhere.

Work was proceeding with the extension of the Liverpool Street – Shenfield electrification to Chelmsford and Southend (Victoria). Various other schemes had been under consideration, and planning upon them had reached different stages of development. It was proposed that under the plan all these schemes should be adopted, unless any unforeseen difficulties should emerge as planning proceeded. The list was as follows:

	Approximate route mileage
London, Tilbury and Southend line	85
Liverpool Street to Enfield and Chingford	20
Liverpool Street to Hertford and Bishop's Stortford	35
King's Cross and Moorgate to Hitchin and Letchworth, including the Hertford loop	60
Glasgow suburban lines	190
Total	390

In addition, it had always been the intention that as soon as circumstances permitted, all the main line routes of the Southern Region east of a line drawn from Reading to Portsmouth should be electrified. In conjunction with the diesel services to be introduced this would effect the elimination of steam traction from all the lines of the Southern Region in the area mentioned.

It was the intention to electrify two major trunk routes, and one of lesser traffic density under the plan. The main line of the Eastern and North Eastern Regions from King's Cross to Doncaster, Leeds and (possibly) York, and the main line of the London Midland Region from Euston to Birmingham, Crewe, Liverpool and Manchester, would comprise the two major schemes. The subsidiary main-line scheme would consist of the extension of the existing electrification from Liverpool Street (which would soon reach Chelmsford) to Ipswich, including the Clacton, Harwich and Felixstowe branches. By these schemes there would be a virtual elimination of steam from important areas of the country.

Under the plan a much wider extension of diesel multiple-unit working was envisaged. This would include three principal types of service:

city-to-city express services,
secondary and cross-country routes,
branch lines.

The total number of multiple-unit diesel vehicles that could be employed on British Railways for the services listed above was estimated at about 4600 including the 300 already in service or on order.

It was envisaged that the programme for the construction of diesel shunting units in replacement of steam locomotives would be completed in 1957, and a further programme was in course of preparation. It was considered that the complete elimination of shunting and trip working by steam locomotives should be achieved over the next fifteen years. The total number of steam locomotives that would be displaced by this conversion was approximately 1500. They would be replaced by about 1200 diesel locomotives, additional to those already authorized. By the end of the period covered by the plan it was anticipated that about 2500 main line diesel locomotives would be in use. Finally, and of great importance, some 31 000 passenger carriages would be built under the scheme.

The number of diesel shunting locomotives built between nationalization in 1948 and the announcement of the modernization plan in 1954 was 258. Under the modernization plan between 1955 and 1964 a further 1780 were built; during the same period the number of main line diesel (electric and hydraulic) locomotives built was 2551.

It will be realized from the foregoing that the modernization of British Railways mainly centred around new equipment, and that no basic change was envisaged in the scope of railway services. It was anticipated that the substitution of electric and diesel traction for steam, the concentration of marshalling yards, increased mechanization of goods depots and re-signalling together with other improvements would collectively result in reducing operating costs and attracting increased

Fig. 10.1   Multiple unit diesel train fitted with Leyland equipment

traffic. On the face of it, so it was said, there appeared to be ample scope to enable the railway once again to be self-supporting; a critical examination at that time, using work study techniques, would have proved the fallacy of this contention unless the plan took into account the need to streamline the railways as a whole and eliminate all duplication of services.

At the British Transport Commission Headquarters, there was considerable activity in setting up a high level organization to bring the scheme to fruition in all its various facets within a period of fifteen years. A small team of specialist advisers, collectively called the General Staff, was appointed with Major-General L1. Wansbrough Jones, the Secretary-General, as their chairman. It was the function of this high-powered team to examine the multifarious schemes submitted by the general managers of the six Regions forming BR, and to pass them forward for Commission approval if and when they were satisfied with their viability.

Simultaneously with the start of this new organization at Commission Headquarters, I was asked to see the Deputy Chairman, Sir John Benstead, on 11 March, 1955, and he informed me that the Commission wished to second me to headquarters as soon as practicable to formulate the policy to be followed to enable the modernization and re-equipment plan to be developed quickly so far as mechanical and electrical engineering was concerned. Sir John informed me that he had just seen Sir Allan S. Quartermaine, the recently retired Chief Civil Engineer of the Western Region and a Past President of the Institution of Civil Engineers, and the latter had agreed to undertake a corresponding assignment covering civil and signal and telecommunications engineering. Sir Allan and I were duly introduced and after a useful discussion we went our respective ways; we occasionally met during our perambulations and formed a mutual regard which I am happy to say has continued into our retirement.

Arrangements were made for me to begin work at BTC Headquarters on 21 March, 1955, and on

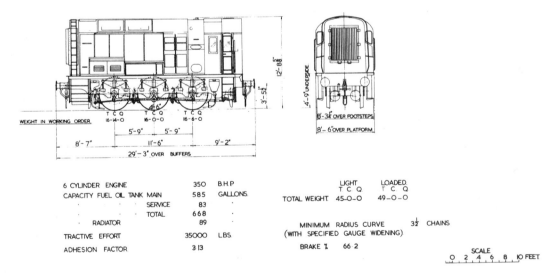

6 CYLINDER ENGINE		350	B.H.P
CAPACITY FUEL OIL TANK	MAIN	585	GALLONS.
· · · ·	SERVICE	83	·
· · · ·	TOTAL	668	·
·	RADIATOR	89	·
TRACTIVE EFFORT		35000	LBS.
ADHESION FACTOR		3·13	

	LIGHT T C Q	LOADED. T C Q
TOTAL WEIGHT	45-0-0	49-0-0

MINIMUM RADIUS CURVE   3½ CHAINS
(WITH SPECIFIED GAUGE WIDENING)

BRAKE %   66·2

SCALE
0 2 4 6 8 10 FEET

Fig. 10.2   BR Standard 350 hp diesel–electric shunting locomotive

the following day W. P. Allen, the Manpower Adviser, handed to me the following Remit:

1. Your duties will consist of the following:
   (a) In conjunction with the General Managers, to take such steps as are necessary to encourage recruitment from the following sources:
       (i) Universities
       (ii) Polytechnics
       (iii) Technical Colleges
       (iv) Public, Grammar and Secondary Schools
       (v) Appointments Bureaux of the Ministry of Labour, the Services and the Professional Institutions
       (vi) Engineers with experience obtained in industry, railways abroad, or in the services.
   (b) To recommend means of increasing the productivity of present and potential staff.
   (c) To recommend methods of technical training of recruits, and of junior staff and craftsmen already in the service.
   (d) To make any other recommendations which appear to be appropriate and necessary to obtain for British Railways the technical staff required for the execution of the Modernization Plan.
   (e) Having considered the assessments of the Regions of the number and grading of professional and technical staff required
       (i) immediately
       (ii) ultimately
       to advise upon their acceptance by the Commission in the light of
       (iii) volume of work in hand in each Region
       (iv) future commitments of each Region.
2. Sir Allan Quartermaine and you will work in direct contact with the General Managers of the Railway Regions and their departmental Chief Officers, who will be advised of your appointments and duties.
   You will have placed at your disposal the services of the Training and Education section of British Railways Central Staff. You will deal with the Commission through the General Staff (Technical and Manpower Advisers).

My investigations necessitated talks with the General Managers, Chief Mechanical and Electrical Engineers and other senior officers in each of the six Regions. I made a strenuous effort to complete the assignment and copies of my report were in the hands of the Chairman, the Deputy Chairman, members of the Commission and the General Staff within four months. The date of my report was a very significant one to me, namely 25 July, 1955 – my wife's birthday. There was so much ground to be covered that inevitably it was a fairly weighty report which ran to seventy pages and twenty-four appendices. Some of the appendices took the form of diagrams whilst others were detailed statements showing the estimated requirements of each Region. It was well received and, following discussions with me, almost all my proposals were ratified.

The calibre, number and responsibilities of additional professional and technical staff which I agreed with the officers concerned were, of course, of fundamental importance to the modernization plan. I recognized that when it was completed not all of them would be required. My recommendation for the setting up of a Diesel Training Centre at which all technical staff, designers, headquarters and works assistants, workshop and motive power supervisory staff should attend appropriate courses was of high priority. At a meeting of the General Staff which I attended I was asked where I considered the new Diesel Training Centre should be located. I advocated extensions to the BR School of Transport at Derby because it had the right atmosphere and because there were two large works as well as the design and research departments, all of which would be vitally concerned. My proposals were implemented and after more than twenty years in operation the Centre is as active as ever and I understand continues to give an invaluable service to all levels of staff concerned. Thanks to a carefully selected team of instructors led by James Caldwell, who subsequently became chief locomotive draughtsman, in the first instance and their worthy successors it is doubtful whether there is anything in the engineering industry which is comparable. It was an extremely practical set-up.

In looking back on the entire modernization plan I would say that the most rewarding and most spectacular project was the electrification of the LMR main line from Euston to Birmingham and Manchester (more recently extended to Glasgow). In the days of the LMS Pacific class of steam locomotives, the 400¼ mile journey from Euston to Glasgow took 6¼ hours. With an electric locomotive the journey time was reduced to 5 hours, and this compared favourably with the overall time by air travel, taking into account the time required to get to and from the airports. The planning of the 25 kV overhead electrification scheme was largely the work of two of my colleagues, Stanley B. Warder, Chief Electrical Engineer, and J. Alan Broughall, his Principal

Assistant, both of whom were located at Commission HQ. The Electrical Assistant on the spot, under J. F. Harrison, Chief Mechanical and Electrical Engineer of the LMR, was Alec H. Emerson, who later became the Chief Mechanical and Electrical Engineer of the LM Region, and who was a really first class administrator.

During the early stages of the modernization plan, and as a direct result of it, a sequence of events occurred which significantly affected the course of my career in the ensuing decade. I have referred to the appointment of the General Staff and the manner in which they functioned. The Technical Adviser was the genial John Ratter, a railway trained civil engineer who later succeeded Sir Landale Train as the technical member of the Commission. The Commission decided that the General Staff should be strengthened with a Production Adviser and to fill this position someone was brought in from outside the railway service shortly before I had completed my report. Within a month after I had submitted my report, and having attended a meeting of the General Staff to discuss certain items, I was invited to London to see Sir John Benstead, Deputy Chairman of the Commission, who I knew quite well. He saw me with three other members of the Commission, Lord Rusholme, Sir Alec Valentine and Sir Cecil Weir, together with W. P. Allen, the Manpower Adviser. I was informed by Sir John that the Commission were considering me for an appointment as Assistant Production Adviser. I was aware that none of the other advisers had an equivalent assistant. I had not met the newly appointed Production Adviser but I had read his background in the Press and he was clearly a contracts officer, and therefore could scarcely advise and take the initiative on production matters. I've always held the view that nobody can be good at everything. We all have our limitations and I certainly have my full share. For the new Production Adviser to be superimposed over all the technical officers, and function effectively, was in my view impossible; it would be difficult enough for an experienced railway officer steeped in production techniques to be placed in this newly created position and win over the goodwill of experienced technical officers. I respectfully told the Selection Panel that had I been offered the Adviser's post my reaction would be different but, in the circumstances, I much preferred to carry on in my present position. Job satisfaction was always worth more to me than

money. Sir Alec Valentine, a member of the Commission who later became the Chairman of London Transport, asked 'Are you telling us, Mr Larkin, that you would not be happy in the job?' I replied 'Yes, that is really the position; and I have never met the newly appointed Production Adviser.' Before leaving the building I sensed that the Panel were disappointed in my response. A month later W. P. Allen spoke to me and told me the Commission were disappointed in my not wishing to accept that key position. He knew me well and said it had been left to him to see me and ascertain whether I had had second thoughts. I told him I was less inclined than ever to take it. He said he understood and said I should hear no more about it. Within eighteen months the Production Adviser was asked to leave the Commission. He never had an Assistant nor was the Production Adviser's position ever filled again. Not many months after this incident I was again requested to see the Deputy Chairman. I was told beforehand that I was the nominee of the Chief Regional Officer of the LMR, Colonel J. W. Watkins, who some time later became a member of the Commission, for the newly created position of Director of Work Study to the British Transport Commission. Again I appeared before a panel headed by Sir John Benstead and the nature of the post was explained to me. I learned later that I was the last of five nominees to be interviewed. If the job was offered to me and I accepted I would be head of a new department concerned with all the divisions of the BTC. Clearly it would be a sizeable job and it would be pioneering work with which I could accommodate myself. In that respect it presented no problem. For myself I had to weigh up the possibility of becoming somewhat remote from BR and I wanted to avoid disruption of my home life.

The interview was perfectly straightforward and pleasant; I did not however enthuse and this did not go unnoticed. Once again I felt I was in the unfortunate position of not being over-anxious to fill the job and from questions put to me this was correctly interpreted by the panel. A few weeks elapsed and Colonel Watkins rang me at Derby from Euston and said that Sir John wished to see me again. It had been arranged for me to have coffee with Sir John in Colonel Watkins' office. The latter asked me to come to his office early and after a chat he said he would leave me with Sir John. He expressed the hope that I would accept, although he felt my selection would be a great loss for the LMR. Sir John said the Commission wanted me to take this appointment, and he hoped I would accept it. We had a full and frank discussion and he offered such favourable conditions that it would have been foolish to decline.

One of my intimate colleagues at Commission Headquarters, who had learned of these happenings, said to me, 'You are a braver man than me to let the Commission know how you felt'; oddly enough we always knew him as a fair but tough, outspoken individual. Another one smilingly said on meeting me soon after I took up my appointment, 'Here's the man who knows how to steer his boat.'

In retrospect I have never had any regrets in moving. I feel I have lived a very full and interesting life. The pity of it is that life moves on too quickly and we cannot accomplish as much as we would wish.

CHAPTER 11

DIRECTOR OF WORK STUDY, BRITISH TRANSPORT COMMISSION

To the majority of people the term 'work study' seems to conjure up all sorts of mysteries. Work study may be described simply as the critical examination of any work with a view to making the most economical and effective use of men, materials, equipment and buildings. It is not confined to highly repetitive operations; it can be applied to jobbing, maintenance or similar work in which there is little or no repetition of particular operations. Improvements do not necessarily have to be obtained by the installation of new and costly mechanical equipment; improvements of some magnitude can often be secured by analysing the process and operations carefully, eliminating unnecessary work and motions, and instituting simple practical work-reducing methods. There is just as much scope for work study in offices and non-technical departments as there is in technical departments.

Work study is a tool or technique of management and not a substitute for good organization. Where work study techniques, such as network analysis or activity sampling, are not applied, decisions are often based on what was thought to be true – not uncommonly referred to as 'guestimating'. The function of work study is to obtain the facts and to use those facts as a basis for improvement. Much of the work is technical, but equally as much of it is the application of common sense.

BRITISH TRANSPORT COMMISSION

OUTLINE ORGANISATION

OF DIVISIONS

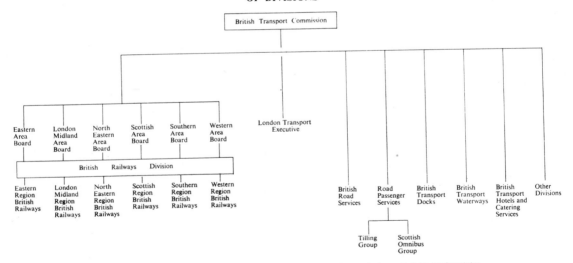

NOTE.—" Other Divisions " include Pullman Car Co., Thos. Cook and Son Ltd., and certain other organisations controlled by the Commission.

Fig. 11.1 Outline organization of divisions, British Transport Commission (controlling a total of approximately three-quarters of a million staff)

Fig. 11.2   The Grove, Watford, Hertfordshire, which became the BTC Work Study Training Centre in 1956

I took up office as Director of Work Study to the British Transport Commission on 1 May, 1956. I had previously received the following letter from Colonel James W. Watkins, my General Manager, a long serving railway officer for whom I had a high regard:

> I am pleased to inform you that approval has been given to your appointment as Director of Work Study at Commission Headquarters.
>
> I should like to congratulate you on obtaining this appointment and wish you every success in carrying out the duties of such a responsible post. At the same time I must express my appreciation of all that you have done for the London Midland Region and its predecessors during your association with them.
>
> I am very pleased you have accepted this post although we shall be very sorry to lose you on the Region.

As Director of Work Study I was given the following responsibilities:

1. to provide a specialist advisory service in work study to the British Railways Regions and to the other Divisions of the Commission,
2. to establish a central pool of experience relating to the application of work study to transport problems,
3. to advise on the co-ordination of relations with the Trade Unions on this subject,
4. to organize a Work Study Training Centre at The Grove, Watford, Hertfordshire,
5. to advise the Divisions and Regions on the use of industrial consultants.

The Grove, Watford, where the Training Centre was to be established, was formerly the home of the Earl of Clarendon. This Georgian mansion is a substantial edifice of red brick, three storeys high, and steeped in history. Records of the manor of The Grove go back to the fourteenth century and show that it was held by many distinguished families until it passed into the hands of Thomas Villiers, who, for diplomatic services on the Continent, was made Earl of Clarendon. The present house was built during his ownership by Sir Robert Taylor in 1756, without the top storey, which was added later (1780). It was purchased before the Second World War by the LMS to serve as their headquarters if the international situation made it advisable to move from Euston. This move actually took place, and the building became the administrative centre of the Company throughout the War, after which it was used as a Training Centre for certain divisions of the British Transport Commission until it was decided to use it as the Work Study Training Centre.

Work study had been in operation to a very limited extent on British Railways, London Transport and the other divisions of the British Transport Commission for several years. For instance, at some of the main works, method study had been well developed by planning engineers, who formed part of the production planning organization. Prior to my appointment further progress had been made within the Commission's undertakings. Many investigations had been, or were being, made by industrial consultants. In the civil engineering departments, particularly on the Southern Region of British Railways, considerable success had attended the introduction of work study incentive schemes for permanent-way maintenance staff. Nevertheless we were still only on the threshold of a vast

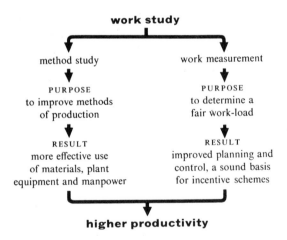

Fig. 11.3 How work study operates

development. Industrial consultants, and the larger firms who were practising work study techniques, considered that the British Transport Commission, with their 700 000 staff, had in the value of their assets and the wide diversity of their interests, probably the largest work study problem in the world. Added to this, the £1600

million modernization plan for British Railways was a challenge to all.

In moving to Commission Headquarters at Marylebone I realized that senior management had first to be won over before I could have any success in the field of work study, and the best way was to start off with some short appreciation courses. I therefore gave priority to the adaptation of The Grove as the Work Study Training Centre. Concurrent with this and the provision of laboratories in adjacent buildings to carry out practical work, I gave a great deal of attention to the appointment of the team who would help to run the Training Centre, the responsibility of selection being one to which I attached great importance. I was not disappointed in my choice.

The principal courses which we planned were of three types:

Two-day appreciation course; specially designed to give, in a minimum space of time, a picture of the full scope of work study. They were attended by the highest level of management, including General Managers, Chief Officers at the Commission and Heads of Departments from all Divisions.

One-week appreciation courses; designed to give a fuller appreciation of the techniques of work study and their purpose and were attended by Assistant Heads of Departments and Area and District Officers from all Divisions.

Ten-week courses; comprehensive work study courses for senior staff who were required to initiate work study schemes as well as control the work study staff who carried out the detailed investigation and preparation of such schemes.

These were the main courses for which the Training Centre was provided, and covered all grades of senior staff irrespective of Division or department. Other grades of staff, including full-time work study personnel, were trained in six Regional Schools which were set up for the purpose.

More specialized courses were devised, as required, and these included short courses for assistants concerned with new works projects, design of product and maintenance of equipment.

The emphasis in the training courses was on practical work, and the course members investigated industrial and transport projects. This was

Operation ○	When something is being done, changed, created or added to. For example, issuing a ticket, picking up a spanner, filling in a form, giving an order.
Inspection ▢	When something is checked or verified but not changed. For example, checking the label on a parcel, or checking the length of a piece of timber.
Transport ⬠	When something moves or is moved. For example, a parcel carried from platform to storage area or an Inspector walking from the Inspector's room to the platform. The distance travelled may be recorded to the left of the symbol.
Storage ▽	When an article is stored. For example, tickets in the ticket rack, or material held in store awaiting issue and use.
Delay D	When something is delayed or its progress interfered with. For example, parcels in a barrow awaiting unloading, or a passenger waiting in a ticket queue.

Fig. 11.4 Symbols used in method study

done in the laboratories where suitable processes were reproduced, at selected Commission installations, and in nearby factories and other establishments where we generally found the management most co-operative. Initially the training scheme provided for about forty course members so that two courses could be run simultaneously. Ultimately, the residential accommodation was increased and additional lecture rooms were provided, enabling four courses to be run when desired. The laboratories were well equipped and the whole establishment took on the air of a first class residential college.

The first Principal, Arnold Kentridge, and his team of instructors, who included Peter Corbishley, Paddy Doyle (a former sapper colonel in the Army) and Ron Brown, did a really first class job. From the outset we made a point of inviting the Presidents and General Secretaries of the major Trades Unions with whom we negotiated staff agreements to attend the same courses that our own senior officers were attending and this arrangement was a psychological success. These included Ray Gunter, MP for Southwark and President of the Transport and Salaried Staffs Association, and Minister of Labour in the first Wilson government, and Sidney Greene (later Lord Greene), General Secretary of the National Union of Railwaymen. Both told me subsequently that they were greatly impressed with what was being done, and Sidney Greene provided me with a helpful write-up for publication in *Project*.

In order to keep all Divisions of the Commission well informed in the development and implementation of work study schemes, I formed and chaired the British Transport Commission

TABLE 11.1   SELECTING A JOB FOR IMPROVEMENT

What jobs need improvement most?	
A bottleneck job	because it is holding up other work
A very tiring job	because one of the main aims of work study is to make work easier
A dangerous job	because through work study it can be done with greater safety
A chasing-around job	because any job which involves a lot of movement from place to place offers scope for study
An over-and-over-again job	because any savings, however small in themselves, will quickly mount up to something really worth while

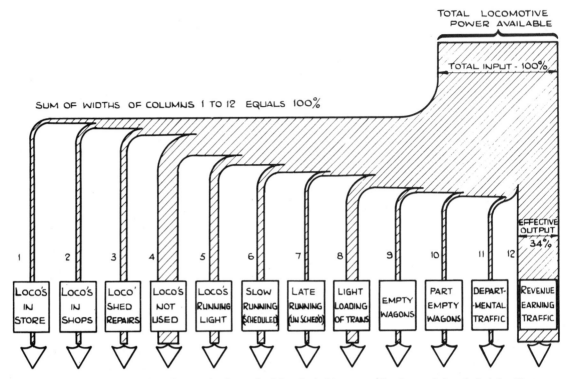

Fig. 11.5 *Locomotive productivity diagram showing productivity of only 34 per cent. The diagram is hypothetical, but illustrates the type of situation which arose. A critical examination points to areas of activity which could be improved, giving, say, upwards of 50 per cent productivity*

Work Study Development Committee which met quarterly, each Division, as well as the six Regions of British Railways, delegating a senior officer as their representative. The services of my small but very experienced Headquarters team of consultants were always in demand and the consultants took the initiative in many worthwhile pilot investigations.

On each Division of the Commission we adopted the British Standards Institution scale of 0 to 100 to measure the level of productivity. It was considered that a 75 rating was required to justify normal pay, and that if there was an increase of 25 points, bringing the level of productivity up to 100, i.e. up to standard, there was justification for an incentive bonus of 33⅓ per cent.

A critical examination using work study techniques often revealed an initial performance of, say, not more than 40. If this performance was raised to 80, the output per individual was doubled yet it did not reach standard performance and therefore did not strictly justify a bonus payment. This was where management had to

find a compromise solution over payment in the light of the facts revealed by work study. But management did have a solid foundation on which to work; without this schemes could have become quite phoney and costly.

One of our earliest visiting speakers to The Grove was the Chief Planning Officer of John Laing, the main contractors for the M1 motorway. He talked to the course members about the initial planning of this gigantic engineering project, and his audience, including myself, were much impressed with the critical path analyses which his firm had used. Yes, they knew their work study and were practising it.

I found that many people confused the terms productivity and production. An increase in the former reduces the cost per unit of product, whereas the latter is generally achieved by increasing the staff or man-hours worked *pro rata* to the increase in output required, and if the effort of the individual does not improve, no reduction in price is achieved. Capital investment may increase production, but not in itself will it increase productivity. New equipment should not

TABLE 11.2 WORK MEASUREMENT. Undesirable factors which lead to performances averaging well over standard and steps to be taken to bring them into line with accepted practice

	Factor	Attributable to:			Cause	Action
		WS	M	O		
1	Defects in schemes resulting in loose standard times.	X			Insufficient experienced staff available. Errors in compilation of standard times.	Take earliest opportunity to re-study.
2	Inadequate Work Specifications.	X	X		Insufficient detail.	Review and redraft Work Specifications.
3	*Allowance – Excesses* Rest allowance	X[1]		X[2]	[1]Errors in using RA tables. [2]Operators using rest allowance for work; also using travelling time for rest.	[1]Correct errors. [2]To note and if common to the group consider revision.
	Process Allowance	X		X	Unloaded operator doing extra work.	Reduce allowance and show separately from measured work. Load with additional work.
	Apprentice Allowance		X	X	Apprentice performing work not authorised.	Reallocation of work and reduction of overall time allowance.
4	Cumulative improvement of quality resulting in reduced work content.	X			Lack of appreciation of the effect of improvement on work content.	Investigate frequency and reduce man-power if practicable.
5	Changes in working arrangements and specification and no advice to Work Study Staff.		X		Liaison between Work Study and Design Staff inadequate.	Improve communications.
6	Failure of Staff to observe rules and regulations.		X	X	Short cuts regardless of safety.	Strict enforcement by Management.
7	Exceptional effort and/or skill.			X	Ability.	None – merely to note, because it is accepted that a particular individual, as opposed to a group of men, may achieve a relatively high performance.
8	Familiarisation with the job.	X		X	Development of rhythm of working and memorisation of job.	Careful measurement and planning prior to work evaluation.
9	Improvements in tooling and other methods undertaken by the operator.	X		X	Insufficient Method Study.	If practicable adopt improvements.
10	Incorrect booking by the operator.		X	X	Carelessness, deceit or ignorance.	Progressing & Inspection. Periodical audit. Disciplinary action.
11	Lowering of Standards.		X	X	Acceptance due to deliberate intent. Emergencies.	Draw attention of Management.

Note: WS = Work Study, M = Management, O = Operator

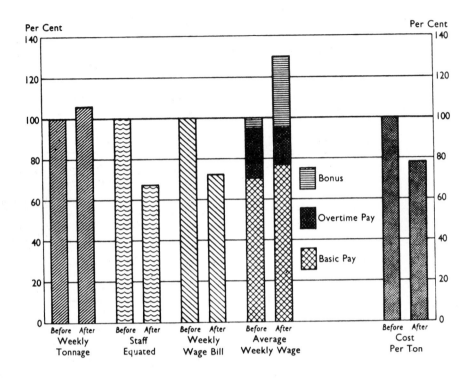

Fig. 11.6   Manchester London Road Parcels Depot, before and after start of work study incentive schemes

be installed until a high level of productivity has been achieved with existing facilities. With work study the staff are not normally required to work harder (indeed, sometimes less hard), but more consistently and with repetitive, wasteful operations eliminated.

Throughout my appointment as Director of Work Study I had contact with consultants from various organizations. They were always appearing somewhere, doing their best to persuade management to utilize their specialized services. They were seeking and obtaining assignments for some time before my organization was fully functioning, but their engagement largely faded out as time went on. Some of these outside consultants did a worthwhile job, but others cost a great deal and achieved very little. I would normally recommend the use of specially selected and well trained personnel from within the organization. Of course I recognize that for a relatively small organization it might be simpler to bring in management consultants. But changing circumstances necessitate continuous monitoring

of any worthwhile scheme which might be introduced and for this purpose no one is more suitable than one's own trained staff who are readily available – and much cheaper.

Russell M. Currie, a pioneer in this country in the field of work study, head of the work study organization at ICI and at one time President of the Institute of Work Study, introduced me to Earl Mountbatten and the three of us had some hard things to say about people in high places who should give a tangible lead to raise the level of productivity throughout the country.

In 1959 I had a visit from Dr Omond M. Solandt, Vice-President of the Canadian National Railways. He had wanted me to join the Canadian Railways on secondment for three months to advise on the introduction of work study and associated management techniques. He had said that if I were agreeable he would see Sir Brian Robertson, Chairman of the British Transport Commission, and seek his approval. I told Dr Solandt that whilst I much appreciated the honour I felt that with the Commission's three-quarters of a million staff I already had a job which demanded all my attention. I was not wrong in this assessment.

In 1961, Ernest Marples, then Minister of Transport, set up a Committee of Inquiry into BR affairs under the Chairmanship of Sir Ivan Stedeford. One of its members was Dr Richard Beeching, PhD, Technical Director of ICI, Britain's largest private undertaking, and in view of the prominent part he took as a member of the Stedeford Committee, it was no surprise to learn that he had been seconded from ICI for five years to succeed Sir Brian Robertson, whose term of office was coming to an end. This coincided with the winding up of the British Transport Commission and the establishment of separate autonomous Boards for the various Divisions, including one for British Railways. Dr Beeching asked me to tell him something of my activities. We had an interesting conversation during which I referred to BR's modernization plan. Dr Beeching said he was surprised to hear me refer to the modernization 'plan', and I, sensing what he implied, replied, 'You don't regard it as a properly integrated plan, but a collection of unco-ordinated individual schemes submitted by the Regional General Managers'. He said, 'Precisely, there does not appear to me to have been any fundamental re-appraisal of the shape and form of the future railway system and the commercial outlook is far too superficial'. I realized that here was a man of independent approach who first needed to know what railway traffic was potentially worthwhile and what should be discarded before deciding on new methods of conducting a modern railway system. He was well aware that heavy road transport had already taken a monumental slice of traffic away and that many millions of private cars on the roads had eaten into passenger traffic, especially on the branch lines. He told me he intended to set up a small working party to follow up certain lines of enquiry before committing himself to the approval of some weighty projects. He asked me to make nominations. I gave his request careful thought and the following day submitted four names. One of them, David Bowick, is now a Vice-Chairman of the Board and Chief Executive of BR. Another member of the team was Philip Satchwell, one of my headquarters assistants who normally functioned in the Regions as a consultant, and who later became Local Services Planning Manager at Board Headquarters.

I made reference in the previous chapter to the fact that the modernization and re-equipment plan centred mainly around new equipment and that no basic change was envisaged in the scope of railway services. With hindsight such an approach was a fundamental error and one which Dr Beeching was quick to follow up even before he became chairman. Of course, by the time he took office much of the plan was well under way and some of his decisions were influenced by expenditure which had already been committed.

The days of railway monopoly of both passenger and freight transport still governed the minds of the planners even though those days were no longer a reality. As a mere engineer, albeit with forty years service on the railway at that time, I had felt for many years that the railway system had not moved with the times and that in the light of road traffic development – and congestion – drastic attention needed to be given to the re-vitalizing and strengthening of the commercial aspect. Both freight and passenger services needed to be critically examined because railway receipts were shrinking fast, and yet running expenses, especially in a labour-orientated industry, were all too rapidly increasing. To the best of my knowledge there was no co-ordinated attempt in the formulation of the modernization plan to streamline passenger services between one Region and another which would have avoided the duplication of services or even necessitated their withdrawal. Inevitably many schemes were submitted and authorized which had been in the minds of management long before the railways were nationalized in 1948 and bore little relation to a heart-searching analysis as to whether they were still viable. In my early days on the railway, the freight receipts represented about 70 per cent of the total. Today, shrinking rail traffic receipts present a very different figure and, with a much smaller total, the proportion of passenger receipts is now higher than those of freight. It is a sign of the times, and one wonders whether the present congestion and carnage on the roads will have to be suffered for ever. Additional motorways seem only to effect a degree of improvement disproportionate to their enormous building and subsequent maintenance costs.

During his first visit to The Grove Dr Beeching asked me to submit an extension scheme which would enable us to increase the number of 'students' attending courses. This I did, and since my days the Centre has been re-named 'BR

Management Services Training Centre'. As such it provides intensive courses for various senior grades, in various aspects of management planning including all that is involved in computer techniques. It has now been functioning for well over twenty years since I had the privilege of first setting it up.

In 1962, in response to my request to Dr Beeching for a message to the staff, I received the following:

> I am writing at a time of change in our affairs, both nationally and for the railways. People at all levels, the man in the street and on the railway, in management and in the Government, have a number of major decisions to make about the future.
>
> The need for decision – whether it concerns the Common Market, the pay pause, or the future of the railways – is clear. We must decide quickly on the best means of competing successfully with the rest of the world in the battle for exports, without which we cannot maintain, let alone increase, our standards of living or levels of employment. This need for decision brings with it various doubts and fears, but the way of resolving all these doubts and fears is a straightforward one. Nationally, and on the railways too, the way is to improve the quality and reduce the cost of our product. If we are to survive satisfactorily, economies are not enough; we must sell more and increase our revenue. In other words, we must produce more sales value per man employed.
>
> In railway terms, this means that we must be more selective in the service we provide and we must improve overall performance by better use of manpower and more intensive and effective use of rolling stock and all other forms of equipment. All these factors affect our level of productivity – a level which must be very greatly raised if the railways are to stay in business. Only by reducing our costs and improving the services we continue to provide will we increase our revenue.
>
> Everyone can and must help in doing all these things, but the essential responsibility for getting things done rests on the management – technical, operating and commercial alike.

Sixteen years have elapsed, and his message must be just as relevant now as it was then. Nor is it, I suggest, peculiar to British Railways.

In 1962 I was destined to vacate my position as Director of Work Study and take up the position of Deputy General Manager of the newly created BR Workshops Division. I left the field of work study with the knowledge that whatever had been achieved to date was only a beginning and that tremendous scope remained for increased produc-

tivity in every activity connected with the railways. The pace had to quicken if the railways were to survive. I could never stress too frequently that transport added nothing to the quality of the goods carried. It only added to their cost.

I cannot do better than reproduce the thoughts I put on paper at that time. The write-up was published in the quarterly work study journal which I had started entitled *Project* and in which one of my Headquarters assistants, Geoffrey Lund, took a prominent and enthusiastic part.

> After six years as Director of Work Study I have been reviewing the progress we have made and the future development of the ways and means available to us for studying work.
>
> In the widest sense the job of the Railways Board is to provide rail services which meet the nation's needs and to achieve a viable railway system. To help management reach their objectives, there are two separate yet inter-related aspects of work study. The first is what I might call the bread-and-butter of our job – the investigation of lines, depots, stations, offices and workshops, examining each job, studying the methods and measuring the work content so that we improve productivity – the input/output ratio – of the unit we are investigating, of labour, materials and services. The second aspect is the use of work study as a tool of management to help in planning the way ahead.
>
> So far as the first aspect is concerned, we have made considerable progress. On British Railways in the past six years the number of men whose work has been studied has grown from 5000 to 58 000. We have carried out pilot investigations in every type of activity with which British Railways are concerned. It is a unique achievement. But we must accelerate the work and strive for improved quality.
>
> The number of trained work study staff has in the same period increased from approximately 100 to 1740. The rate of net savings, covering both labour and equipment, averages £100 per annum for each man whose job has been covered, after taking into account the payment of incentive bonus and the cost of staff to maintain the schemes. The greater part of the staff covered are paid incentive bonus based on measured work, so increasing their earnings, the higher wages per man being offset by the employment of a smaller number. We are thus making progress along the road towards a viable railway system operated by a smaller number of better-paid staff. Although these are substantial achievements, we still have a very long way to go.
>
> One aspect of considerable importance is that we have not yet achieved acceptance of work analysis and the integration of work study into management –

a position which efficient industries in America reached over thirty years ago. We have to keep constantly in mind that work study of itself accomplishes nothing. It is only when management takes full advantage of the help work study can give that real results become possible, and indeed certain.

Thus the second aspect of work study, as I have said, is its use as a tool of management in carrying out the job of planning the way ahead. Here it is not so much a matter of improving detail methods as to finding out whether a particular function is necessary at all; not so much whether we can improve methods as of designing units so that they cost less to operate and maintain. For instance, instead of building bigger and better marshalling yards, how far can we order our trains and traffic flows so that they do not require marshalling?

A good example of the use of work study has been in the introduction of concrete sleepers and long-welded rails. When the adoption of these was under consideration, it was largely the anticipated savings in maintenance cost found to be possible by work study which justified the increased cost of materials and installation. Having put in the new track, we have now established by further study, that the maintenance and inspection periods can be progressively lengthened, so achieving additional savings in maintenance costs.

There can be no doubt that the most important fields for work study are in traffic organization. This is the railway proper, all other work being ancillary to it. Work study in its widest sense is already being used in the identification and solution of the fundamental problems of traffic working. In this the critical examination technique – one of work study's greatest assets – is proving of special value.

This technique has been developed as a discipline to guide investigating teams along strictly logical paths to the various possible solutions to a defined problem. It is then necessary to evaluate the practical solutions and so find the one which is the best under the existing circumstances or constraints.

Critical examination can be used on various scales, according to whether a manager is employing it as an aid to decision-making or whether an investigating team is using it as a guide to the course which the investigation should take. In either case it is a most powerful and flexible research tool, comparable to an electronic microscope or to a hand-glass according to the scale on which it is employed.

Common to both aspects of work study is the technical development and production of accurate synthetic data. This is work being done by all Regions and departments to standards and specifications laid down by the Director of Work Study. The data is indexed under functions and types of work. The basic times are obtained under closely defined conditions, and from the data, job and task times are collated for any purpose for which they are needed. This serves the double purpose of ensuring uniformity and of avoiding duplication of investigation work. There is considerably more scope for the use of the data in planning, in labour control and in design work.

Work Study must win recognition as being closely involved in every aspect of management. While it does so, particular emphasis must be placed on its application in the traffic field, as I have suggested, in the planning of new projects and in the achievement of the highest efficiency standards in workshop operations. These are the areas of the railway business in which we can achieve the most rewarding results – for work study as an activity, for the railways as a whole, and for the people who work for them.

Throughout my tenure of office as Director of Work Study, I had three additional allied responsibilities. The first of these was to be the Chairman of the British Railways Suggestions Committee. This was composed of senior Headquarters officers representing each major activity of the railways, together with a senior officer from each Region of British Railways. We met each month and suggestions which had been vetted in the six Regions and were considered worthy of our attention were carefully reviewed and financial awards made. The second was to attend the British Railways Productivity Committee meetings under the chairmanship of John Ratter, Technical Member of British Railways Board. This Committee included three Board Members, Alec Dunbar the Manpower Adviser, three General Managers, two or three Senior Officers like myself, and the senior Trades Union Officers of the major Trades Unions.

Apart from the visits of the British Railways Productivity Committee to newly developed installations, it was customary for an annual visit to be made to an overseas railway. These included Germany, Holland, Sweden and Switzerland. Such visits were always well organized, extremely informative, and well worthwhile. It was during our visit to Switzerland that Roland Bond and I were invited to ride on the footplate as our special train went through the world renowned St Gotthard Tunnel.

My third commitment was as the representative of the Nationalized Industries on the Government sponsored British Productivity Council. This Council mainly consisted of members of the CBI and TUC.

1961 was National Productivity Year, during which there was a very successful National Conference held at Eastbourne. I attended this as the representative of the Nationalized Industries and was introduced to the Duke of Edinburgh who took a lively interest in all that was being done.

By the time I left the post of Director of Work Study, my successor was appointed as Director of Work Study, British Railways. Hence I was the first and last Director of Work Study to the British Transport Commission.

CHAPTER 12

BRITISH RAILWAYS
WORKSHOPS DIVISION

The Transport Act of 1962 saw the end of the British Transport Commission and the creation of separate Boards for its various Divisions. It was at this period that the British Railways Board came into existence and for the first time in the development of the railways the main workshops were transferred from the control of the six Regions and a separate Workshops Division created.

Under the reorganization which followed the Transport Act of 1962 the General Manager of the new Workshops Division reported directly to the Board, and was invested with a status similar to that of the Chief Regional Officers of the six Regions. The reorganization was the last of a series spanning half a century of railway history, and it is instructive to examine briefly the changes which preceded it.

Under the Railways Act of 1921 each of the four railway companies which were formed included a nucleus of main line companies which constituted the major elements in the new undertakings, the rest being subsidiary companies.

The order in which Table 12.1 is arranged coincides with the relative size, the first-mentioned being the largest of the four networks. Investing Day was 1 January, 1923. The first general manager of the London Midland and Scottish Railway, which absorbed my Company, the Midland Railway, was Sir Guy Granet, a former general manager of the Midland Railway. Within three years he had come to the conclusion that the organization was too big to be run by one individual and from 1927 an Executive Committee, comprising a President and four Vice-Presidents, was introduced. The President was Sir Josiah Stamp – later Lord Stamp – an outstanding economist and a former director of ICI, and within a short period Lord Stamp became Chairman too. He was still in office when tragically he met his death in April 1941.

Throughout the Second World War the railways were under Government control and it was not surprising that a newly elected Labour Government decided to go ahead in 1945 with full nationalization. Accordingly, for better or for worse, this irrevocable step was taken by the Transport Act of 6 August, 1947, and Investing Day was 1 January, 1948. The question of nationalization had been going on for a century or more and it had finally been resolved. It is interesting to record that the Chairman of the London and North Eastern Railway at that time was William Whitelaw, grandfather of the likeable and trustworthy Willie Whitelaw, Secretary of State for Northern Ireland in the Edward

TABLE 12.1   FORMATION OF MAIN LINE COMPANIES

New Railway Company	Constituent Companies	Subsidiary Companies	Total
London Midland and Scottish Railway	8	27	35
London and North Eastern Railway	7	26	33
Great Western Railway	7	26	33
Southern Railway	5	14	19
Totals	27	93	120

Heath Government and Deputy Leader of the Conservative Party under Mrs Thatcher. The total number of locomotives taken over was 20 030, comprising 448 different types.

In 1952 a Government White Paper was followed by the Transport Act of 1953 and a further reorganization of railways took place.

In 1960 the British Transport Commission organization came under the scrutiny of the Select Committee on Nationalized Industries, under the Chairmanship of Sir Toby Low. At about the same time the Minister of Transport, Ernest Marples, was being assisted by a Special Advisory Group, chaired by Sir Ivan Stedeford. The group included Dr Richard Beeching, Technical Director of ICI. At this time there were 450 000 employees on the six Regions of British Railways with a total route mileage of approximately 16 000 and track mileage of 44 000.

Within a few months of Dr Richard Beeching becoming Chairman of British Railways he brought in as a Member of the Board – with the approval of the Minister of Transport – Sir Steuart Mitchell. Dr Beeching's object in doing so was for Sir Steuart to carry out a survey of all the main Locomotive and Carriage and Wagon Works, totalling twenty-eight, with a view to their control being transferred from the six Regions

and centralized under one authority responsible directly to the Board. It transpired that Sir Steuart had carried out a rationalization of the Royal Ordnance factories in his capacity as Director General.

At this time I was not in any way involved and I continued to function as Director of Work Study, in which position there was unlimited scope for me to be kept fully occupied for the rest of my working life.

Sir Steuart Mitchell set about his survey, involving visits to each of the main works, and towards the end he had two or three conversations with me. I had been closely associated with the works over a longer period than most active railway engineers and he wanted to seek my views on a number of points which had occurred to him.

Soon after his report and recommendations had been approved by the Board, Sir Steuart became Vice-Chairman to Dr Beeching and continued to devote most of his attentions to the new Workshops Division which he was required to set up. In September 1962 Dr Beeching sent for me and said that Sir Steuart Mitchell had been talking to him about me and would like me to join the new organization. I had not expected to receive this invitation, as several senior appointments had

TABLE 12.2 STOCK OF BR MOTIVE POWER UNITS, 1948–1964

| Year | Locomotives (Standard gauge) | | | Multiple-unit vehicles Power cars and trailers | |
	Steam	Electric	Diesel and diesel-electric	Electric	Diesel and diesel-electric
1948	20 211	17	69	4235	40
1949	19 790	17	102	4606	39
1950	19 598	10	128	4597	39
1951	19 103	33	148	4560	36
1952	18 859	58	211	4597	36
1953	18 584	65	260	4571	39
1954	18 420	71	320	4638	72
1955	17 955	71	456	4685	181
1956	17 522	71	609	4948	455
1957	16 954	71	803	5013	1351
1958	16 103	72	1201	5270	2422
1959	14 452	85	1800	5854	3252
1960	13 271	135	2550	6442	3833
1961	11 687	158	3179	6916	4011
1962	8764	178	3683	6982	4087
1963	7047	194	4060	7021	4145
1964	4970	198	4462	7004	4120

Key

Horwich .... works continuing

Gorton .... works closing down

C .... activity on carriages

L .... activity on locomotives

W .... activity on wagons

An encircled letter indicates that
activity is to be discontinued

① .... one works where there
were previously two

② .... 2 works closing

2 .... 2 works continuing

Fig. 12.1 Map showing the reorganization of British Railways' Main Works

already been made in the new Workshops Division and I had anticipated being left in charge of the BR work study programme. I asked Dr Beeching in what capacity I was required, and he said that, whilst he did not rule me out as General Manager, he felt he had to look around outside the Railway organization for a younger man. He suggested therefore my being appointed as Deputy General Manager and if this was acceptable he would like me to go and talk the matter over with Sir Steuart. This I did, and I was appointed, with mixed feelings, in my new capacity, on 14 September, 1962. By this time many of my old works colleagues were already working in the embryo Workshops Division headquarters in senior positions. These included Frank Pepper as Assistant General Manager, Irvine Forsyth as Production Manager, R. C. S. Low as Technical Manager, E. R. Brown as Locomotive Manager, S. A. S. Smith as Carriages Manager, W. Vandy as Wagons Manager and John F. Cameron, one of my own senior work study assistants, as Personnel Manager. All did a first class job and it is good to know that John Cameron, the youngest of all of them, was appointed a member of the London Transport Executive in 1974.

I was fortunate in having Beryl Phasey – my extremely competent secretary throughout my years as Director of Work Study – transfer with me to my new post. She was most efficient and, although earmarked to become Dr Beeching's secretary, a short time later she married Derek Finch and resigned. She was succeeded by José Pipon who also gave me excellent assistance and I had no worries over correspondence, keeping appointments or taking minutes at meetings. José Pipon is now Mrs Peter Mundy and I owe it to her for kindly volunteering to type the manuscript of these memoirs.

Shortly after my appointment, I saw Sir Steuart's report on the main workshops. In total there were twenty-eight main works, and of these he had recommended that twelve should be closed, the remaining sixteen be re-equipped at a cost around £18 million, and the workload be re-allocated. A very substantial saving was anticipated by the time the scheme was completed. It was an impressive report and one which would take a few years to implement. Not unnaturally there were some railway officers who regretted the separation of the workshops from Regional control, but I was of the opinion that the advantages far outweighed any disadvantages.

The considerable reduction in workshop staff which was envisaged did not surprise me. I was very conscious of the millions of capital which had been allocated to new locomotives, diesel rail cars, and coaching stock under the modernization plan initiated by Sir Brian Robertson, and it was crystal clear to me that the volume of new building and maintenance of locomotives and rolling stock would inevitably be permanently reduced. The renewals of diesel-electric power units and all the electrical equipment would need to be obtained from contractors and these items represented a high proportion of the cost of a diesel-electric or electric locomotive. In the days of steam locomotives BR designed and manufactured almost everything, but it was clearly out of the question for them to give any serious thought to attempting to compete with the outside engineering industry which had invested many millions of pounds in research and development work. My former chief, R. A. Riddles, who was the Mechanical, Electrical and Road Motor Engineering Member of the former Railway Executive – and had retired some years previously – said to me that in his view British Railways would have saved a lot of money if they had retained steam locomotives until they were able to electrify all the lines they wished to retain and only use the diesels, say of about 350 hp, for shunting work. It is an interesting comment, the economics of which can never be proved.

I attended the meeting on 19 September, 1962, which Sir Steuart held with the employees' side of the Railway Shopmen's National Council; understandably the news of the proposed closures and reductions in staff went down very badly and there was angry reaction from the Trades Union representatives. Although Sir Steuart presented the Railways' case in a masterly way one can well imagine the atmosphere at this first meeting. Within a few days protest marches were held at several of the works to be closed and there were long processions through the towns concerned.

For some months, there was no appointment of a general manager and Sir Steuart Mitchell kept in close touch; I decided to visit each works and, with the works manager present, explain to the employees' representatives how we intended to implement the proposals. Although I experienced a mixed reception I endeavoured to give the men solid reasons why the decision had to hold. Difficult though these meetings were, I realized the necessity for them and will always feel they served an extremely useful purpose.

One of the early questions to be resolved was the location of the Workshops Division head-quarters to control sixteen main works and several smaller depots employing a total of around 60 000 staff. We made a careful analysis and almost every sign pointed to Derby, with its concentration of railway activities. When I spoke to Sir Steuart he said that it was for me to decide, so I went ahead. The first difficulty encountered was the lack of a suitable railway-owned office block. It was suggested to me that a two-storey wooden building should be erected adjacent to the impressive Research Centre. I felt it would hardly be in keeping with a headquarters which was to be the equivalent of a Regional headquarters. My attention was drawn to a sizeable new office block in Derby, not finished inside, in what was to be called Main Centre. Through the good offices of our Estate Department, I followed it up and we took it on a twenty-one-year lease, with an agreement that we did all the interior work – making of offices, plumbing, central heating, electrical work and decorating. It was centrally situated and very convenient for the staff. Subsequent to my retirement British Railways decided to concentrate additional specialized activities at Derby and the Chief Architect of BR, Dr Fred Curtis, designed a complex of buildings called the BR Technical Centre, at Derby, on the outskirts of the town but advantageously on railway property and adjacent to the Research Department. Provision was made for the Work-shops Headquarters and after four years' occupa-tion the Main Centre lease was transferred to Derby Borough Council.

I chaired the various selection panels for making senior appointments in the new Work-shops Division and took the initiative in a number of policy matters. These included a standard pattern of works organization for each of the works, and determining the responsibilities for each post. Another priority was the need for the standardization of production planning docu-mentation to ensure adequate financial control, and most of the new system was in operation by the time I made my farewell. I had an experienced team for this work and they did a great job. There was plenty of scope for all of us in the new organization. Some works were being closed and the land and buildings offered for sale, whilst other works were being modernized and re-

equipped to deal with diesel-electric and electric locomotives, rail cars, new designs of coaching stock, wagons and containers. Fourteen years had elapsed since BR came into existence and it was the first opportunity for rationalization on an unrestricted scale.

Out of the twenty-eight main works, employing a total of 60 000 staff, only sixteen were to continue, following reorganization, with a staff of approximately 40 000. A few years later two of these sixteen works were closed, namely Barassie in Ayrshire, and Inverurie in Aberdeenshire. Barassie works were built in 1901 by the former Glasgow and South Western Railway (later part of the LMS) and were used for the repair of wagons and containers. Inverurie works were also built in 1901 by the Great North of Scotland Railway (later part of the LNE) and were used for repairing locomotives, carriages, wagons and containers. Both works were in a very good state of repair and well equipped, but it was found that the more extensive reorganized works at St Rollox, Glasgow, could fully meet all the locomotive and rolling stock repair activities for the Scottish Region.

Although sixteen main works were to continue productive activities, not one of them would function precisely as before. There was a complete rationalization of activities and all the attendant problems which arose had to be resolved between one works and another without impairing output. After all, British Rail could not close down even for one day. Output had to be maintained and problem after problem had to be resolved in proper sequence. Experienced col-leagues in the organization made a superb contribution. These were eventful days which had no parallel in the long history of main works, extending over one and a quarter centuries. Until this major reorganization took place BR had no grade of workshop supervisor higher than Chief Foreman. Some of these Chief Foremen con-trolled several hundred highly skilled artisan staff and I took the opportunity of re-designating a select few of them in the largest of the works to the grade of Shop Superintendent. It gave them supervisory status more in keeping with their considerable responsibilities and the new grades had high psychological value.

The Department of Applied Economics at Cambridge University, under its Director, Professor W. B. Reddaway, became very interested in the inevitable redundancy at the

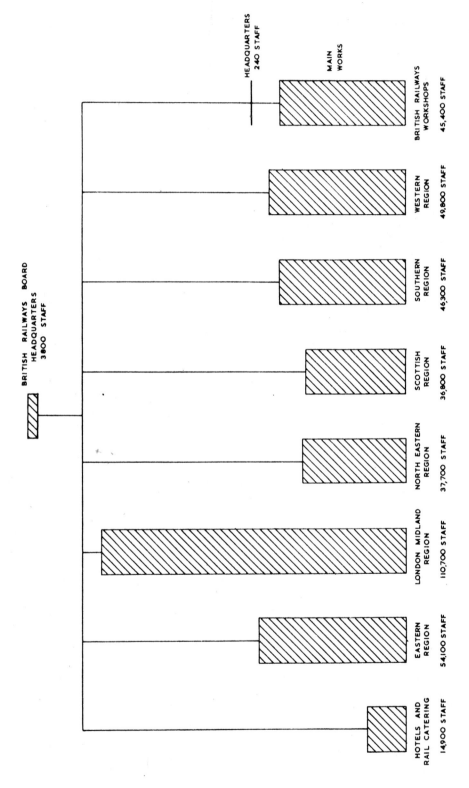

Fig. 12.2   Relative size of BR Regions and Workshops Division, 1965

various works and arrangements were made for Mrs Dorothy Wedderburn, Senior Research Officer at Cambridge University, to head a team of twelve to carry out a survey at two of the main works due to be closed.

Mrs Wedderburn's Report, published in July 1965, was a substantial one, running to 240 printed pages. On the whole the story was a cheering one for those who were anxious to ascertain whether the people and institutions of this country could show sufficient flexibility to make economic progress possible. One unexpected feature emerged clearly from this research and other researches: the Ministry of Employment's Exchanges, which are available free of charge to both employers and workers, played only a minimal role in the workings of the labour market. The picture of haphazard and disorganized methods of bringing employer and employee into contact remained surprisingly similar to those portrayed in Beveridge's classic account, some sixty years previously.

The Preface to the Report included the following:

It is difficult to express adequately my gratitude to the Railways Board and particularly to Sir Steuart Mitchell, the main author of the Workshops Plan. He immediately welcomed the idea of this study and gave freely of his own time for discussion and for comment upon the results. Not only did we receive every facility for carrying out the field work from the Railways Board but they also contributed generously to the cost without attaching any conditions. Mr Larkin of the Workshops Division at Headquarters always made us feel that nothing we asked was too much trouble for him. At Faverdale and Gorton we received the help of many people too numerous to name, but we must mention the two Works Managers, Mr Hillier and Mr Campbell, who had the unenviable task of managing the two works we studied during the run down and closure period and yet found time to make arrangements for us. On the trade union side I am grateful to Mr Brassington, Assistant Secretary of the NUR.

Those who conduct surveys are always indebted to the people who come in the sample and are willing to give up their time to be interviewed. The workshop men from Gorton and Faverdale made the team feel very much at home. Many other people in Manchester and Darlington – trades union officials, local authority officials and ordinary local people – talked freely to us and helped to fill in the background of the story. The Ministry of Labour, both locally and nationally, and the National Coal Board also supplied essential background material

and assistance. This was the first survey to be analysed on the HEC 1202 computer kindly made available jointly to the Department of Applied Economics and to the Cambridge Language Research Unit by ICT.

A separate Survey covering the whole of the Workshops Rationalization Plan, which was announced in September 1962, was undertaken by Dr Lesley Cook, also of the Cambridge Department of Applied Economics, and this too was a notable contribution to an extremely difficult problem. Dr Cook reported:

When a complex multi-department, multi-works, joint product enterprise like the main railway workshops has to contract, enormous problems have to be faced and heart-rending decisions taken. Great works have to be closed and several thousands of long service employees dismissed in towns largely dependent upon these works. The Plan seemed, to many, drastic, harsh and ruthless. There had been a long period of uncertainty and it was known that something had to be done but the actual plans came as an unpleasant surprise because they were unexpectedly far reaching. One reaction was that they were unnecessarily ruthless. Why, it was asked, was there such a hurry to do so much? Why had the axe been wielded so furiously?

The plans covered the five year period 1962–67 and during that period, but mainly by the end of 1965, the number employed was to be reduced from 62 000 to 42 000 and the number of separate main works establishments from twenty-eight to sixteen; in addition, three large works were to be substantially reduced. Examination of the nature of the problems exposes many reasons why so much contraction was planned and so suddenly announced, but that something had to be done was already obvious and changes were already being made.

The main workshops of British Railways constitute a very large organization. In 1962 over 60 000 people were employed. This is comparable with the boot and shoe industry or the hosiery industry. The railway workshops are however highly specialized; their main activity, two thirds, is the maintenance and overhauling of locomotives, carriages and wagons. The other third of the work is the building of new stock, which constitutes about one sixth of the total, and 'other activities'. The latter cover work on a range of items such as mobile cranes, chains, batteries, furniture, points and crossings equipment and some road vehicles.

In 1962 the Workshops Division was created and the main workshops came under a central organization. It is important to recognize that they were then for the first time looked at as a single business and that for the first time also their capacity was looked at from a national rather than a regional point of view.

The number of main railway workshops* can be measured in two ways. In 1962 there were 47 individual main works which were distinct organizations carrying on a particular range of activities but they were not wholly independent of each other. In many cases a single Works Manager controlled two of these workshops and the number of separate and independently managed units was 29. The 29 main units were located in 24 towns, for in Derby, Darlington, Glasgow, Eastleigh (Hants) and Swindon there were two independent workshops. Thus in 1962, 62 000 people were employed in 24 towns in only 29 independent organizations – an average size of over 2000, which is high.

The typical size was about 3000 employees. In 1962 there were ten of this size including the two adjacent works at Swindon and only one, Crewe with 5970, was substantially larger. The eleven largest employed 42 000 out of a total of 57 000 in the workshops grades of employees. A further six workshops employed between 1400 and 2250 men each and a total of 11 000. The remaining eight had less than 1000 employees and, in this industry, were regarded as small; between them they only employed 4000 men out of the total of 57 000 in the workshops grades. Thus 53 000 men were employed in seventeen large organizations.

Many of the 29 separate main works comprised two distinct works, one doing one activity (for example, the repair and maintenance of locomotives) and the other doing work on either carriages or wagons or both.

Looked at in terms of activities, there were 20 wagon works employing a total of nearly 12 000 men, 15 carriage works employing a total of 11 000 men and 14 locomotive works employing a total of 20 000 men. The building of new stock was done at 4 out of the 20 wagon works, 5 out of the 15 carriage works and 6 out of the 14 locomotive works. Although the works are large the number of units passing through per day or per week is relatively small.

Dr Cook concluded that the '. . . Main Workshops Plan was an impressive policy document designed to meet a very difficult and unhappy situation. It could not be popular but it could have been very much more controversial'.

The Preface to the Report included the following:

This work is the result of what I believe to be a

---

* A main workshop is defined as one where heavy repairs can be undertaken. There exist large numbers of small workshops which do light and running repairs and maintenance.

---

unique opportunity to study a major industrial reorganization while it was taking place. Industries and firms have contracted but they have not before announced their long-term plans and given all the assistance needed for an independent study to be made. The work would not have been possible if the British Railways Board had not been willing both to give full co-operation and to agree to complete freedom to express independent views. The complexity of the problems of contraction are not immediately apparent and many aspects are, I believe, quite unfamiliar.

I am very deeply indebted to Sir Steuart Mitchell, the Vice Chairman of the British Railways Board, and to Mr E. J. Larkin, Deputy General Manager of the Workshops, and to the many others I met during the course of the work.

At the beginning of 1963, H. Owen Houchen was appointed as General Manager. He came to BR from British Overseas Airways Corporation and I found him a very likeable and understanding individual. When Sir Steuart Mitchell retired – Dr Beeching was still Chairman – Owen Houchen became a Member of the Board, and my colleague, Roland Bond, formerly Chief Mechanical Engineer of BR and later Technical Adviser to the Commission, succeeded him as General Manager of the Workshops Organization.

Since my retirement from British Railways, the Workshops Division has been renamed British Rail Engineering Limited (from 1 January, 1970) and has been given Government approval to undertake contracts for outside organizations. The first managing director was a very old friend, A. E. Robson, some ten years younger than myself, who had followed me on my retirement, with the designation of Assistant General Manager, but with a remit giving emphasis on production. By the time he joined the Workshops Division in 1966, the new organization had been in existence for four years and the expenditure authorized for new layouts and equipment was well under way. The rationalization programme was completed in 1968. On his retirement in 1974 another esteemed friend, Sidney Ridgway, became the managing director and during his term of office some sizeable overseas railway contracts were secured which was good for British Rail, particularly as a balancing load for the works involved. It may well be that these contracts and others will expand as time goes on.

A brief history of the thirteen main works which today cover all the requirements of British

Rail in the field with which I was so closely associated is given below, the works being arranged in alphabetical order. During the past decade the total staff in these thirteen main works has been reduced to around 32 000.

ASHFORD WORKS

It was in February of the year 1846 that the Board of Directors of the South Eastern Railway decided to purchase 185 acres of Kentish farmland on which to lay the foundations of a 'Locomotive Establishment'. In the summer of 1847, in the shape of a cluster of seventy-two labourers' cottages, there arose the first signs of a new railway project and the story of Ashford Works had begun. Towards the end of the same year, the inaugural meeting of the Ashford Works Mechanics' Institute took place, at which the chairman of the Board stressed that the construction work was not merely of a fine and well-equipped locomotive works but of a complete village. In the autumn of the same year, official news was given that the railway's locomotive depot at New Cross would be transferred to the new site at Ashford. During 1848 work had begun on the first new locomotive to be built at the works. In the autumn of 1850 the creation of the carriage and wagon works was seen at Ashford. By this time the adjoining Railway village, known at first by the name of Alfred Town, had been expanded by another sixty houses and the gas works was making an appearance on the site. When the old railway companies were grouped in 1923, Ashford became one of the three main works of the Southern Railway and dealt with the construction and repair of locomotives, carriages and wagons. The construction of new coaches was transferred to Eastleigh and, in the main, carriage repairs to Lancing in the year 1929, and since then the main activity of the carriage and wagon works has been the building and repair of wagon stock. The total staff employed is slightly in excess of 1000.

The last locomotive built was the main line diesel-electric locomotive No. 10202, which was completed in the autumn of 1951. Locomotive repairs ceased in 1962 and activities have since been confined to wagon construction and repairs as well as repairs to many types of mobile cranes.

A reorganization programme took place between 1964 and 1966 for progressive working and to accommodate the construction and repair of modern rolling stock. Besides fulfilling their requirements for British Rail, Ashford Works have already made their mark in the building of large-capacity steel wagons for the Middle East.

CREWE WORKS

Originally built for the construction and repair of locomotives, wagons and carriages for the Grand Junction Railway (later the LNWR) the works commenced production in 1843. At that time covered an area of only 2½ acres, but from this small beginning it gradually developed to cover 136½ acres, of which 44 were covered by buildings.

From 1845 until December 1958 – when BR class 9F No. 92250, the last steam locomotive constructed at Crewe, was turned out – the works built over 7000 locomotives for the LNWR, LMSR and British Railways.

Construction of diesel locomotives commenced in 1957 with a series of diesel-electric shunters, and from June 1959, when the first main line diesel-electric 1160 hp type 2 No. 5030 was built in the works, various types of diesel-electric and diesel-hydraulic main line locomotives have been constructed at Crewe.

Extensive modernization and re-organization of the works was started in 1964 and after completion in 1968 at a cost of nearly £2 million the activities were concentrated and contracted to an area of 89½ acres. It remains the largest locomotive works centre on British Railways.

The main functions of the modernized works are building and overhaul of diesel and electric main line locomotives. In addition the works manufacture and repair a variety of mechanical signal appliances and signal gantries, wagon springs and lifting tackle used by British Rail. The works also produce steel castings in the only steel foundry belonging to British Rail Engineering.

DERBY CARRIAGE & WAGON WORKS

At the time of the formation of the Midland Railway Company in 1844 Derby boasted one works which built both locomotives and rolling stock. 1876 saw the establishment of a separate carriage and wagon works to satisfy an increasing demand for freight and passenger rolling stock. In 1923 the works became an integral part of the London Midland and Scottish Railway Company until nationalization in 1948. Extensive modernization and re-organization of the works started in 1963 and were completed in 1967 at a cost of

Fig. 12.3   Integral coach construction jig, Derby

Fig. 12.4   Typical locomotive erecting shop at Derby

£1¼ million; included in the modernization were new buildings, plant and equipment.

Many new developments have been adopted by the works during their history including the 'Standard' wagon in 1882, flow-line wagon production in 1921 and the all-steel passenger carriage in 1948. During the 1950s and early '60s both diesel and electric multiple units were built for short and medium range passenger traffic under the railways' modernization plan. In 1971 the building of fully air conditioned passenger carriages for inter-city services became the main activity. The works also builds freight containers and overhauls and repairs carriages, wagons and

Fig. 12.5   Diesel maintenance depot, Derby

diesel multiple units as well as manufacturing components for repairs carried out at regional depots. All these activities require a staff of some 4000, employed in a wide variety of skilled trades, and a total works area of 104 acres.

DERBY LOCOMOTIVE WORKS
Derby Locomotive Works are situated to the east of the main North/South railway line through Derby Midland Station, about half a mile from the city centre.

The first workshops were built in 1840, occupying a total area of 8½ acres. The present works cover 51 acres.

1851 is the earliest date on record of locomotive construction at Derby, and between 1851 and 1957, a total of 2937 steam locomotives were constructed. Between 1932 and 1967, 1010 diesel locomotives were built.

The present functions of the works are the repair and overhaul of diesel main line and shunting locomotives, the reconditioning of diesel multiple unit engines and transmission equipment and the overhaul of breakdown cranes and track maintenance vehicles.

I understand that an increasing part of the resources of the works have now been geared to the production of new coach and wagon bogies including the manufacture of the prototype bogies for the Advanced Passenger Train. These bogies are principally for British Railways, but a significant portion are for other concerns.

DONCASTER WORKS
Built in 1853 for the Great Northern Railway Company, the original works with ten shops covered an area of 11 acres. The present works cover 84 acres.

The works has built many types of locomotives, some of historical interest including the Gresley streamlined Pacific *Mallard* which holds the world speed record for steam traction of 126 mph. The last steam locomotive to be built left the works in October 1957. More recently diesel locomotives, diesel-electric shunting locomotives and 25 kV ac electric locomotives have been built. Since 1965, wagon repairs have been undertaken at the main works which previously were undertaken at the 'Carr' wagon shops two miles away.

Today the main function of the works is the repair and overhaul of diesel main line and shunting locomotives, diesel multiple units and wagons. In addition the works manufactures container lifting frames and repairs, overhauls and tests rail and mobile cranes, fork lift trucks and lifting tackle. A considerable amount of fabrication and machining work is also undertaken for outside customers.

EASTLEIGH WORKS
Originally there were two railway works at Eastleigh. The carriage works was opened by the London and South Western Railway in 1891 on a site north of the present works. After the formation of the Southern Railway in 1923

Eastleigh carriage works' main activities were the building of new carriages and containers, and the repair of carriages, wagons and containers. In 1945 construction of all-steel suburban electric carriages began alongside the construction of all-steel carriages for main line steam routes. After nationalization in 1948 various types were built to British Railways' design including main line and semi-fast electric units for Kent coast lines, also diesel-electric units for the Hastings line and for the Hampshire services.

The locomotive works was opened on the present site in 1910 and, with the railway grouping in 1923, Eastleigh became one of the three main locomotive works on the Southern Railway. Some of the notably successful classes of locomotive built were the King Arthur, Lord Nelson, Schools, Battle of Britain, West Country and LMS 2–8–0. In passing it is worthy of mention that my son is the proud possessor of one of the handsome nameplates from the locomotive *King's Wimbledon* (4–4–0 three-cylinder passenger engine No. 30931, one of the forty SR Schools Class locomotives, designed by R. E. L. Maunsell; built at Eastleigh, 1935; withdrawn from service, 1961; total mileage 1 015 426). The nameplate from the opposite side of the locomotive is in the safe keeping of King's College School, Wimbledon. It is now worth a lot more money than I paid for it when the locomotive was broken up at Ashford Works in 1961. From 1945 to 1958 the repair and rebuilding of steam locomotives was the main activity with repair facilities for diesels being added later. In 1962 the works took over the whole of the Southern Region's repair work on steam, diesel and electric locomotives, as well as motors from multiple-unit stock.

Extensive modernization and re-organization were completed in 1968 as part of the Workshops Plan. This included closing down the carriage works and the provision of new buildings, plant, equipment and staff amenities within the former locomotive works.

Today the works handles repairs and modifications to Southern Region diesel-electric locomotives, electric locomotives, electric and diesel-electric multiple-unit carriages and locomotive hauled vehicles. It covers an area of 41 acres of which 11 acres are covered buildings.

GLASGOW WORKS

Glasgow Works is situated to the north-east of the city centre in the once famous steam locomotive building district of Springburn. Erected in 1856 – rebuilt and enlarged in 1882 – the works built and maintained rolling stock for the Caledonian Railway Company. The original workshops – known as St Rollox Works – occupied an area of 31½ acres.

Locomotive building ceased in 1926 and a year later re-organization took place. Locomotives and coaches were then only maintained and repaired and all wagon repairs were transferred to Barassie Works – which closed in 1972. Between 1964 and 1968 – when Cowlairs Works closed – a major re-organization was effected to incorporate the workloads of both works. The main function of the works, which now covers 42 acres, is the repair and overhaul of diesel and electric multiple units, diesel-electric locomotives, coaches, wagons (since 1972), rail and road cranes, chain lifting tackle and relays for the Signal and Telecommunications Department. The works also undertakes the repair of containers.

HORWICH WORKS

Horwich Works are situated at the edge of the Lancashire industrial area and are within easy reach of Manchester, Liverpool and other important manufacturing towns in the north-west. Erected in 1885–87 as a locomotive building and repair works for the Lancashire and Yorkshire Railway Company, the works covered an area of 160½ acres. Locomotive repairs began in 1886 and a total of 50 000 locomotives had been through the works by 1962. The year 1888 is the earliest date recorded of new locomotive construction at Horwich and the last steam locomotive was built in 1957. A year later, the works began building the first of ninety diesel-electric shunting locomotives which ended in 1962 when the works were re-organized.

The present function of the works, which now covers 150 acres, is the repair and overhaul of electric multiple units, wagons, containers and Chief Civil Engineer's equipment. Wagon sheets (PVC/nylon), laminated springs and iron castings are manufactured, and the works also undertakes private work for customers at home and overseas. A £1½ million modernization scheme for the mechanized iron foundry will enable it to produce higher quality castings at a rate approaching 50 000 tons per annum.

Horwich Works also control Worcester sheet works which manufacture mainly canvas sheets used on rail and road vehicles by British rail and private customers.

SHILDON WORKS

Established in 1883 by the Stockton and Darlington Railway the works are situated in south-west Durham adjacent to the Teesside industrial belt. It was from a point near the works that the Stockton and Darlington Railway commenced its first services in 1825. Over the years the works have been gradually extended, and between 1965 and 1967 were extensively re-organized and modernized at a cost of £800 000.

Shildon Works are the largest wagon works of British Rail Engineering and are equipped for the construction and repair of mineral and freight wagons both for British Rail and outside customers at home and overseas. Many vehicles of new design have been proved and manufactured at Shildon, notably the 'Presflo' air discharge cement, 'High Capacity' coal and 'Freightliner' wagons. The repair shops have capacity for overhauling and repairing up to 800 wagons per week. A large proportion of the drop stampings and forgings required by British Rail are manufactured in the Shildon forge. The present area of 43 acres includes a roofed workshop area of 12 acres.

SWINDON LOCOMOTIVE AND CARRIAGE & WAGON WORKS

Swindon – the town on the hill – was mentioned in the Domesday Book in 1085, and was an ancient market town when the Great Western Railway was being constructed in 1840. In June, 1841 the line from London to Bristol was completed and passed close to the old town, 77 miles from London. Daniel Gooch, then Locomotive Superintendent, recommended Swindon as a suitable site for a new central locomotive repair depot because of its proximity to the junction with the Cheltenham branch and its location at a point on the Great Western line convenient for locomotive working. On February 25, 1841, the directors authorized construction of the works and by January 1843 they were in full operation. Much of the stone used in building the workshops was obtained from the boring of Box tunnel. From a small beginning the works grew in size until eventually it covered 826 acres of which 77 were roofed. In 1962, when the railway workshops were transferred from the control of

the Regions in which they were located and placed within the Workshops Division, Swindon's financial allocation was £2.3 million and the reorganization was completed at the end of 1967. The works was reduced in size, all activities being accommodated in an area formerly occupied by the locomotive works and covering 104 acres, with 32 acres roofed. The first diesel hydraulic main line locomotive was built at Swindon in 1958 and the last steam locomotive built for British Railways, No. 92220 (*Evening Star*), was completed in March 1960. Swindon Works no longer constructs new rolling stock. The main function of the modernized works is the repair and overhaul of diesel main line and shunting locomotives, diesel multiple unit vehicles, service vehicles, wagons and containers. The works repairs Civil Engineer's plant and equipment, such as track-laying machines, and manufactures springs and non-ferrous castings. BRUTE trolley equipment, now widely used for handling parcels traffic, is also built for all Regions of British Rail.

TEMPLE MILLS, LONDON

Temple Mills Works has a background and experience of wagon repairs dating back to its construction in 1896. In 1956 major reorganization resulted in several new shops being built and in 1963 Temple Mills works became part of British Railways Workshops Division. Over the years the works has developed prototype vehicles and become involved in repairs on Freightliner vehicles and containers, commencing in 1964. In 1974 the need for refurbishment facilities at the works became apparent and two shot blast areas were developed. The facilities and quality of work have attracted private customers, and transportation costs have been minimized by the close proximity of the works to Stratford and other London 'Freightliner' terminals. The present area of 22 acres includes a roofed workshop area of 6 acres. The total staff employed is 400 and approximately 200 wagons and 30 containers are repaired each week.

WOLVERTON WORKS

Wolverton Works are situated at the northern boundary of the new city of Milton Keynes situated approximately halfway between Euston and Birmingham. The original buildings were erected as the locomotive works of the London and Birmingham Railway in 1838 and occupied an area of approximately 2¼ acres. After the formation of the London and North Western Railway in 1865, when all locomotive work was transferred to Crewe Works, Wolverton concentrated on building and repairing carriages and wagons, and this continued after the advent of the London Midland and Scottish Railway in 1923.

In 1962, under the British Railways workshops reorganization plan, new rolling stock construction ceased and the principal activity became carriage repairs. There sometimes has to be the exception to the rule and Wolverton Works has continued to have the distinction of looking after the Royal train, whether it be new or repair work. Their work is all *par excellence* and the works personnel can be justifiably proud of their skills. Now the works is one of the largest railway carriage repair centres in Europe and covers an area of 73 acres. The main function is the repair of electric trains and all types of locomotive-hauled coaches. Other activities include container repairs, construction and repair of road vehicle bodies, manufacture of lead–acid batteries and glass-reinforced plastic components, and general engineering and joinery work for private firms.

YORK WORKS

Originally known as York Carriage Works, the works were established on the present site in 1884 by the North Eastern Railway Company.

In the early days of carriage building at York, timber arrived at one end in the form of logs and went out at the other end as coaching stock. Since then there have been several transitional stages, ranging from composite steel and timber underframes with timber bodies to steel underframes with timber bodies, and also steel underframes with composite steel and timber bodies. Subsequently all-steel coaches were introduced.

In 1958 construction was undertaken of 25 kV ac multiple-unit electric stock for the overhead line system. Since then other types of multiple-unit electric stock have been built at the rate of approximately four vehicles per week for the Southern Region's 750 V dc third rail system. The works have more recently been involved in prototype construction of carriages designed specifically for handling heavy commuter traffic.

The repair shops have capacity for overhauling and repairing up to fifty carriages per week. These are locomotive-hauled carriages and include Pullman cars, sleeping cars, catering vehicles, Post Office and service vehicles. Extensive modernization and reorganization of the works, started in 1965, was completed in 1967 at a cost of nearly £1 million. Included in the modernization were new buildings, plant and equipment, staff amenities, centralized stores facilities and new reception sidings. Old and redundant shops were demolished. The present area of 45 acres includes 12 acres of covered buildings.

CHAPTER 13

MANAGEMENT CONSULTANCY

When I was approaching the normal retiring age, to take effect from February 1965, the British Railways' Board invited me to continue in office. Although I felt as active as ever it was a request which I had not bargained for and I naturally had to give it a good deal of thought. After all, I had been working non-stop, through a whole range of widely different jobs, with a fair dose of administrative and senior managerial posts, for over fifty years.

Apart from my dearly loved family, my work had always taken precedence over all of my voluntary outside activities and I felt I should not lightly turn down the invitation. My general health throughout my working life had, fortunately, always been good. Indeed, I had only been away from the office for two days through illness since my son, Garth, was born in 1946. I did, however, learn from the Board's Superannuation Officer that for maximum pension I should retire on the day before I was 65. Accordingly I made this point and the Board therefore agreed that my resignation should take effect from 10 February, 1965, and that on my birthday, 11 February, I should be appointed as a Consultant and continue with some of my former duties as well as undertake special investigations. To the best of my knowledge, I am the only railway engineer on BR to have received this distinction. With school leaving age now having been raised to 16 years of age and the likelihood of earlier retirement for everyone it must be a British Railways service record for a BR Headquarters engineer which is unlikely to be equalled.

During 1965 Sir Steuart Mitchell resigned as Vice-Chairman of the BR Board, and the General Manager of the Workshops Division, Owen Houchen, was appointed a member of the Board. The latter's position as General Manager of the Workshops Division was filled by Roland C.

Bond, the Board's Technical Adviser. This presented no problem to either of us and as I anticipated we had a perfect rapport.

As the months slipped by and Christmas 1965 was approaching I agreed with my wife that I should arrange to relinquish my appointment with BR. Roland Bond very kindly urged me to stay on for a further period but in the end we agreed that I should leave on 31 January, 1966. And so the curtain finally came down.

From my colleagues and former staff in the Chief Mechanical and Electrical Engineer's headquarters office at Derby, from those associated with Work Study at Board headquarters in London, from the many works managers and from the workshops headquarters staff at Derby and at Board headquarters in London, I was delighted to receive a handsome silver tea-set and tray, the latter being inscribed with the following words:

Presented to *Edgar J. Larkin* by his colleagues and friends on his retirement from *British Railways* after 52 years service

January 1966

These presentations were made by Roland Bond at workshops headquarters at Derby and by Owen Houchen in the committee room at Board headquarters in London. To me they will always remain very memorable occasions. From my colleagues in the senior management mess at Board headquarters, Marylebone, London, I received a leather suitcase together with an 8 ft general purpose fishing rod, in four parts, for easy transportation. From my competent secretary, José Pipon, I received a book entitled *Where to Fish*. All these gifts were gratefully appreciated.

On the eve of my leaving British Railways I received a request from the Ministry of Overseas Development inviting me to carry out a detailed

Fig. 13.1   Farewell presentation by Roland C Bond, General Manager of British Railways Workshops Division, on behalf of all BR colleagues, February, 1966

survey of the main works of the Turkish State Railways (TCDD) and make recommendations for their reorganization, coupled with the introduction of diesel motive power and certain main line electrification.

Following discussion with my wife I agreed to visit Turkey and carry out a preliminary survey, to see what was broadly involved. I flew to Ankara, capital of Turkey, via Athens, on a British European Airways flight on 1 February, 1966. I was met at Ankara airport by a Turkish railway officer who spoke no word of English, and a young female interpreter who was employed as a secretary in the railway headquarters offices in Ankara. At the end of an intensive week I had visited three of the main works, namely Ankara, Eskisehir and Adapazari, and two motive power depots. Throughout I was accompanied by Hasïm Akduman, a headquarters workshops officer who had taken his engineering degree at Stanford

University, USA, and who spoke English fluently. He was an excellent and well-informed companion. I quickly realized that a great deal of technical assistance was required by the Turkish authorities and I decided to assist further if it was desired that I should do so. Accordingly, before I left for London on 9 February, 1966, I drew up an agreed memorandum signed by the Director-General of the Turkish State Railways and his Deputy. This read as follows:

Re-organisation of the Workshops of TCDD

1. The Workshops Plan to be based on operational needs and established technical standards of manufacture and maintenance of rolling stock.
2. The relationship between Motive Power Depots and Main Works to be defined.

Capacity
3. To determine the capacity for each activity at present undertaken in the Workshops of the

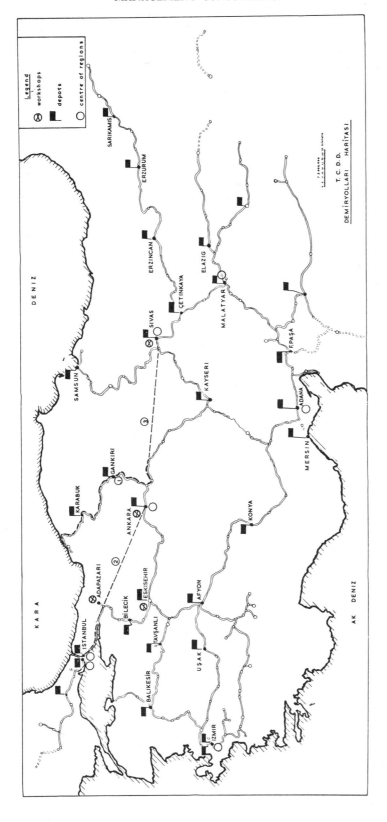

Fig. 13.2 Outline map of Turkey showing the location of the main works and motive power depots of the Turkish state railways (TCDD) 1966

Fig. 13.3   Adapazari Carriage Works

Turkish State Railways to meet railway operational needs.

4. To determine the most economical distribution of Workshops.
5. To take into account the need for capital expenditure, scope for disposal of redundant assets and other relevant factors.

Facilities

6. To determine the facilities required in each of the Continuing Works and any New Works recommended in the Workshops Plan.
7. To study the facilities available in all Works and make recommendations as to the retention, transfer or disposal of these facilities.
8. To give recommendations with supporting financial justification for any new facilities, including plant, equipment and buildings which are desired.

Productivity

9. To study the productivity of land, buildings, equipment, materials and manpower, and make recommendations for the improvement of productivity by:
   (a) Changes in the organization of the management structure of works and headquarters offices.
   (b) Training of management, engineers, supervisors, craftsmen, apprentices, semi-skilled and unskilled staff, and office personnel, to meet the future requirements of TCDD.
   (c) Changes in the method of payment of staff, including the introduction of incentive

systems of payment if these are considered to be of value in improving the level of productivity.

Technical Assistance from Great Britain

10. The investigation will require the assistance of three specialist engineers for approximately one month in Turkey to assist with specified problems. The Consultant will take the initiative in approaching the United Kingdom Railway Advisory Service [UKRAS] (representing the British Government), to obtain the loan of three experienced engineers from British Railways.
The Consultant would hope to come to Ankara with the specialist engineers about the middle of April 1966.

Procedure

11. Following the submission of the Consultant's Recommendations to the Director-General of TCDD, the Consultant will visit Turkey to explain and amplify any or all of the Recommendations. This could be early in July 1966.
The Recommendations will be arranged under two main headings, namely:
   (1) proposals which do not involve capital expenditure, and
   (2) proposals for which capital expenditure is essential.
After full discussions with the Turkish Railway authorities in Ankara and any desired amendments to the proposals have been resolved, the Consultant will take the initiative to implement the Plan so far as (1) above is concerned, with

the assistance of the appropriate Headquarters Officers and Works Managers of TCDD.

So far as (2) is concerned, the procedure will be as follows:

(a) With a view to facilitating the detail planning of the agreed physical re-organization schemes at each Works, the Director-General of the Turkish Railways will, at a later date, approve the secondment of one or more senior Railway officers at Ankara headquarters to work closely with the Consultant and co-ordinate and implement, as expeditiously as possible, the agreed Recommendations.

(b) Additionally, the Director-General of the Turkish Railways will approve the temporary appointment of a project team at each Works consisting of three engineers, namely a civil engineer, a plant engineer and a production engineer. The Works teams will be responsible to the Works Managers and will be required to prepare detailed information and plans in conformity with the Recommendations following the Consultant's report.

(c) The detail scheme for each Works, including a time scale for implementation, will require the approval of the Works Manager and endorsement by the Consultant before submission to the Director-General for financial authority.

Visits to England

12. The Consultant will take the initiative in providing appropriate contacts and facilities throughout the British Isles which will be valuable to the Turkish Railway authorities. He will make Recommendations to the Director-General for some Senior Engineers and Works Managers of TCDD to visit selected establishments of British Railways to enable them to see clearly what is required. These visits, each of about a fortnight's duration, will prove of high value in improving the efficiency of TCDD.

The Consultant will enlist the assistance of the United Kingdom Railway Advisory Service of the Ministry of Transport, as well as British Railways, to make these visits possible.

It might be advantageous for these visits to take place after the Recommendations have been received in Ankara and before the Consultant makes the suggested visit in July 1966.

It was an assignment of great interest and after seeing Sir Hugh Parry at the Ministry together with Bernard M. Strouts of the United Kingdom Railway Advisory Service, I agreed to undertake the Survey.

In my opening discussions with Feyzi Ozïl, the Chief Officer for Planning at Ankara head-

quarters, I gleaned some useful background information about TCDD. There were 4765 miles of standard 4 ft 8½ in gauge track, of which 17 miles were electrified at 25 000 V, 50 cycles. Additionally there were 76 miles of 5 ft gauge and 77 miles of 2 ft 5½ in gauge.

The motive power fleet and total rolling stock were as follows:

Number of locomotives:

Steam	858 (German, Swiss, British and American manufacture)
Diesel	48 main line (3 diesel-hydraulic, 45 diesel-electric)
	117 shunting locomotives
	3 electric locomotives

Number of carriages: 1167
Number of multiple units:

Diesel	58
Electric	30

Number of wagons:

Open	6880
Closed	8906
Tank	182

In July 1953 the Turkish Railway administration acquired the status of a Public Corporation and together with the acquisition of the existing railways the Turkish Government began a programme of new railway construction which had extended the railway service to almost every part of Turkey. Construction had continued without interruption since 1923 with an average of 62 miles of new line annually. Further railway construction was planned and by 1963 the Turkish Ministry of Public Works had completed surveys for almost 1364 miles of additional railway lines and had made preliminary surveys for nearly 2170 more.

Projects high on the list included the construction of a difficult 19 mile line joining the present Black Sea port of Zonguldak with the port of Eregli, which is the site of Turkey's major steel producing plant, and a 174 mile east–west link between the two existing TCDD routes to the Black Sea coast which would provide a shorter and better route for some 45 000 tons of iron ore to be transported annually between the mines and another steel mill at Karabuk.

The most important railway construction project in recent years had been the Turkey–Iran rail link built under the auspices of the Central Treaty Organization (CENTO). This was part of the CENTO plan to link Turkey, Iran and Pakistan by rail.

A 62 mile extension to Tatvan was opened by the Turkish Prime Minister in October 1964 when it was stated that the link was expected to be completed by 1967 and it would then be possible to go from London to Teheran by train.

The Turkish State Railways were rated as the largest Turkish industry and employed 60 000 personnel. They included four main works, employing in total some 10 000 men and an additional 6000 men in the motive power depots. At the time of the survey in May 1966 the TCDD had prepared two five-year development plans, in conjunction with the Ministry of Transport and the Ministry of Planning, to cover the entire railway system. The first covered the period 1963–67 and the second 1968–72.

I found Turkey an enchanting country. It is about 3½ times as big as the British Isles, but with only half the population. Ankara became the capital of Turkey before the Second World War in the time of Kemal Ataturk. He considered that Istanbul (previously Constantinople) was too near the border and he chose Ankara to take its place. Kemal Ataturk's tomb and memorial in Ankara provide the outstanding piece of architecture in the City, but in my humble view it will take centuries for Ankara to compare with Istanbul in interest.

I made three further visits to Turkey; the first of these commenced on 22 April, 1966, and I arranged with British Railways to have with me, on secondment for two months, the services of three professional engineers. These were R. Hitchings, who at that time was Assistant Works Manager at Horwich Works, Dennis J. Lees, Production Engineer at Doncaster Works, and Harry Roberts, Assistant Works Manager at York Works. They were each extremely knowledgeable engineers and specialists in particular fields. We worked at top speed and for long hours throughout the two months and between us we made detailed surveys of the four main works. We made many friends among the railway officers and we were given an official welcome by the British Ambassador to Turkey. The social side, inevitably short because we had much work to do, was full of interest and much enjoyed by all four of us.

Turkey extends into both Europe and Asia, with most of the country, including the capital Ankara, in Asia. Before the Second World War French was the second language in the country, but it is now English and some of the senior railway officers and all the works managers spoke English fluently. We had no time to learn much Turkish and found it impossible to converse with the average Turk. It is a country in which one can see extreme wealth and poverty side by side. The Turks can boast, however, of being rich in minerals and being largely self-contained. Their fruit and vegetables are all *par excellence*; I have never seen better melons, which could be bought at the side of the road very cheaply.

On completion, my report was printed and six copies sent to Turkey. Copies were also sent to the Ministry of Overseas Development and the Locomotive and Allied Manufacturers Association (LAMA) in London. In Turkey the report was well received and accepted in principle, and this acceptance also included a high proportion of the detailed recommendations.

The main proposals provided for the following:

1. An improved Headquarters organization to give closer technical and financial control.
2. A modern rationalized organization for each of the main works. This had the advantage that when management, technical, clerical or supervisory staff were transferred from one works to another, they would operate a standard procedure common to all works. Furthermore, senior assistants could readily be brought together from different works with common problems to resolve.
3. A standard Job Specification for each management position at works level.
4. Radical changes in shop layouts and equipment at each works, necessitated by the changeover to diesel and electric traction, coupled with a measure of rationalization to facilitate more economic production.
5. The introduction of modern types of machines and workshop processes.
6. Arrears of buildings maintenance.
7. Improved heating and lighting schemes.
8. Improved amenities.
9. Introduction of initial examination and finished work inspection with appropriate pre-printed documentation enabling management to control effectively the volume and quality of work undertaken.
10. A reduction in the time locomotives and rolling stock were undergoing repair as well as the number on the works at any given time.
11. The introduction of machine printed and centralized documentation for new locomotives and rolling stock as well as for all manufacturing activities.

12. A considerable improvement in the level of productivity by raising operator performance through such management service techniques as method study, work measurement and network analyses.

13. Closer financial control at all levels, covering new manufacture, repair work, estimating and workshop expenses.

14. A much wider and improved curriculum for the training of apprentices in the Training Schools, and the initiation of a systematic programme of vocational training courses for management, technical, workshop supervisory and artisan staff.

15. Other recommendations which, taken collectively, would materially assist in the more efficient and more economic running of TCDD.

A knowledgeable railway engineer, who had looked after me on my first solo visit to Turkey, Hasïm Akduman, from Ankara headquarters, accompanied the team throughout our tour, and his never-failing courtesy is something to remember.

For my third visit to Turkey, I combined business with pleasure. I had been asked to discuss my Report with the Director-General and Senior Officers of the Turkish State Railways. I also had the great pleasure of having my wife Freda and my son Garth and daughter Anthea accompanying me, and whilst I spent a week with the Turkish officials explaining any aspect of my Report on which they desired further clarification, my family were conducted around the capital. We also visited Istanbul, Adapazari and Meneksha on the shores of the Sea of Marmara. On leaving Turkey, all four of us spent a week in Greece and Italy staying at Athens and Rome in turn, before returning home.

On my fourth and last visit in February 1967, I travelled alone to Ankara to have further discussions with the Railway administration at their request. On my last day with them, when I met the Turkish Minister of Transport, I was accompanied by Miss Marian Clay of our Diplomatic Service, the extremely competent liaison officer from the British Embassy who had been so helpful to me and my colleagues and who drew up an excellent resumé of the final discussions.

During 1969 the British Minister of Overseas Development sent a technical officer from Beirut – the diplomatic and administration centre for Middle East commitments – to report on progress made. A copy of his report was sent to me for comments. It was a favourable report which emphasized that the Turkish railway management needed further technical assistance to implement some of my many proposals. Within a year or so the French Government, under President de Gaulle, had offered such favourable financial aid in the purchase of capital equipment that the British Government could not, or would not, compete, much to the dismay of British industry. This was the time when Britain lost its opportunity to provide any diesel or electric traction to Turkey. Early in 1972, however, there was a change in Turkish policy and I was asked whether I would consider making another visit to Turkey and ascertain what further assistance they needed and would welcome from Britain. Regretfully, I found it necessary to decline the invitation because we had recently moved home and were in the middle of certain structural improvements. Furthermore, I was not anxious to be away from home again and leave my family behind.

Following my Report on the TCDD, I was invited by a well-known group of machine tool manufacturers in England to visit both the Middle East and South America. They suggested my carrying out short surveys of the railway workshops in various countries, following which they would send their own technical staff with a view to implementing my recommendations. I just had to decline because I began to think I should never retire!

In addition to my consultancy work for British Railways and the Turkish Railways I also conducted a relatively short survey of the supervisory training required in the Shipbuilding Industry. The request came to me through Sir Steuart Mitchell, Chairman of the Shipbuilding Training Board and the former Vice-Chairman of BR under Dr Richard Beeching (later Lord Beeching). It was a fascinating assignment. I visited the largest shipbuilding firms, some middle-sized firms, and some quite small firms engaged in boat building. The amount of training already given was negligible and there was very wide scope. I formed the impression that the Board had to cater for what were virtually two separate industries, namely shipbuilding and boat building. It was crystal clear that lines of demarcation between grades as to the work that each should perform were always in dispute on the shipbuilding side of the industry. This situation contrasted sharply with the boat building side of the industry where lines of demarcation were scarcely ever known.

Some interesting facts emerged from the survey. Although there were about 33 per cent more boat building and repair firms than shipbuilding and repair firms, the staff employed in boat building and repair work amounted to only 7 per cent of the number engaged in shipbuilding and repair work. There were 15 shipbuilding establishments employing over 2000 persons and these accounted for no less than 41 per cent of the total shipbuilding labour force. Furthermore, of the 373 establishments employing under 11 persons, 258 were boat builders. Although there are considerable differences between new manufacture and repair work, whether one is dealing with ships or boats, the differences between ship work and boat work are much more apparent. Boats, although in these days not necessarily limited to timber construction, are certainly limited in their overall size – say

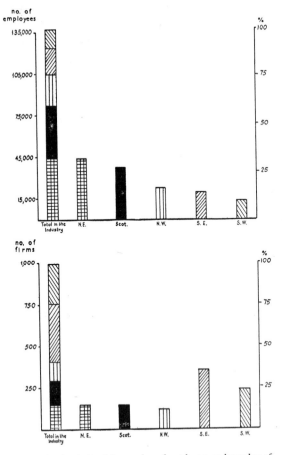

Fig. 13.4 *Analysis of the number of employees and number of firms in the shipbuilding industry, 1966*

60 or 70 feet in length. Furthermore, boat-building establishments are for the most part relatively small family businesses in which the owner operates the simplest of organizations often with only a working foreman, who is paid by the hour, or by one or more working chargehands; the owner is in daily contact with his men, actively directing and working with them as he considers necessary.

Shipbuilding and boat building are both highly competitive businesses, influenced, no doubt, by the fact that there is scarcely ever enough work available to go round. The Geddes Report of 1966, published shortly before I carried out my survey, provided a comprehensive analysis of the future needs of the industry. Shipbuilding is part of industry, and industry is part of society; society is always changing and this means that managements' attitudes must also change. It seemed to me that a major step forward would be the elimination of the peaks in employment and the avoidance of the need for men to move so frequently from one firm to another by running on a 'more even keel'. Supervisor training could well provide a satisfactory solution for this and many such problems.

It was generally accepted by management at all levels that staff relationships, using the term in its widest sense, were the most complex and difficult part of its responsibility. For this reason alone the supervisor had a great role to play in ensuring *esprit de corps*, in ensuring loyalty to the organization and in helping to ensure that:

(1) the quality of the product would give satisfaction to the customer;
(2) productive wages costs were held at an economic level, thus securing continuity of work coming into the firm;
(3) minimum overhead expenses were incurred;
(4) promised delivery dates were maintained.

No two supervisors in the shipbuilding industry have precisely the same responsibilities. For a variety of reasons their duties and responsibilities often vary within the same organization. There is, however, common ground in all cases and this can conveniently be stated under three headings, in so far as they are all concerned to a varying extent with men, materials and equipment. As masters of their craft they were not unduly concerned about the use of materials and equipment. They were, however, all concerned with the difficulties of dealing with men.

Primarily, the foremen are leaders of men, though they have important technical and craft responsibilities. They hold key positions in the shipbuilding industry and gave me every impression of being men of excellent calibre and dedicated to their work.

In the small boat-building firms, skill as a craftsman and ingenuity in making the best use of general purpose machines or other tools are said to be of prime importance, whilst in the larger shipbuilding establishments, greater ability of an administrative type is required.

In all cases it could be said that the foreman was the vital link between the manual workers and the management. Indeed it was also true that the foreman represented the management in the view of the manual workers who tended to interpret his attitude as that of the organization.

The supervisors' reactions covered a wide range, but to summarize:

(1) they were forward thinking and were not at all interested in the historical background of their industry;
(2) they wanted better communications to help them in their current daily tasks;
(3) they wanted to know more about human relations and how to deal with men in differing circumstances (a most pressing problem with the majority of them);
(4) they wanted to know more about Trade Union law;
(5) they wanted to know how their own organization operated;
(6) they wanted to know how costs were arrived at;
(7) they wanted to know the latest methods and techniques associated with their own trade;
(8) they wanted to know more about incentive schemes.

I sincerely hope that some tangible progress has been made during the ensuing years. There was very considerable scope for systematic training when I made the survey in 1967, and it would take many years to reach a stabilized position.

In 1969 the Minister of Employment and Productivity set up a joint committee to recommend the responsibilities and duties of work study personnel throughout industry. The committee included representatives from the Industrial Training Boards and the TUC together with Government Assessors and representatives from certain well-known firms. The Chairman was the talented G. Alan Hutcheson, Managing Director of NUMAS (National Union of Manufacturers' Advisory Service) and a former engineer-pupil under me at Derby in the early 1930s. Alan Hutcheson had been Chairman of the British Standards Institution Committee on Work Measurement; he and I had kept in touch with each other over the years and because of my close association with work study for a decade, he invited me to become an unattached member of the Committee. The report of the Joint Industrial Training Boards' Committee was published by HMSO in 1971 and it set out the suggested responsibilities and duties for the three grades of work study personnel which we recommended.

My last activity in the field of consultancy was to interview experienced engineers for senior positions in both Australia and New Zealand. The request came to me through my good friend Charles S. McLeod, formerly Chief Industrial Relations Officer at Railway Board headquarters, who was acting for an Engineering Consultancy located in Manchester. Most of the interviews took place in London and Glasgow. Some of the applicants were first-class candidates for the vacant positions. An interesting feature was the need to interview the applicant's wife as well. This arose because of previous experience in which candidates for overseas posts had been accepted, a medical examination had taken place, all preliminaries completed with the immigration authorities, and then, at the last minute, the wife of the selected candidate had refused to emigrate. Although it was a wise precaution, it did not seem to prove necessary in the case of those applicants whose wives turned out to be Australian or New Zealand born. My last assignment was to recommend an applicant as works manager for the largest firm in New Zealand. They employed 8000 staff and the output of the factory was impressive. The firm had tens of thousands of acres devoted to the growing of pine trees and they were cutting down these quick-growing trees at a rate which produced no less than 3000 tons of paper a day. The firm were, I understand, growing a succession of new trees at the same rate. Assuming I never do any more active consultancy work, these interviews will serve as a very personal and happy finale to my contribution in that field.

CHAPTER 14

THE WORLD OF SWIMMING

In my spare-time activities I have obtained my greatest pleasure from swimming, and in retrospect my interest in this sport might modestly be described as an object lesson in enthusiasm.

My father too enjoyed the sport and I still treasure one of his school swimming prizes, a book entitled *In the Wilds of Africa*. At first reading it captured my imagination – mainly because I have always been fond of animals and

Fig. 14.1 Members of Derby St John's Swimming Club, winners of the Express Cup for Life Saving, 1920. (Left to right: H Hitchcock, D Neil, S Phillips (seated), J H Norman (Founder and Honorary Secretary), E J Larkin (Captain))

wild life generally – and as far as I can remember it is the only book I have ever read twice.

I can only recall my father taking me to the Derby swimming baths on one occasion; I was eight years old, and he literally threw me in at the deep end. However, he was there to support me, and I have never regretted my rather unpleasant introduction to water.

Alas, my father was so keen on drying me before he dried himself that he developed a cold. This in turn led to pleurisy and pneumonia and after only a week in bed he passed away. Although I was only 8 he had, it seems, fired my enthusiasm to learn to swim and within a year I was able to do so.

I became a junior member of St John's Church Swimming Club, Derby, in 1915. The following year there was a dearth of seniors – they were mostly in the Forces – and I was voted on to the Committee. In 1917 I was appointed Vice-Captain and in the next year became Captain, continuing in that capacity until 1923. On relinquishing the Captaincy I was made a Vice-President.

I played water-polo regularly in the Derby and District League – we won the championship in 1927 – and I competed in Club and Derbyshire Swimming Association competitions with moderate success. On one occasion I won a free-style swimming prize in the Derby Hospitals Gala which took place in the lake at Alvaston Sports Ground.

In 1917 I obtained the life saving Bronze Medallion, in 1919 the Teacher's and Honorary Instructor's Certificates and in 1920 the Award of Merit of the Royal Life Saving Society. I was Captain of the St John's S.C. team that won the Express Cup for Life Saving in 1920. Subsequently I officiated as a judge at various centres in the Midland Counties Life Saving Championships, as well as examining candidates for the Award of

Merit and the Diploma of the Royal Life Saving Society, which was affiliated to the Amateur Swimming Association.

It was in the 1920s that I gave a number of ornamental and fancy swimming displays, some solo and others in conjunction with my brother, William, and Elsie Offen, a school teacher whose performances as the Derby Women's Champion in all strokes have never been surpassed. She was also a Midland Counties Champion. In our joint displays, Elsie executed all the modern strokes to perfection, my brother did a variety of fancy diving and I did ornamental and trick swimming. My brother and I generally wound up our joint display with some comic stunts.

In 1921 I became an individual member of the Amateur Diving Association, later merged with the parent body, the Amateur Swimming Association. The following year I coached my brother, who is eight years my junior, to win the Midland Counties Junior Diving Championship at Nottingham. His prowess in the art became well known and he featured prominently in many competitions in the East Midlands.

In 1924 the Derby LMS Swimming Club was formed. I was the Co-founder, along with W. J. Blake, the Welfare Supervisor of the LMS, and I was appointed the first Honorary General Secretary. I was Chairman of the Club from 1927 to 1935 and later became President. Since my departure from Derby to London I have remained a Vice-President and I have observed that all the Rules of the Club, which I drafted over fifty years ago, still hold good.

The first President of the Club was Sir Henry Fowler, KBE, who was the Chief Mechanical Engineer of the LMS Railway. He was a great sportsman, having been a Derbyshire County Hockey team player in his time. In the Club's first year he volunteered to swim for the team in our match against Chesterfield Town Swimming Club – and he certainly did, but we lost! We did, however, win the water polo match. Afterwards he took the team to see the grave of George Stephenson, the inventor of *Locomotion* in 1825 and of the *Rocket* in 1829 and possibly the greatest name in railway history. His grave is in the churchyard of Trinity Parish Church, Chesterfield – not All Saints' Church, which has the well-known crooked spire.

The temperature of the water is an important factor in all forms of swimming and diving. I recall that the Miners' Strike of 1926 occurred during my active days as a competitive swimmer. Without heating, the water was freezing cold and ten minutes in the water was more than ample! At the other end of the scale was Stonebridge Park Cooling Lake at one of the LMS Power Stations where the temperature of the water was 80° F and extremely enervating when playing water polo.

Over the years, the Derby LMS Swimming Club has gone from strength to strength, much of it due to its honorary secretary Frank Cripps, with a long list of successes including the overall swimming championship of British Railways. The club celebrated its Golden Jubilee Dinner on 19 February, 1974, when as Co-Founder I was privileged to be present and was invited to say a few words about those earlier days.

At the time when I was Chairman of this club I was on the Amateur Swimming Association list as a starter and judge, and on the local list of water-polo referees, and was also a member of the Derby Swimming Club Selection Committee; for good measure I also had the privilege of being the Auditor to the Derby Family Swimming Club.

I was elected to represent the Derby LMS Swimming Club at the Council Meetings of the Midland District of the Amateur Swimming Association, an area for the purposes of swimming organization covering no fewer than nineteen counties. In due course, I was elected to the Midlands Executive and at a later period I became one of its six Vice-Presidents. For many years I was the President of the Derbyshire Swimming Association, an active organization which co-ordinated all the Derby and District Swimming Clubs and organized the County Championships. The ultimate honour for me was to become President of the Midlands in 1955, the year I somewhat reluctantly left Derby.

The Queen Street Baths at Derby, not far from the Cathedral, were opened on 30 July, 1932; they were a considerable advance on their predecessors in the town. In the early stages of their design, I tried hard to have the depth of water under the diving boards increased from 8 ft 6 in to 10 ft, because I knew it was a 'must' if we were ever to stage a national diving championship – if only from the one-metre springboard – but regrettably my efforts were to no avail. In the end Derby had to wait until 1974 before it embarked upon a more advanced swimming establishment which conformed to international requirements; it was a case of the old maxim 'better late than never!', and I understand that my old swimming opponent, Alderman Jack Bussell – always a much faster swimmer than myself – officially opened the new project by diving in when he was mayor of Derby.

On 10 August, 1932, less than a fortnight after the opening of the Queen Street Baths, I was instrumental in forming the Derby Diving Club. The energetic and capable Secretary was E. M. (Maisie) Grasett, who has been the Chairman of the Derby Borough Magistrates for many years.

In 1966 the Derby Diving Club produced a Women's National Springboard Diving Champion in Janet Dickens, whose mother and father were prominent Derby swimming champions of their day.

During the 1930s I found that my interest in both springboard and firmboard diving was fast increasing and I did a considerable amount of coaching as Captain of the Derby Diving Club. I was appointed as the Midland Counties' Representative on the Amateur Diving Association and when the merger with the Amateur Swimming Association took place in 1934, I was elected to the newly formed Amateur Swimming Association National Diving Committee.

At the time when I was attending meetings of the ASA in the 1930s at the Hotel Great Central, Marylebone, I never imagined that the day would come when this building would become the Headquarters of the British Transport Commission and that I should hold office there for the final decade of my working life.

On many occasions I acted as judge or the referee at the National Diving Championships held in various parts of the country, including the Empire Pool, Wembley.

I realized that in British diving circles there was no-one of the calibre of the Americans, and in 1935, with the support of the ASA, I invited 'Pete' Desjardins, winner of both the Spring- and High Board Championships at the 1920 Olympics in Amsterdam, to do a fifteen-week tour of the British Isles. He was acclaimed as the leading diver in the world, and although he had become a professional I undertook to manage the tour as an amateur; I was anxious, like many others, to see the standard of diving in Britain improve. Desjardins had an unsurpassed record; not only had he won both major events at the Olympic games – never before had this been accomplished – but also, in the Springboard Championship, had averaged no less than 9.2 points from each judge, and in two of his dives had scored the maximum of 10 marks from each. These scores were truly remarkable.

Desjardins performed in England, Scotland, Wales and Ireland, and, whenever convenient, I compèred his displays. The tour was such an

Fig. 14.2 'Pete' Desjardins, the 'little bronze statue' from Miami Beach, former USA and World Springboard and Highboard diving champion performing a 1½ forward somersault

outstanding success that I arranged for him to visit England again in 1936. This second tour was equally successful, and I planned a third and final visit in 1937, when he performed with Marian Mansfield, the USA Women's Springboard Diving Champion and a member of the American team at the 1936 Olympic Games in Berlin.

'Pete' Desjardins also made a diving film for Gaumont British, and gave several radio broadcasts; I wrote the script for him when he appeared on the well-known BBC radio programme of those days, 'In Town Tonight'.

During the last tour I arranged a special demonstration, at 'Pete's' suggestion, for physical training colleges, sporting celebrities, leading swimming and diving officials and coaches and top level competitors to attend by invitation only. This unique gathering of about 500 took place at the Marshall Street baths near Oxford Circus in London, and for added interest I invited each of our national swimming champions to give a demonstration of their own stroke – one length in slow motion and one length at racing speed. The combined demonstration was a great success, and afterwards I received scores of appreciative letters from many eminent personalities, saying how much they had enjoyed such an educational display.

In 1936 I was one of six appointed to form the nucleus of International Diving Judges and I remained on this select panel for over twenty years. I was also on the equally small panel of Referees for national and international diving competitions.

Towards the end of the 'thirties I was asked by Harold Fern, honorary secretary of the ASA, whether I would be willing for my name to go forward as the British nominee for the Secretaryship of the Fédération Internationale de Natation Amateur (FINA), the international federation which controls the laws of swimming and the Olympic Games. It was a tremendous honour. He said if I would allow my name to go forward he felt there would be no opposition from any European country. Naturally I gave the matter most careful thought. I felt it was a job I could carry out, but common sense told me that the commitments imposed, including meetings in various countries, could seriously affect my position on the Railway. In the event I declined this great honour and happily I have never regretted it. As far as I can remember an American was appointed at this particular time.

With the other members of the Diving Committee I assisted in the production of the first Amateur Swimming Association Diving Manual and also prepared the first edition of a leaflet which described the English Header, my proof copy of the former being dated 13 June, 1937.

In 1937 I volunteered to write a comprehensive manual of swimming, covering every aspect of the sport, with the object of any royalties accruing being devoted to the Olympic Games Training Fund, at that time in the capable hands of Captain Cummins. When the war began I had already written a substantial part of each of the eighteen chapters I had decided upon; I felt that there was a real need for such a book. However, my war-time commitments prevented any more progress being made and at the end of the war the situation materially changed. No longer was there a paucity of books on swimming. Authors of varying quality, on various aspects of swimming, sprang up everywhere and I regretfully came to the conclusion that the impact of a comprehensive manual had markedly declined. In these circumstances I abandoned my previous good intentions.

In 1938 I was invited to take a team of swimmers and divers to Scotland for a week and give lecture-demonstrations in Ayrshire, under the auspices of the local education authority. In all we performed before several thousand children and adults at the pools, as well as at the schools and academies in Ayr, Cumnock, Kilmarnock, Troon and elsewhere. This all went exceedingly well, so much so that we were asked to go again the following year and stay for a fortnight. Unfortunately this was not possible because it involved most of our annual holidays and we reluctantly had to decline.

Organized sport of all kinds was severely restricted during the 1939–45 War, as it had been during the 1914–18 War, and it was not until 1948 that Great Britain staged the Olympic Games at the Empire Pool Stadium, Wembley, when I had the honour of officiating in the Olympic Championships. Peter Heatly of Edinburgh was the current National Spring Board Diving Champion of England and he was one of Great Britain's representatives; he later became the Chairman of the Organizing Committee for the highly successful 1970 Commonwealth Games held in Edinburgh in recognition of which he was awarded the CBE, and in 1972 he was Chairman of the Diving Committee for the European Diving Championships held at the new Crystal Palace

Sports Centre in London where he invited me to meet him and where we had lunch together during the Championships.

A short time before the 1948 Olympic Games, I was invited by the BBC to give a ten-minute talk on Diving. Harry Walker, a colleague of mine who was a headmaster in Birmingham and who was President of the ASA in 1963 and who compèred BBC national and international swimming events for a total of nearly thirty years, was my interviewer. I remember his saying, 'Edgar, in a dive do you award any points for the return to the surface?' I replied, 'No, the dive is finished as soon as the head or feet, whichever is appropriate, have gone below the surface of the water. A diver can be awarded 10 out of 10 points from each of the judges even though he may never return to the surface again!'

Whilst I was President of Derbyshire Amateur Swimming Association I took an active part in securing the 1949 National Swimming Championships for Derby, the first time in the history of swimming that the Centralized Championships had been staged in an inland town. This was arranged in conjunction with my extremely competent Midland colleagues, not least K. B. Martin, MBE, and C. W. Plant, both of whom became presidents of the ASA. During the Championships, I was invited by Harry Walker on behalf of the BBC to give a short account of the organization work involved. I was subsequently honoured to receive a Public Presentation of Crown Derby china and a testimonial from the Mayor, Alderman Charles Bowmer, for this modest contribution to the town's prestige.

In the world of swimming, as well as in many other national sports, there is often the lighter side to the more serious task of organizing top level Championship Meetings, International Contests, Selection Trials and National Coaching Sessions. A few personal, and unconnected experiences readily come to mind.

On one occasion when I was compering a diving display by two former world champions, 'Dutch' Smith and 'Pete' Desjardins, both Americans, at the Empire Pool, Wembley, I found the amplifying equipment faulty, and the General Manager, Paul Herbert, asked me whether I would prefer to use a megaphone. I started to do so but after my first announcement there was an urgent telephone message from Sir Arthur Elvin, Chairman of Wembley Stadium, to the effect that the use of a megaphone would be adversely reported on by the Press, with loss of prestige, and that he would rather I use the faulty equipment!

I was invited during the mid-thirties to arrange for a prominent team of swimmers and divers to give a display at the official opening of the delightful thermal open air pool at the New Bath Hotel, Matlock, Derbyshire, owned by Trust Houses Ltd. This I agreed to do but to my dismay the management had arranged for a mannequin parade to take place in the middle of the display. They had six models, each of whom changed her costume six times. That was fine but it lasted nearly an hour and my team of swimmers were still in wet costumes and only half-way through their display. They were national champions so you can well imagine their reaction in having to wait to complete their programme and get thoroughly chilled in the meantime. Fortunately for me none was any the worse after a good meal!

Each year the Bologna trophy was competed for between England, Scotland and Wales. It was held under the auspices of the Inter-Countries Committee. I was Master of Ceremonies at Birmingham on one occasion after the war and there was a capacity house including the Lord Mayor. By a slip of the tongue, I announced this important three-cornered contest as the 'Boloney' Competition. I knew the event was being broadcast and so I quickly followed up by saying, to the amusement of the audience, 'I apologize, my Lord Mayor, Ladies and Gentlemen, I can assure you this is not all boloney as you will soon realize!'

CHAPTER 15

AUTHORSHIP AND LECTURING

My first effort at writing a paper – or at least the equivalent of one – occurred soon after I had turned 18 years of age, when I was serving my apprenticeship. The Bursar at the Derby and District College of Technology, where I was studying mechanical engineering as a part-time day and evening class student, was organizing a Students' Association debate with the title 'Is Novel Reading a Waste of Time?' He asked me whether I would be one of the two leading contestants and argue the case that novel reading was not a waste of time. I said that I was willing to have a go but that I should find it much more acceptable if I could take the opposite point of view and say that novel reading *was* a waste of time. At that age I was much too involved in working a 54 hour week, coping with engineering and mathematical text books, attending classes, and undertaking a fair measure of homework to do much reading. Indeed there was little opportunity for me to do anything else except sleep and eat and, indeed, there were times when I dozed off for a short period in my evening classes. Novel reading for me was out and this early background has given me an attitude all through life of having no inclination to read novels. It may well have been my loss but there is much truth in the old adage that what one has never had one never misses. In any event my alternative suggestion was accepted for the impending debate and I prepared my paper in the affirmative, that novel reading *was* a waste of time. In due course the debate took place and in the outcome the vote favoured my opponent. It was noticeable to all that nearly all the women students were opposed to my point of view.

Another of my early experiences in writing was through the medium of St John's Church, Derby. Not long after I was 21 years of age, the Vicar of the day, the Reverend A. T. Humphreys, asked me whether I would take over from him the Editorship of the Parish Magazine. At that time I was already a Sidesman, a member of the Parochial Church Council and captain of St John's Swimming Club. I suppose the vicar thought, as so often happens in any form of voluntary organization, that it is the busy man or woman who can always take on an additional responsibility. However, his main reason was that the magazine was increasingly in debt each year and he hoped I might reverse the trend. I was young and I accepted the invitation as a challenge. At the end of four years when I left the Parish to live in Allestree, I had managed to turn a deficit of £20 – a lot of money in those days – into a balance of about the same amount. This happy situation was achieved only by a lot of hard work. It was an extremely useful medium for me to improve my ability to write on a variety of topics and I have never regretted the time that was taken up in the production of the magazine.

This introduction to a modest form of journalism fired my enthusiasm and by the time I was 30 I had done quite a considerable amount of writing, mostly perhaps, in my work as an experimental draughtsman in the form of report writing. My recollections are that this was a field which gave me a good deal of satisfaction. There was scope for some original presentation; it was a form of pioneering work and all through my life nothing has ever suited me more or given me greater satisfaction than setting a precedent. It is far more rewarding than looking for one.

In 1930, the same year that I left the locomotive drawing office to become Superintendent of Apprentices in the Derby locomotive works, the Local Education Authority for Derby invited me to conduct evening classes in machine drawing at two of their evening continuation schools, namely Ashbourne Road School (which had been my own day school) and Reginald Street School, situated directly opposite the swimming baths which I knew so well. It was my first experience of teaching an engineering subject. I started in September 1930 and my remuneration was the princely sum of 15 shillings (75p) for each of two hours, extending from 7.00 pm to 9.00 pm. It was a modest start but apart from supplementing my all too meagre salary at a time when I contemplated getting married, it gave me confidence in addressing a sizeable class of teenagers.

The following year I was invited to take an initiation class at Repton Public School, eight miles from Derby, for senior boys who were contemplating becoming engineers. This took the form of tuition in orthographic projection and the basic principles of machine tools. I knew the school well because I had for some years judged the school diving championships, and had met, among others, the Headmaster, the Reverend Geoffrey Fisher, who later became Archbishop of Canterbury.

I usually met the boys, never more than six at a time in the Art School where the likeable middle-aged art master was Foxley Norris, a bachelor son of Dr Foxley Norris, Dean of Westminster; I recall his telling me of the secluded position his father had allotted to him in the Abbey to paint a picture of the coronation of George VI on 12 May, 1937. On occasions we went into the school workshop and discussed the functions of the machine tools. My association with Repton School was an extremely pleasant experience and it was satisfying to know that some of the boys eventually took up apprenticeships with the railway.

Within a few weeks of my accepting the invitation to teach some of the sixth formers at Repton School, I received an invitation to teach Machine Design and Drawing for the Higher National Certificate in Mechanical Engineering at the Derby and District College of Technology, which I had attended for many years during my apprenticeship days and subsequently. I was therefore committed for two evenings a week and in view of this I resigned from taking the two elementary classes of the previous year. I continued to attend at Repton School on one evening a week until 1939 when my commitments with contracts which we were undertaking for the Government in the railway workshops necessitated my giving up this enjoyable association.

After teaching Machine Design and Drawing at the Derby and District College of Technology for two years, I was invited to initiate the new Section C Syllabus of the Institution of Mechanical Engineers examination, which was called Works Organization and Management and had replaced Industrial Administration. I regarded the invitation as worthwhile and readily accepted the challenge of initiating the new course. Although I was a locomotive engineer by training, I found that having left the drawing office and having become a works assistant with responsibility for the building and maintenance of locomotives, I became increasingly drawn to the techniques of production engineering. It was in this field, together with the use of modern management techniques, that I developed my forte. It is in the area of production engineering, perhaps more than any other branch of engineering, that job satisfaction can be experienced to the full. If I could live my working life all over again, I could only wish for a repeat – or if possible even more of this fascinating type of work, with all its vicissitudes. The preliminary planning involved in the manufacture of any product, the daily contacts with the workshop supervisory staff, the inevitable frustrations which arise – all are ingredients in the working life of a production engineer.

I was asked by Arnold Rimmer, Head of the Mechanical Engineering Department at the College and Assistant Scout Commissioner for Derby, if I would recommend someone to take over my Machine Design class if I were prepared to take on the new Works Organization course. An old drawing office colleague, Eric Langridge, obliged by taking the Machine Design class. He had everything in his favour – ability and temperament. He was an extremely competent locomotive designer who on retirement was Locomotive Development Assistant in the Chief Mechanical and Electrical Engineer's Head-quarters office of the British Railways LM Region at Derby. For good measure he was an accomplished concert pianist.

As with my appointment at Repton School, where I was succeeded by a railway colleague, Ellis R. Brown, I also found it necessary in 1939 to give up my Technical College appointment and my place at the College was taken by Frank Bloor, an engineer employed by Rolls-Royce in Derby. Since my retirement a railway colleague of mine, Charles Garratt, then works manager at Eastleigh works, who subsequently became works manager at Crewe locomotive works and later at Derby locomotive works, kindly arranged for me to have lunch with Frank Bloor when the latter was Principal of the Eastleigh Technical College in Hampshire. Until then I did not know that Bloor had taken up full-time technical teaching. What a pleasure it was after all those years to meet him again, and what memories we were able to recall after an interval of no less than thirty years!

During this period and, indeed, right up to my retirement from British Railways, I often found myself called upon to give talks and lectures on different subjects to various organizations. It involved me in a fair amount of work, but not unduly so because I only undertook to give a talk on a subject in which I felt I was reasonably experienced and which would not involve too much time in preparation. I started off in 1931 with a lecture entitled 'Locomotives' at Manchester Central High School. How such requests arise in the first place one can seldom be sure. I came away, however, with the feeling that the talk and long discussion were appreciated by those present and that I had reasonably upheld the prestige of the LMS Railway.

In 1932, I read a paper in Birmingham on 'The Training of Engineers' before the Institution of Locomotive Engineers, and as a Committee Member of the Derby Society of Engineers a couple of years later I read a paper to the Society entitled 'Production Planning'.

In the early 1950s I gave addresses at the annual school-leaving ceremony in the historic Guildhall in Derby, at the prize-giving ceremonies at Derby Central School for Boys, and at the Herbert Strutt Grammar School in Belper, Derbyshire. On each occasion my basic message was that nothing worthwhile was easy to accomplish. To be successful in any sphere of activity meant a full measure of hard work. The rewards, however, for such hard work were great and I stressed that one should never be guilty of lost opportunities. I also managed to sprinkle a little humour into my addresses.

In 1951 I gave a talk in Bradford to the Yorkshire Branch of the Engineering Employers' Association, at their request, on 'Productivity and Incentive Schemes'. This was an extremely well attended meeting and there was an excellent discussion.

The following year I was asked by my friend Charles Forrest, Managing Editor of the *Derby Evening Telegraph*, whether I would take the lead in opposing Sir Jack Longland, Director of Education for Derbyshire and a well-known radio broadcaster, in a debate entitled 'Does the Ratepayer get value for money in Education?'. The debate took place at Derby School and I presented the negative case – that the ratepayer did *not* get value for money in the field of education. Why I was invited I shall never know because the debate had been organized by the Derby Rotary Club and I had never been a member. It might possibly have been because I had expressed certain views from time to time. The line I took in opening the debate was that over the years I had interviewed many hundreds of boys and a few girls, and that in the course of these interviews I had all too often been extremely disappointed with the level of education. It was not, I suggested, the fault of the children, but was largely due to their school timetable. I gave many examples and blamed the school curricula which, in my view, were far too varied with too small a percentage of time left for basic subjects. I have always maintained there is no short cut to experience and insufficient time was being allocated to essentials such as English Grammar and Arithmetic, both of which were needed all through life. One could visit any modern school, as I had done, to find that many thousands of pounds had been spent in providing special rooms full of expensive equipment for what could only be described as fringe subjects. I held the view, and still do, that vocational training was and is a matter for the employer and that the employer, not the taxpayer or the ratepayer, should provide these facilities for the successful operation of his business. After all, it is the employer who is in the best position to know what is required.

During a very lively and refreshing discussion I made a point which I had often made in the past. In a cautious manner I said that most teachers had never left school and that in my view an essential ingredient to qualify for a teacher's certificate to teach in a senior school should include the proviso that twelve months should first be spent in industry – preferably on the shop floor. I was sure that it would pay dividends, because the fully qualified teacher, given the right industrial experience, would see in all sorts of ways what an employer required of his employees – not least the will to work combined with good manners. Most of the audience, numbering about 150, were school teachers, and when it came to the vote it was clear that the result was likely to go against me. In the event it was about 2:1 in favour of Sir Jack Longland's side. It was, however, a worthwhile effort and I came away with no regrets for the contribution I had made.

For National Productivity Year in 1961, sponsored by the British Productivity Council, I was invited to give a talk on 'Productivity' by the Derby and District Chamber of Trade. At that time I was Director of Work Study to the British Transport Commission and located at the Commission's headquarters in London. The large room at the St James' Hotel in Derby was crowded to capacity and I received an enthusiastic welcome. I only wished that all the good intentions which were expressed during the discussion would come to fruition. After a lifetime's experience as an engineer, I remain firmly of the opinion that there was and still is great breadth of scope almost everywhere for an appreciable increase in the level of productivity.

When Brigadier C. A. Langley was Chief Inspecting Officer of Railways under the Minister of Transport, he was President of the Junior Institution of Engineers, in which capacity he invited me to read a paper on 'Productivity' and I was happy to meet his request. I have always had a great admiration for the Brigadier, who served so much of his Army career at the famous Longmoor Military Railway Camp, Hampshire. He was the author of several military textbooks on transport and I always thought that his annual reports on Railway Accidents for the Ministry were models in presentation. Like me, he was a firm believer in using graphs and simple diagrams in his reports.

In 1960 I was invited by the British Transport Commission to read a paper at the International Railway Association Congress in Brussels, entitled 'Work Study and Productivity'; the Congress was attended by senior railway officers gathered together from countries far and wide.

To obtain certain factual information beforehand, I carefully prepared a questionnaire which I sent to most of the railway administrations throughout the world. To their credit, all of them replied. Two of them stand out in my mind in a peculiar way. The American and Russian replies were different but it was equally difficult to make any sense out of either of them! The American reply was altogether too confusing because the co-ordinating organization in the USA tried to summarize some two hundred independently owned railway companies – for better or for worse

the railway systems are not nationalized in the USA – each of whom operated their own independent schemes. The Russian reply told me virtually nothing and I was left in no doubt that they had not begun to use modern management techniques, nor did they understand them, on the Russian railways. I did not take the view that they were evading my questions. It was crystal clear to me that although there were two or three railway systems in the world which understood the advantages of using modern management techniques to improve productivity, and practised them to a varying extent, none was so advanced as British Railways. On British Railways there was no lack of basic knowledge of the modern techniques to be adopted, but unfortunately in a staff-orientated industry there was not always the urge to use them.

I have already said that I was invited to 'read' my paper in Brussels. In actual fact this was an occasion where the paper had been circulated previously and taken as read, and I was allocated twenty minutes to introduce the subject. Following this the Chairman of the Conference opened the discussion and this lasted most of the day. The Conference was efficiently organized, with English translated simultaneously, for broadcasting purposes, into French and German.

I have never liked the use of the word 'expert' because I feel it is too hackneyed and means nothing, but I recall Sir Brian Robertson, who was attending the Conference as Chairman of the British Transport Commission, saying, in furtherance of a question which had been raised with me, 'We should recognize that Mr Larkin is an expert in this field and I think we should accept his observations'. Well, even the so-called 'expert' in any subject is not infallible but I was appreciative that my Chief was backing me up.

It was one of those happy occasions when my wife was invited to accompany me to Brussels and a delightful programme was arranged for her, along with the other visiting ladies; it was an occasion to remember.

Throughout the years, I found myself writing short articles and Press reports on various swimming events. During my time as a draughtsman I wrote several short technical articles, and when I returned to the works I remember writing a three part article running to about 6000 words entitled 'The Building of a Locomotive'. This was published in three consecutive editions of the LMS railway monthly magazine.

From 1934 to 1939 I wrote a regular monthly feature in the *Swimming Times* magazine which I called 'Around the World'. To obtain my information I wrote to prominent swimmers in various parts of the world. The founder editor, the indefatigable Bertram W. Cummins, sent me many letters from his correspondents saying how much readers appreciated the information I was able to impart. Forty years have passed and I still see articles appearing from time to time in the *Swimming Times* under the same title of 'Around the World'.

Some years before the Second World War it was suggested to me by Arnold Rimmer, Head of the Engineering Department at the Derby and District College of Technology, that my lectures in Works Organization and Management would be good material for writing a book of the same title and that it would be in great demand. After some thought I accepted the suggestion and rephrased the lectures for that purpose. It involved many hundreds of hours work in my spare time and extended over a period of nearly six years. Sir Isaac Pitman and Sons undertook to publish the book, which ran to approximately 500 000 words with 400 illustrations, and the first edition appeared in 1940. I invited Dr Alfred W. Richardson, Principal of the Derby and District College of Technology, with whom I had formed a close friendship over the years, to write the Foreword, and he readily agreed. The second edition appeared in 1945 following which the publishers invited me to write a book suitable for apprentices. As I was very interested in the subject I accepted the invitation. I entitled the book *The Elements of Workshop Training* and prepared it in two parts, Workshop Theory and Workshop Training. First published in 1945, it ran to two editions and then finally a second impression. I was also approached in 1945 by the editor of the *Works Manager* magazine to be the co-ordinating editor for an engineering handbook which it was proposed to publish covering a wide variety of relevant subjects. After full consideration I decided not to accept this assignment. I was no longer a bachelor and had family responsibilities which had greater interest for me, and I knew that many long hours of work would have been involved.

Subsequently, I wrote, on request from Sir Isaac Pitman and Sons, a complete section consisting of six chapters covering various aspects of Systematic Management, which was intended by the publishers to form an integral part of a comprehensive manual on Radio Technology. The publishers experienced difficulty with the main author of the book and decided not to proceed with the publication. Although they graciously offered me my royalties, I informed them I would prefer to waive them having regard to the circumstances which had arisen.

Some of the varied reports which I have prepared as part of my railway work or in a consultative capacity, have been appropriately referred to elsewhere in these memoirs. Apart from this autobiography, on which I started work in 1972, the foregoing chapter is a fairly comprehensive résumé of my spare time activities in this field.

CHAPTER 16

TROUT AND SALMON FISHING

Fishing is one of the largest participant sports in the British Isles – nearly four million anglers. Throughout most of my life I have been happy to be one of those four million. There is certainly plenty of scope for fishing in the British Isles with our countless streams, rivers and lakes and our extensive coastline.

It was the renowned Izaak Walton (1593–1683), one of the most lovable of English writers, who wrote the classic work *The Compleat Angler*. Masterly and original though it was, I have often thought that if he were around today he would have to learn his angling all over again. The quality and variety of equipment now available is in a different category from that which he used and recommended.

Although as a young man I did my fair share of coarse fishing with line and float and enjoyed it, I found later that mainly winter fishing, often sitting for long periods on a stool, was not quite my cup of tea. For years now I have given up coarse fishing in favour of what I have found to be the more delightful pastime of trout and salmon fishing. I have had considerable success with the former, but have been confined almost entirely to near misses with the latter. Even so, my ardour for salmon fishing has in no way diminished; anticipation remains as rewarding as ever. To me, the catching of fish is incidental; I'm well satisfied if I know there are fish around even though they don't seem to like me.

My interest in fishing started when I was about ten years of age and, despite some lack of continuity during my working life, fishing has undoubtedly been my principal relaxation – especially since I retired from full time employment in 1966 – in contrast with my swimming activities which frequently involved a good deal of hard work.

Since my retirement I have been a member of the Enton Fly Fishers Club at Witley, Surrey. There are four lakes, all beautifully landscaped, and I have had many many hours of pleasure in pitching my skill against the wary brown and rainbow trout. On the last day of the 1972 season, I was fishing alone very quietly from a boat on what we call the Upper Lake which covers an area of 9 acres. I hadn't caught a fish when quite unexpectedly a large trout jumped near to the boat and fell back into the water. Almost immediately afterwards it jumped again and this time landed in my boat; as quick as lightning I grabbed my net and placed it over this very lively fish. It was a most unexpected situation and if it hadn't been the last day of the season I would have returned it to the water. In the event, I decided to keep it and when I weighed in found it to be a rainbow trout of 2 lb 2 oz. Although this somewhat exclusive Club has been established since 1912, there is no record of any other member having had this unusual experience.

Through my interest in fly fishing for trout, I was fortunate enough to make the acquaintance of Colonel T. Hawker who lives at Longparish in Hampshire near to the River Test, England's most famous chalk stream in which to be a riparian owner one has to fork out about £30 000 for a quarter of a mile of river.

Game fishing is confined to trout and salmon; there are three distinct varieties of trout – the brown trout, the rainbow trout and the sea trout. It is lawful to catch trout between April and October, the actual period varying according to the appropriate Fishing Board. In most fishing clubs and in private waters, it is customary for trout fishing to be restricted to fly fishing, sometimes using only artificial dry fly, whilst in others artificial wet or dry flies may be used. Dry flies are designed to float on the surface and wet flies and nymphs are designed to sink. They are usually made from pheasant feathers or from the feathers of other colourful birds. Many anglers make their own artificial flies.

Salmon fishing has a longer season than trout fishing, most rivers in the British Isles starting in February and finishing in October. There are restrictions on some beats as to what type of tackle an angler may use; otherwise spinning, in which one uses an artificial minnow or other lures, such as a prawn, or else wet fly fishing, are commonly practised. For myself, I like a stretch of water where one can try the fly or use a spinning rod according to circumstances.

My former chief, Sir Steuart Mitchell, who was Vice-Chairman of BR Board under Dr Beeching, was an ardent trout fisherman, but despite his Scottish ties he took a dim view of salmon fishing because he thought it so unrewarding – too many hours without any sign of a salmon being anywhere near! For myself, I have found the challenge irresistible.

I must mention Longford Brook, Derbyshire. This is a well-known stream containing trout and grayling in goodly numbers. The late Charles Penney, managing director of International Combustion Co. Ltd at Derby, bought the fishing rights of a stretch of this delightful stream. He subsequently found he didn't like fishing and he invited two of his business acquaintances, one of whom was me, to fish the beat. On the last occasion I went, which was shortly before I came to London, I had the pleasure of taking the family with me. I caught two trout and my daughter Anthea, who at that time was only 4 years old, wanted to carry the fish to the car. We started for home and I asked Anthea to show me the fish. To my surprise she could only produce one fish and although I retraced my steps through two fields I couldn't find the other. Anthea's remark was priceless, 'If you had caught more fish, Daddy, you wouldn't have missed one.'

Since 1957 I have annually spent a week fishing with Peter Corbishley, a former member of my staff, in various parts of the British Isles – trips which have become quite an institution and have covered many well-known rivers. I have spent many happy times fishing with other good friends, including George Warland, a neighbour in Surbiton and an authority on the design and manufacture of press tools for the motor-car industry, and Sidney Ridgeway, Managing Director of British Rail Engineering Ltd.

Much of my salmon fishing has been done on the River Deveron in Aberdeenshire, which is very accommodating and has a great deal to commend it. For the most part one can fish from low banks and if desired there are plenty of places in the Huntly area where it is possible to wade across the river and fish to advantage from the opposite bank. If one comes to the conclusion that the salmon are not interested, there are plenty of brown trout to be caught.

On one occasion on the Deveron at Rothiemay – the birthplace of James Ferguson, the eighteenth century astronomer – I was amazed to have a large fish take my lure on my first cast; unfortunately the salmon was only on for a matter of seconds and after surfacing it was clear away. I examined the lure and found that the small plastic mount which prevents the triple hooks from sliding up the body was missing; the hooks had slipped up into an ineffective position and the salmon had only to open its mouth a second time and release

Fig. 16.1 *The author with a grilse salmon caught in a gorge on the River Findhorn in the forest of Darnaway, Invernesshire, 1973* (Photo by P Corbishley)

itself. How careful one has to be in checking one's tackle. It has often crossed my mind that I have bought enough tackle to catch most of the salmon in Scotland but it is mainly the salmon which seem to have the laugh and not me.

In April 1978, when fishing a three mile beat on the River Deveron owned by John Brown, who at his retirement was Director General of guided missile development at the Ministry of Defence, I caught my largest fish ever. It was a 17 lb salmon measuring just over three feet in length, with a girth of 18 inches, and it was a perfect specimen.

Fig. 16.2   A British Railways Inter-City 125 High Speed train – winner of the 1978 Design Council Award for Engineering – crosses the Tay Bridge on its inaugural run from Edinburgh to Dundee, Aberdeen, Inverness and Perth in April 1978. Whilst fishing the Conniecleugh stretch of the River Deveron the author had the unexpected pleasure of seeing this magnificent train passing north of Huntly, only a few hundred yards from the river. The full operational service on the east coast main line between London and Edinburgh takes under four and a half hours

CHAPTER 17

HOSPITAL ADMINISTRATION

The National Health Service came into being under the National Health Service Act 1946, and the effective date for implementation was 5 July, 1948. The main purpose of the Act was to provide a comprehensive health service for the entire population of England and Wales. There were three main parts, which established:

(1) the Hospital Service, with Regional Boards and Hospital Management Committees;
(2) the Executive Councils, which were to provide contracts and means of employment for General Practitioners, dentists, chemists and associated professions;
(3) the Local Health Services, such as environmental health and sanitation, district nursing and midwifery, school health services, and the provision of ambulances.

The organization was directed from a central department within the Ministry of Health, with England and Wales being divided into 15 regions, each with an appointed Regional Board. These Regional Boards had the main function of appointing consultant medical staff and of planning the major capital developments for the service. Other duties included providing a management consultancy service for the Hospital Management Committees, over which they also had some control in respect of finance and manpower. The Act placed the day-to-day management of the hospitals in the hands of the Hospital Management Committees, which were appointed by the Regional Boards for sub-divisions of the regions.

In 1952 I was invited to become a member of the Derby No. 1 Hospital Management Committee. Nearly all the hospitals in Derby, as well as some in the County, came under the control of this Committee, which in turn was responsible to the Regional Hospital Board at Sheffield. It was felt, apparently, that as the railways were the largest employers in the town there should be a representative of the railway management on the Committee. After a good deal of thought I accepted the invitation. I found that the members of the Committee included well known local businessmen, employers, representatives of large organizations, Trades Union Officers, local Councillors and Medical Consultants, a total of sixteen including the Chairman. I served on the Management Committee and also on the Finance and Establishment Sub-Committee, both of which met monthly.

In 1955 I was surprised to be asked by the Sheffield Regional Hospital Board to become the Chairman of the Committee. At the time the Vice-Chairman of the Committee was James Rudd Ratcliffe, Derby's Senior Consultant Surgeon. He was such an able man and so keenly interested in the work of the Committee that I wondered why he had not been appointed as the Chairman. I learned, however, that the Minister of Health preferred a layman as Chairman of these committees, and in any case, J. R. Ratcliffe himself preferred to remain as Vice-Chairman. In the event, I think it proved a very satisfactory combination. I found Mr Ratcliffe a tower of strength. His regular attendance at all important meetings and his wide experience of hospital work were a source of inspiration. He served on the Committee from its inception in 1948 until 31 December, 1966, a splendid record of voluntary public service. His wife Joyce was an unsuccessful Conservative parliamentary candidate on one occasion and one of their two sons married the daughter of a railway colleague of mine, Fred Umpleby.

Four full-time officers served on the Derby No. 1 Hospital Management Committee. They were B. H. Chubb, MBE, MSc(Econ), FHA, the Group Secretary; W. C. Hubin, the Treasurer; W. Bagshaw, the Supplies Officer; and B. G. Masters, the Group Engineer. The brother of B. H. Chubb was the Welfare Supervisor on the Western Region of British Railways.

Under the National Health Service Act, the Management Committee had full power to receive donations and legacies of money or property upon trust for purposes relating to hospital services or research. These funds were used to provide amenities which could not be met from Exchequer Funds, as well as to finance improvements beneficial to patients and staff.

When I left Derby to move to London in 1956 I had to resign as Chairman and was succeeded by Captain John Spencer, formerly Clerk to the Shardlow and Repton Urban District Council. He held the Chairmanship for no less than ten years – a longer period than any of his four predecessors. His successor, Alderman Arthur Lamb, who was a valuable member of the Committee when I was Chairman, was the last Chairman to hold office before the hospital service was reorganized.

The Management Committees throughout England and Wales had their final meetings in March 1974 before being wound up after a total of more than 25 years' service. In most areas House Committees had been discontinued some years earlier following a report suggesting that there should be greater delegation of administrative functions to officers and that the members should maintain their interest in the hospitals and services by visiting, rather than formal house committees receiving reports.

During my time as Chairman, I had many pleasant functions to carry out in addition to Committee work. These included the nurses' annual prize-giving ceremonies at the different hospitals, official openings of improvements and extensions, the appointment of matrons and hospital secretaries, accompanying the Mayor during his visit to some of the hospitals on Christmas morning, and attending the occasional radio broadcast or other function.

There were nineteen hospitals under the control of the Derby No. 1 Hospital Management Committee during the time I was Chairman, with a total of 2227 beds (see Table 17.1). In addition there were nine school clinics, two chest clinics, two schools (the school of Occupational Therapy and Derby School of Nursing) and the area laundry.

There was a steady development of many important patient services during the years, particularly in respect of pathology, which provided an area pathology service for psychiatry, radio-diagnostics, anaesthetics and paediatrics.

TABLE 17.1   HOSPITALS UNDER THE CONTROL OF DERBY No. 1 HOSPITAL MANAGEMENT COMMITTEE

Hospital	Bed complement	Classification
Ashbourne Maternity	11	GP maternity
Babington	171	Geriatric/GP maternity
Bretby Hall	112	Orthopaedic/Pre-convalescent
Derby City	306	Medical/Surgery/Maternity
Derbyshire Children's	92	Paediatric/Surgery
Derbyshire Hospital for Women	71	Gynaecology
Derbyshire Royal Infirmary	426	Medical/Surgery/RT
Etwall	94	Pre-convalescent
Grove	84	Geriatric
Derwent	165	Paediatric/Surgery/Chest/ID/Pre-convalescent
Draycott	37	Pre-convalescent
Holbrook	22	GP maternity
Manor	367	Geriatric
Nightingale	56	Maternity
Parwich	47	Pre-convalescent
Queen Mary Maternity	41	Maternity
Ripley	24	Acute
St. Oswald's	81	Geriatric/GP medical
Wirksworth	20	GP maternity

There was also considerable expansion of out-patient clinics of all types in the extended departments at the Derbyshire Royal Infirmary and the Derbyshire Children's Hospital. The former, which is located on the London Road, Derby, is much the largest hospital complex in Derbyshire, and proudly displays the statue of Florence Nightingale (1820–1910) who was a native of Derbyshire.

As a member and one-time Chairman of the Derby No. 1 Hospital Management Committee during the 1950s, I found my hospital work most rewarding and I like to think that I had made a modest contribution to the splendid work of a dedicated team. Even so I always had the feeling that if I had been a retired man I could have done a great deal more. Without any doubt it was the most responsible voluntary position I ever held. After all, the Committee was directly involved with the spending of substantial sums of tax-payers' money.

CHAPTER 18

INDUSTRIAL TRIBUNALS

For many years, industrial disputes throughout England and Wales could be referred to the Industrial Court sitting in London, on terms of reference agreed between the two sides. A decision of the Industrial Court was binding.

During my first twelve years as a senior officer in the Headquarters' office of the Chief Mechanical and Electrical Engineer of the LMS Railway and – following nationalization of the railways in 1948 – of the London Midland Region of British Railways, there were occasions when I was called upon to give technical evidence before the Industrial Court, which was located in George Street, Westminster, opposite to the Houses of Parliament.

The first President before whom I appeared was Sir William Morris, QC, and the second, appointed some years later, was Sir John Forster, QC. They were two very different men; for example Sir William insisted that anyone required to give evidence should stand up, whereas Sir John started the proceedings by telling the witnesses they could retain their seats, if they so desired, when giving evidence. I well recall one occasion with Sir William in the Chair when a senior colleague was on his feet giving evidence. At one point he paused, bent down and asked me in a whisper about a particular point; I was replying to him, equally quietly, when Sir William roared out, 'If Mr Larkin has anything to say to the Court, will he please stand up!'

The case I best remember involved the manning of a newly installed mechanical press for manufacturing oil pipe and steam pipe clips at the Crewe locomotive works – the largest locomotive centre in the country. These steel clips had hitherto been made under a steam hammer at the particular works by a skilled smith. The object of the mechanical press was to use a semi-skilled operator and at the same time speed up output.

Despite the fact that the mechanical press took practically all the skill out of the work, the engineering Trades Unions objected strongly to the appointment of semi-skilled operators to perform the work. The Unions maintained that work which in the past had been regarded as skilled must continue to be performed by a skilled craftsman, irrespective of any fundamental change in the method of manufacture. The new press had been installed in the works for over a year and the engineering unions had refused to allow it to be operated as proposed by the railway management. It was an incredible situation and the railway company had taken the initiative to resolve the matter at the Industrial Court. This was done on the usual mutually agreed Terms of Reference.

For the purpose of my evidence, I had arranged for a young apprentice pattern-maker to make me a small wooden model of the press. I held this up in the Court and, addressing the Tribunal, said: 'Gentlemen, this is what I call skilled craftsmanship. A boy of 17 who is serving his apprenticeship has made this model of the mechanical press by interpreting a small undimensioned sketch in the manufacturer's brochure.'

I proceeded to demonstrate the operation of the press and said, 'Almost anyone could learn to operate the press in a few hours because the dies in the press automatically ensure the correct manufacture of the clip.'

The Chairman, Sir John Forster, said, 'I think what you are telling the Court, Mr Larkin, is that the Archangel Gabriel couldn't influence the quality of the work done in the press.'

I replied, 'That is so, Sir.'

The sequel was interesting. The Tribunal deferred their decision, as was customary. Surprisingly they subsequently advised both parties that they would like to visit Crewe locomotive works and see the new press demonstrated. This was duly arranged and the shop foreman operated the press. The members of the Tribunal were clearly amazed at the simplicity of the press and in due course their findings were published. They came down firmly in favour of employing a semi-skilled operator and so the new press, after standing idle for nearly two years, was put into commission. It was sad to think that such a lot of unnecessary time had elapsed before the press had begun to show a return on the capital expenditure involved. A further and no less important point which occurred to me was that no skilled smith – one of the oldest and most highly respected trades in the engineering industry – would have had any interest in operating a press which removed the necessity for him to use any of his craftsman's skill and experience. Clearly the case should never have arisen. Space does not permit my referring in any detail to the several other cases in which I gave evidence at the Industrial Court over more than a decade. The feature which stands out in my mind is that in every instance where the railway management decided to take a stand on the merits of particular circumstances, the railways' view was accepted by the Industrial Court.

In January 1966, at the end of my 12 months as a Consultant with British Railways, I received an invitation from the Ministry of Employment to serve as a member of the Industrial Tribunals for England and Wales. I assumed I had been nominated by the Chairman of British Railways, at that time Sir Stanley Raymond, or by Alec Dunbar, Member of the Board who dealt with such matters, and I accepted the invitation. Actually I learned that two of us were nominated, the other being Major-General Wansbrough-Jones who, under Sir Brian Robertson, Chairman of the former BTC and later, under Dr Richard Beeching, Chairman of British Railways, had held with great distinction the office of Secretary-General to the Transport Commission and later Secretary to British Railways. He and I had first met in the drawing office at Derby over 50 years previously when he was a sapper in the Royal Engineers on secondment. We were both born in 1900 and one of his quips was to say to me, 'Edgar, 1900 was a great vintage year!' He died at the age of 73 after a very distinguished career. He had an outstanding, dynamic personality with great drive and clarity of decision, and I shall always remember him with affection.

The Industrial Tribunals had no jurisdiction over cases of alleged breach of contract of employment which had to be dealt with through the normal civil courts of the land. They were first set up under the Industrial Training Act, 1964. Subsequently their jurisdiction was extended to cover appeals under a number of other new Acts in the employment field. The law continues to change but the categories of cases which could be referred to the Tribunals during my period of office as a serving member of a Tribunal were as follows.

(1) *Industrial Training Act 1964.*

Under this Act, Industrial Training Boards for various industries were established with responsibility for providing industrial training within each industry. To raise the necessary finance, each Board was empowered to impose a levy on employers. This was done by means of assessments and any person assessed to a levy had a right of appeal to a Tribunal, on the ground that he was not liable to pay a levy, either because he did not come within the scope of the particular Board or because the assessment had not been accurately calculated. If a Tribunal was satisfied that the appellant ought not to have been assessed to the levy, or that he ought to have been assessed in a smaller or larger amount, it rescinded, reduced or increased the assessment, as the case may be.

(2) *Redundancy Payments Acts 1965 and 1969.*

The 1965 Act required employers to make lump-sum payments to employees who were dismissed because of redundancy. It also required these payments to be made in certain circumstances to employees who were laid off or kept on short time for a substantial period. Employers who had to make redundancy payments as required by the Act could claim a rebate of part of the cost from a Redundancy Fund financed by contributions collected from all employers as part of the flat-rate National Insurance contribution. (The 1969 Act reduced the amount of rebate payable.) Various questions about entitlement to payment or about claims for rebate could be referred to the Industrial Tribunals by employees, employers or by the Secretary of State for Employment who had responsibility for the control and management of the Redundancy Fund.

(3) *Contracts of Employment Act 1972.*

This Act consolidated the provisions affecting the contract of employment formerly to be found in the Contracts of Employment Act 1963, and in certain sections of the Redundancy Payments Act 1965, and the Industrial Relations Act 1971. Under Section 4 of this Act if an employer failed to give an employee a written statement of the particulars of his terms of employment, the employee could require the matter to be referred to a Tribunal to determine what particulars ought to have been specified in such statement. Similarly, any question as to the accuracy or sufficiency of written particulars supplied in accordance with the Act could be referred to a Tribunal by the employer or the employee. The particulars decided on by the Tribunal had effect as if they had been included in a written statement issued by the employer.

(4) *Section 44 and Schedule 7 of the Redundancy Payments Act 1965.*

Section 44 of the Redundancy Payments Act 1965 transferred to the Industrial Tribunals jurisdiction over questions which under various statutes (some of which were listed in Schedule 7 to the Act) were directed to be determined by a referee or board of referees. The matters concerned were questions with regard to compensation for persons who had lost their employment because of some statutory enactment, e.g., the nationalization or denationalization of the industry in which they worked or the reorganization of local authority areas. Questions of comparability of a person's employment or the worsening of his position as a result of such an enactment could also be referred to the Tribunals under these statutes. An employee or a compensating authority could apply for a decision of a Tribunal.

(5) *Selective Employment Payments Act 1966.*

Under this Act employers were required to pay a tax, which was collected as part of the flat-rate National Insurance contribution, for each employee. The tax was refunded to employers in respect of establishments in certain industries (mainly manufacturing) which satisfied certain conditions; in development areas a premium was paid in addition. For the purpose of claiming a refund or premium employers had to register the establishment with the Department of Employment or with the Ministry of Agriculture, Fisheries and Food as appropriate. Full or partial refunds could also be claimed in certain circumstances from the Department of Health and Social Security, e.g., for part-time workers or for persons employed abroad.

Appeals could be made to the Industrial Tribunals against the refusal of the appropriate Minister to register an establishment as one qualifying for refund or premium or against his decision to remove an establishment from the Register. The Tribunals could also determine disputes as to the effective registration date and as to the amount of refund or premium payable. Reference to the Tribunals could be initiated by an employer. Towards the end of my service on Industrial Tribunals, the Selective Employment Payments disappeared following a Government decision to abandon the Selective Employment Tax.

(6) *Docks and Harbours Act 1966.*

Section 51 of the Act provided for reference to the Industrial Tribunals of any question concerning (i) whether certain work was dock work; and (ii) whether any place was in, or in the vicinity of, a port to which a labour scheme for the time being applied. A question could be referred to the Tribunals by the National Dock Labour Board, the Licensing Authority, an employer of dock labour, a trade union on behalf of employees, or by a Court.

(7) *The Industrial Relations Act 1971.*

This Act extended the jurisdiction of Tribunals by giving them the right to adjudicate in cases involving what were described as 'unfair industrial practices' (e.g. unfair dismissal) and which were not reserved to the jurisdiction of the National Industrial Relations Court. It also extended and varied certain existing jurisdictions and conferred jurisdiction in cases involving complaints of alleged infringement by an employer of an individual's rights in relation to trade union membership, and complaints about organizations of workers or employers concerning alleged breaches of their rules or alleged breaches of the guiding principles laid down in the Act for such organizations.

Each Tribunal consisted of a legally qualified chairman and two lay members. The chairman was a barrister or solicitor of not less than seven years standing and was drawn from a panel appointed by the Lord Chancellor. In England and Wales there were a President and a number of chairmen, some of whom were full-time and some part-time. The Regulations provided for the President to hold office up to the age of 72. He could resign his appointment by notice in writing to the Lord Chancellor and his appointment could be terminated if he became unfit to discharge his duties or became insolvent. Full-time chairmen were also appointed up to the age of 72. Part-time chairmen were appointed for a period of three years, were eligible for re-appointment, and could also resign by notice to the Lord Chancellor. Thirteen of the full-time chairmen were in charge of Regional Offices of the Tribunals in Ashford (Kent), Birmingham, Bristol, Bury St Edmunds, Cardiff, Exeter, Leeds, Liverpool, Manchester, Newcastle-upon-Tyne, Nottingham, Sheffield and Southampton. Six were attached to the Central Office of Industrial Tribunals for England and Wales, located in Ebury Bridge Road, Chelsea, in London (which was the one where I always attended), three to the Birmingham office, and one each to offices in Bury St Edmunds, Cardiff, Leeds, Manchester and Newcastle-upon-Tyne. Full-time chairmen dealt with interlocutory work in addition to sitting as Tribunal chairmen.

The Secretary of State for Employment appointed members from a panel of persons appearing to him to have knowledge or experience of employment in industry and commerce. They were appointed after consultation with such organizations representative of employers or of employed persons as he considered to be appropriate. Each was an entirely independent judicial member of the Tribunal and decided a case on the evidence. Members were appointed for a period of three years and were eligible for re-appointment.

The Regulations provided that for each sitting the chairman would be selected by the President or by a member of the panel of chairmen nominated by the President for the purpose and they could select themselves. Similarly, the President or a nominated chairman could select two lay members from the panel for each sitting.

The Department of Employment, as the Department responsible for the principal legislation providing a right of appeal to the Tribunals, issued guides to the provisions of each of the Acts concerned in which the right of appeal was explained. In addition, the Department published explanatory leaflets for issue to parties to proceedings setting out in simple terms the procedure of the Tribunals.

Tribunals sat regularly at the Central Office in London and at the Regional Offices, and at other centres as required. The procedural regulations for all jurisdictions were very similar. There were, however, certain differences between them. For example, in Industrial Training and Selective Employment Payments cases the hearing was in private unless the applicant requested that it should be in public, whereas in all other jurisdictions the hearing was in public unless in the opinion of the Tribunal a private hearing was appropriate. Another important difference was that in cases under section 106 of the Industrial Relations Act 1971 an opportunity had to be given for the complaint to be settled by the intervention of a conciliation officer of the Department of Employment.

Appeals from a Tribunal in respect of decisions under the Industrial Training Act 1964, the Selective Employment Payments Act 1966, and the Docks and Harbours Act 1966, could be made to the High Court only on a point of law. All other appeals under other jurisdictions in which the Industrial Tribunals were concerned were made to the Industrial Court except those against decisions on applications under section 10 of the Industrial Relations Act 1971, which lay to the High Court. Particulars about the right of appeal, the time for appealing (42 days in England and Wales), and information about legal aid were issued to parties with the written decision. The only circumstances in which a decided case could be re-heard by a Tribunal was when: (i) a case was remitted to the Tribunal by the High Court or the Industrial Court; (ii) it could be shown that there were grounds for review of the Tribunal's decision under the Industrial Tribunals (Industrial Relations, etc.) Regulations 1972; and (iii) there had been failure of natural justice due to serious procedural irregularity.

The staff of Industrial Tribunals were all civil servants, but while employed by the Tribunals they were responsible to the Tribunals alone and not to any Government Department.

I undertook three consecutive terms, each of three years, and when my last term finished in October 1974 I was the oldest member of the panel. Throughout my time on the panel Sir Diarmaid Conroy, QC, was President of the Industrial Tribunals and his deputy was Sir John Clayden, QC, with each of whom I regularly sat. There were about twelve Chairmen at the Central Office, six full-time and the others part-time. Mr Pereira was a well-known and highly respected

Tribunal Chairman who had served as Judge Advocate with the British Army of occupation in Germany. His stories of some of the cases with which he had dealt were always fascinating and recounted without embellishment.

It was fitting that my last Tribunal, which took place on 9 September, 1974, was chaired by the President, Sir Diarmaid Conroy. During the luncheon adjournment he volunteered several interesting statistics. He said that the Tribunals under his jurisdiction, covering the whole of England and Wales, were averaging a total of 10 000 cases a year; of these 30 per cent were withdrawn and 25 per cent were settled outside the Tribunal. The appeal cases were only 4 per cent of the total and not many of these succeeded. One might imagine that with such a volume of cases arising there must have been many which followed an identical pattern. In my experience, however, over a total period of nine years, as well as in the experience of the various Chairmen under whom I served and my colleagues on the panel, no two cases were ever precisely the same and there were always different circumstances to consider. It was customary for the three members of the Tribunal to receive their case papers from the Central Office about a fortnight before the date fixed for the hearing and although one usually formed a broad opinion based on the applicant's claim and on the respondent's sub-mission, it was surprising how frequently one had to change this opinion as the evidence and subsequent cross-examination of both parties and their witnesses unfolded. Whether intentionally or by an oversight in the written submissions, vital evidence which influenced the decision quite fundamentally was often only subsequently revealed at the oral hearing. In some instances the applicant had no witnesses or counsel to assist him, and very occasionally his ability and intelligence were such that he was able to present his case in a most praiseworthy manner, but in most cases one party or both parties had counsel. In the case of manual workers, it was the customary practice for a Trades Union officer to represent the applicant. Where a decision was made in favour of an applicant for redundancy payment, the arithmetic involved to ascertain the average weekly pay could be quite a lengthy calculation.

The atmosphere in the Tribunal was inten-tionally less formal than most courts because it was appreciated that many applicants and their witnesses were unaccustomed to giving evidence in public and the Tribunal desired all concerned to be at ease – or at least as far as was reasonably practicable. All witnesses took the oath – there were variations according to religion. Representa-tives of the Press were seldom absent. At some Hearings the Court was filled with witnesses or other interested parties; law students and overseas visitors were also present on some occasions.

On average a Tribunal would adjudicate on two cases a day. Only in a few instances was I called upon to serve on what was anticipated to be a two or three day case. The longest case on record occupied a total of nine days. It was a very unusual case of alleged wrongful dismissal – it made the headlines – and the applicant was unsuccessful.

The much maligned Selective Employment Act which was repealed a year or so before I completed my third three year appointment was the subject of a test case which came before a Tribunal of which I was one of the members. The firm concerned were well known manufacturers of electric washing machines but also serviced the machines at twelve separate centres dealing solely with repairs. The Tribunal accepted the firm's contention that their service engineers had nothing to do with sales and that if the repair work had been undertaken at their main factory the SET levy would not have been charged. The outcome of the case was of extreme importance to the Minister of Employment. Eminent counsel appeared on each side and after the fullest discussion among the three members, the Tribunal conceded the application by a majority verdict. This resulted in an appeal by the Minister and the Divisional Court reversed the Tribunal's decision. Leave was given to the Appeal Court and this upheld the decision of the Divisional Court. On request leave was given to appeal to the House of Lords but it was my understanding that this final step was not eventually followed up.

There were of course less spectacular cases. There was the bus conductor who claimed he had been persecuted and dismissed because he was a non-union member. The bus company's case was dereliction of duty and they supplied a copy of the bus conductor's staff record over two years, showing a variety of reprimands for such irregularities as shortage of money, for running early, for refusing to wear his money bag, for being truculent with the passengers and for being offensive to various traffic inspectors. The Tribunal found for the bus company.

Another case was an assistant staff manager who claimed that his status had been reduced because he had dealt largely with recruitment and the recruitment content of his work had virtually come to an end because of reorganization. He lost his case because we were satisfied that he was called upon to do other work of equal status.

Applicants for a redundancy payment or alleged wrongful dismissal represented by far the majority of the Tribunal cases. Those cases involving wrongful dismissal were often very tricky and required the utmost patience because there was frequently a clash of personalities involving a number of individuals in the one dismissal, and the 'wheat' had to be separated from the 'chaff' in order to arrive at the right decision. Sometimes, in the light of the evidence before the Tribunal, the employer would offer to re-engage the applicant and if the latter accepted this was a happy solution.

CHAPTER 19

MY MARRIED LIFE

Fig. 19.1 Family group at the author's wartime wedding at Mackworth parish church, Derbyshire, 9 July 1943

This Chapter covers the most important period of my life. Freda Gould Whittingham and I were married at All Saints' Church, Mackworth, Derbyshire, on 9 July, 1943, the anniversary of my father's birthday. This historic church is situated in the middle of a field just off the A52, the main road running between Derby and Ashbourne, about three miles north-west of Derby. At that time I was serving as Vicar's Warden, an office which I held for five years, including one year after we moved from Kedleston Road, Allestree, to our first married home, 'Boscobel', 141 Manor Road, Derby, in the Parish of Littleover.

Freda was born in Duffield, Derbyshire, on 25 July, 1912, and she had lived in that delightful village, five miles north of Derby, all her life. Her father was a retired railway clerical officer. Freda's mother was formerly Mary Keble Blackburn who was born at Brightlingsea, Essex, the only daughter of a Congregational Minister, the Reverend Joseph Blackburn. She had three brothers, two of whom I had the pleasure of meeting. Freda had a brother, Eric, born like me

in 1900, and a sister Kathleen, better known to all her friends as Mollie, who was two years younger than herself. Freda attended the local primary school in Duffield from whence she gained a Whitworth Scholarship for Parkfields Cedars School for Girls, generally accepted as Derby's leading grammar school.

At the time of our marriage, Freda and I had known each other for well over ten years. In the 1930s I certainly had a great admiration for her intelligence, her industry and her high principles. I was still suffering from the loss of Elsie Village in 1931 and there were no thoughts in my mind of developing the admiration which I had for Freda into a close friendship. However, when the Second World War broke out in September 1939, a mutual friendship had begun. There was no engagement ring because Freda preferred not to wear one. We decided to get married and agreed that we would live with my mother at Allestree, Derbyshire, until the War and the bombing

Fig. 19.2 Home No. 1. 'Boscobel', 141 Manor Road, Derby

were over. Ours was a war-time wedding and apart from a few friends who gathered at Mackworth Church, it was confined to the immediate members of the family. A reception was held at the Broadway Hotel, Duffield Road, Derby. We spent our short honeymoon in Scarborough, Yorkshire, which I knew so well, staying at the Pavilion Hotel, one of the several hotels in Scarborough owned by Charles Laughton, the British actor and film star. We continued to live with my mother until our son, John Garth, was born on 12 April, 1946, at the Florence Nightingale Maternity Home, London Road, Derby. A few weeks previously we had purchased 'Boscobel', an attractive and soundly built property erected in 1932. It had been named after Boscobel in Shropshire, where Charles the First hid in an oak tree. The garden covered three-quarters of an acre, landscaped, with three lawns, one of which was a sunken lawn surrounded by a yew hedge. Additionally, there was a grass tennis court which was always a great attraction. There was also a greenhouse in which I grew tomatoes.

Three years and one day after Garth's arrival our daughter Anthea Jean was born, on 13 April, 1949, at the Queen Mary Maternity Home, Duffield Road, Derby. We always recalled those happy days with our two children as being very dear and special to us. Just a month before Anthea was born my mother passed away, on 9 March, 1949, at my sister's home after a long illness. She was 76 years of age. She was buried in the same grave as my father in Nottingham Road Cemetery, Derby. It was a sad time for all of us. My sister, my brother and I retain the greatest affection for her, and the highest esteem for all that she did for us throughout her hard-working life. She was an ardent churchgoer and her knowledge of the Bible left an indelible impression on all three of us.

At birth Garth weighed 8 lb 9 oz and Anthea 8 lb 5 oz – both bouncing babies. Both were a long time before they walked. I remember my chief, George Ivatt, coming to see us on one occasion when Garth was about twenty months old and still crawling. George, who had no family, said, 'He is so good at crawling, I don't think he will ever walk!' Well, he did and in later years competed for his school in many cross-country races. We remembered Anthea in her early years as the one who would invariably wake up and give us an instant smile. Her mother was the same with

me and over the years this has been one of my happiest memories.

School life in Derby for Garth and Anthea took a quite normal pattern. Garth went to Hargrave House School on the Burton Road. The Headmistress was Mrs Mary E. Frank, daughter of the previous headmistress, Mrs Huxley, under whose headship two of my cousins, Gwendoline and Marjorie Hoon, had both received a good education.

Three years younger than Garth, Anthea started at Derby High School for Girls in April 1954 at the age of five. We chose that Church-orientated school because it held a premier position in the town and we anticipated that Anthea could stay there, if desired, until 'O' or 'A' Level. Anthea did not find school much to her liking, but from her earliest days she showed plenty of originality in various activities, not least in her great love and understanding of animals and living things in general.

Freda's mother died at Duffield, Derbyshire, on 28 February, 1955, and her father died in London on 3 January, 1958. We all had a great affection for both of them.

Fig. 19.3 Home No. 2. 'Woodlands', 16 Seymour Gardens, Surbiton

In October 1956 we moved home from 'Boscobel', in Derby, to 'Woodlands', 16 Seymour Gardens, Surbiton, Surrey. We sold 'Boscobel' to Dr Ian Mackenzie, a pathologist at Derby City Hospital, and we purchased 'Woodlands' from Thomas Finn, a dentist in practice in North London. 'Woodlands' was built in 1936 and was a good family house on the former Regency Estate which belonged to the owners of the Café Royal in Regent Street, London. The garden was one and a quarter acres and was said to be the largest in Surbiton. It included an extensive lawn, a delightful water garden, two greenhouses, about thirty well-established cordon fruit trees, two horse chestnut trees and two magnificent *Catalpa bignonioides*, commonly called Indian Bean trees. The latter have superb foliage and are native to North America and the West Indies. These majestic trees were introduced into England in 1726 and there are some at the Palace of Westminster, under the shadow of Big Ben. There was also an aviary and, although I had never kept birds before, I found the ornamental pheasants, the canaries and the finches quite attractive and not a lot of trouble to look after. After a while I rebuilt the aviary and improved the facilities. Although I took on the old gardener, Fred Harmsworth, who had worked there for many years, I still found I had quite a big job in maintaining the garden to a satisfactory standard.

To save a lot of work I converted the kitchen garden to a pheasantry in which I bred ornamental pheasants of various kinds, as well as peafowl. Soon after this conversion, I felt twinges of pain on the left side of my chest; not unnaturally I wondered whether it was my heart. My doctor referred me to Sir Ronald Bodley-Scott, the Queen's physician in Harley Street, London. After a thorough examination he asked me what I had been doing lately. I told him that I had recently wheeled six hundred turves, six at a time, from the front of the house to the new pheasantry which was located about 150 yards away. Sir Ronald said, 'You needn't tell me any more. You have no heart trouble but you have strained a muscle near to your heart and this will right itself within a few weeks, if you are careful. In future you must remember that you are no longer forty and you should not carry out any sustained heavy manual work as you may have done in the past.' What a relief!

The garden included a delightful water garden into which I put a dozen small golden orfe. When we left, fifteen years later, following my retirement, I gave ten of the orfe to the Kingston-upon-Thames Education Authority for one of their new schools. They were almost a foot long and weighed over a pound each.

In the Queen's New Year Honours List of 1962, I was honoured in being awarded the OBE. Although a recipient never sees the citation, I assumed it was in recognition of some of my pioneering efforts in introducing works training schools on British Railways, for initiating a system of production planning in the manufacture of locomotives and rolling stock and for developing work study and associated techniques within the various divisions of the BTC. The great thing about it was that the family were able to share my pleasure. I was invited to attend the investiture at Buckingham Palace on 6 March and I was also sent two invitations for my family to accompany me. I wrote to the Palace authorities and explained that as I had a son and a daughter as well as my wife I should be very grateful indeed if an additional invitation could be sent to me. Happily this was forthcoming. Anthea was twelve and Garth was fifteen and it was a memorable occasion for all of us. The investiture was held in the Banqueting Room and throughout the ceremony the Guards played delightful background music which everyone appreciated. When my name was called, I approached the Queen and bowed. She enquired about my work and I replied that I was the Director of Work Study to the British Transport Commission; I added that my main task was to try and make British Railways more efficient. I was glad she didn't ask me how successful I had been!

In planning our move to London, Freda and I discussed the choice of schools for both Garth and Anthea. We hoped to get Garth into St Paul's School, Hammersmith, or King's College School, Wimbledon. For Anthea we had in mind Wimbledon High School for Girls, because at that time we were looking for a house in the Wimbledon area.

Sir Brian Robertson (later Lord Robertson) Chairman of the British Transport Commission, kindly asked me what my plans were for the family and whether he could help me in any way. I told him that I was already in touch with St Paul's School and King's College School. Sir Brian told me that Monty (Field-Marshal Viscount Montgomery of Alamein) was an Old Pauline and a governor of the school and that he would ascertain from Monty the current position. Sir Brian knew Viscount Montgomery well because Sir Brian had been Chief Staff Officer to the Field-Marshal in Germany and later High Commissioner. I thanked Sir Brian for his good offices and at that stage I went to Germany for a fortnight as a member of a Government team appointed to study technical training in West Germany, of which Sir Cyril English, the ever-helpful Chief Inspector of Technical Colleges at the Ministry of Education, was the leader.

Before going to Germany, I told Freda of Sir

Brian's conversation and said that if there was a reply from King's College School, Wimbledon, whilst I was away, it would be as well if she told the Headmaster that I would deal with the matter as soon as I returned. Freda did exactly this, but the Headmaster at Wimbledon replied that Garth must attend on the day he had given and no other in order to take the entrance examination. Freda, in typical fashion, decided she must take Garth and let him sit for the examination. After a preliminary interview, Garth went into the examination and Freda was asked to come back to the school in three hours' time. The Head saw Freda again and said he had already perused Garth's papers and was satisfied that the school would be able to offer him a place to start in the coming September.

On my return home from Germany, Freda and Garth both met me with a broad smile and told me what had transpired in my absence. I was amazed and then said, 'What do we do now?' Garth himself settled the matter for us almost at once! He said, 'I like King's College School and I've been promised a place already'. In other words, he had done it all himself and this gave all three of us a great deal of satisfaction.

I wondered how far Sir Brian was committed with Viscount Montgomery. Sir Brian was very charming and understanding. He said, 'I had dinner with Monty last week. It seems that as a governor of St Paul's he is allowed to make one nomination a year. If he likes your son (Sir Brian had already shown Monty the encouraging Term Reports from preparatory school) he would be pleased to put his name forward as his nominee for 1956.'

In the light of what I told Sir Brian he said, 'It is for you to decide and if you wish to go ahead with King's College School, I would like you to write to Viscount Montgomery and thank him for his interest and for the offer he has made.' This, of course, was duly done.

Garth started at King's College School, Wimbledon in September 1956 and left at the end of the Autumn Term, 1964, at the age of 18½, having gained entrance to Queens' College, Cambridge, to read law.

He had an encouraging school career, obtaining several prizes in English, History, French and Geography, nine 'O' levels and three 'A' levels, including two at 'S' level. He was awarded an Inglis scholarship prize for English in 1963 and an L. J. Morrison prize for English in 1965. He also

gained the RAF Advanced Training Certificate with Credit, and in the Upper Sixth form was a Map Reading instructor for the Duke of Edinburgh Award scheme. He was an enthusiastic cross-country runner, representing his school on several occasions.

Garth's Tripos Course at Cambridge did not begin until the autumn of 1965, and he spent six months with our solicitor friend Bertram F. Boyles, senior partner with Sydney and Co., Solicitors, London. Garth obtained his BA Law degree and subsequently a post-graduate degree, the LLB (Cantab). He was also awarded a Harmsworth Exhibition to the Middle Temple, one of the four Inns of Court.

For Anthea, it seemed to us that nearby Surbiton High School for Girls was the right place for her and we were successful in our approach. At 16 she obtained four 'O' levels and expressed a desire to leave school and become a secretary. On leaving school, just prior to her 17th birthday, she took a six-week grooming course at the well-known Lucy Clayton's Modelling School in Bond Street. It was an experience she quite enjoyed but she had no wish to take the matter further.

She subsequently successfully completed a full-time secretarial course at The Triangle Secretarial Training College, South Molton Street, London. Following this, she had no difficulty in getting a suitable local job. Later she decided she wanted to work in London and from that time has done so continuously, changing her job without any apparent difficulty whenever she felt she wanted something different. To date she has had a quite wide experience including appointments at the Middle Temple as secretary to an eminent QC, at Westminster Hospital and also at the Cabinet Office in Whitehall.

At 'Woodlands' we kept various animals and birds – many from overseas – for which we had ample room in several outbuildings. The Senegal bush babies of which Anthea and Garth had one each for Christmas one year, were among the most entertaining, but I think Anthea's two favourites were 'Monty', her black stray cat which lived with us for 17 years, and her donkey 'Ardmore', so named because Anthea had seen so many donkeys when she visited Ardmore in Eire. Anthea's many and diverse pets have mostly been females because Anthea says they usually have a more gentle and friendly disposition than the males.

Our family holidays were always a great joy. For two successive years we holidayed in

Skegness on the Lincolnshire coast. We chose this venue because it was our shortest journey from Derby to a seaside resort. We liked the bracing east coast – despite the cool breeze which so often prevailed and made our regular bathing excursions somewhat short – and in the following year we went further north to Bridlington, Yorkshire.

During Anthea's and Garth's schooldays we spent several summer holidays in Cornwall and Devon and all four of us thoroughly enjoyed the West Country, particularly the extensive smooth sands, the sea and the coastline, with plenty of swimming and surf riding.

We also visited Brittany (twice) and one year we spent a holiday with my sister Winifred and brother-in-law Harry Bates and their family, at Knocke in Belgium. Holland was the venue for still another overseas holiday which we all enjoyed. On this occasion we visited Amsterdam, Rotterdam, and the delightful park and bulb gardens at Keukenhof.

In the summer of 1961 we visited Switzerland, although perhaps our most memorable holiday as a family was our visit to Turkey, Greece and Italy in 1966 to which I have referred in chapter 13.

Our last family holiday was in 1970 when we decided to visit the Scilly Isles. We much enjoyed the quiet and uncommercialized atmosphere of the islands and the absence of heavy traffic. I met an old railway associate of mine, Ray Gunter, the former Minister of Employment, who for many years was the President of the Transport Salaried Staffs Association and with whom I had many meetings. Ray, like the former Prime Minister, Sir Harold Wilson, had a holiday cottage on the island of St Mary's.

After much heart searching, we left 'Woodlands' in March 1972 for 'Providence Way', Ramsnest, Chiddingfold, Surrey, deep in the country. After all, Freda was born and lived in the country until we were married in 1943 and I loved it too. We felt the move would be like a breath of fresh air for us in our retirement.

The village of Chiddingfold, lying ten miles to the south of Guildford, on the A283, has a great deal to commend it and is considered to be one of the most attractive villages in Surrey.

'Providence Way' is a bungalow, so named by our predecessor, Pat Scott, because his mother, Pamela Winn, a romantic novelist, always called her own home by the same name. It was originally built in 1922 as a cow house – to quote the title on the architect's plan – on the Chaleshurst Estate, to

Fig. 19.4   Home No. 3. 'Providence Way', Ramsnest, Chiddingfold, Surrey

accommodate four cows and their fodder. For many years Chaleshurst was occupied by Alfred Herbert Tate (Mr Cube), head of the world famous sugar refining firm, Tate and Lyle. The present owners of Chaleshurst, John Fordred and Marjorie Alderson, cleverly converted the solidly built cow house into an attractive bungalow in 1957.

Freda and I instigated several improvements and additions to the bungalow, and outside additions included an artificial stream and a pond of 2000 gallons with a centrifugal pump to re-oxygenate the water and enable large trout to be kept. There was also a donkey stable and fodder storeroom, and we provided a second garage as well as my building an aviary measuring 30 ft by 20 ft. The latter was divided into three sections in which I kept water fowl, parrots, parrakeets, lovebirds, canaries and ornamental pheasants.

Fig. 19.5   The family visits Hampton Court Palace (Photo by Harry H Whittingham, President of Borg Beck division of Borg Warner, Detroit)

Apart from the Aldersons, who resided at Chaleshurst, a quarter of a mile away, our nearest neighbours, with whom we shared our drive, were Richard and Charmian Stiles-Allen. Their large house called 'The Weigh House' had also been converted by the Aldersons from an outbuilding and was located about a hundred yards from 'Providence Way'.

Within a few months of our moving home, in mid-September 1972, Freda told me she was experiencing an occasional twinge of pain on the left side of her chest. I asked her whether there was anything visible and she said there was not but that she could feel a very small internal lump. After seeing our doctor she was sent for an X-ray, and following the X-ray, an exploratory operation was advised. This took place on 2 October at Guildford, to be followed immediately by a mastectomy on the left side which was regrettably found to be necessary.

Freda's recovery appeared to be taking a normal course, but it was clear to all of us, Freda included, that she couldn't carry on as she had done previously. She went to the hospital for her regular check-ups and treatment and at first nothing adverse was discovered. Early in May 1974, however, Freda developed a dry cough and told the doctor at the hospital; he arranged there and then for an X-ray. The cough persisted and to our dismay Dr David Williams, our GP, told Freda that the hospital had reported to him that she had cancer in both lungs. He knew Freda's strong disposition and that she would take the news better than most – me included. He saw me the same day and said that even if Freda responded to the treatment prescribed she could only expect to live for about five years at the most. It was a shattering blow to all of us. Freda had always been so strong and healthy that such an eventuality had never entered our minds. From then on and despite all the medical care it came painfully clear to us that Freda was losing ground. Although she bravely managed to get up each day, she was having increasing difficulty. She scarcely ate any food and by the end of July 1974 her weight had gone down by three stones. It was heartbreaking to see her, yet she never grumbled.

Dr David Williams was kindness itself and we shall always be indebted to him. He arranged for Dr White, the specialist at Guildford, to see Freda at home on 2 August. Dr White talked to Freda and afterwards said to me and to Mollie, Freda's sister who was with us, 'Your wife is not so ill that I have given up hope.' But the original optimistic forecast was not to be, and on 8 August, 1974, Freda passed away. We were all stunned and yet in our hearts we knew only too well that Freda had no wish to live because of her dreadful illness.

The funeral service took place in St Mary's, the Parish Church of Chiddingfold, on 13 August, 1974, and was conducted by the Rector, the Reverend John G. Nicholls, who for many years previously had been the Chaplain at the Tower of London.

It was Freda's wish that she should be cremated and the cremation took place at Guildford Crematorium. Subsequently, it was arranged for her ashes to be placed in a casket, and with the Rector's kindly co-operation, the casket was buried between two trees almost opposite to the south door of the Church. No memorial stone has been erected because we know it would not be in keeping with Freda's nature to do so. Four years have now passed since I lost my beloved wife, and since Anthea and Garth lost a loving and devoted mother. Freda's deep-rooted Christian faith, her high principles in all spheres of life, her modesty, her gracious manner and loving support were always an inspiration to me. Freda was the one person in the world who really made my life worth living; I can never put into words all that she represented. There is no doubt that my life has been immeasurably enhanced by her wise counsel and judgment.

CHAPTER 20

FINALE

I am almost at the end of my story. When I decided to write these memoirs in 1972, I fully expected to complete my story much sooner and in the previous chapter. At that time it never occurred to me that my circumstances in 1978 could be so different. Life is certainly unpredictable for everyone of us.

It is generally accepted that in the world at large the changes and developments have never been so great as in this century. When the General Strike took place in 1926 students from the Universities queued up to register for any kind of duty to help their country. Nothing seemed to be barred. Nowadays undergraduates from far and near parade and demonstrate in their hundreds for almost every conceivable cause. During the miners' strike in 1974 I recall that students at Cambridge had agreed to provide food and accommodation to miners on picket duty. I find it an amazing state of affairs that all these students can really find time to take such an active and time-absorbing interest in everybody else's business and still manage to complete satisfactorily what should be an intensive academic course. I am often left with the thought that as a nation since the Second World War we have grossly overdone the provision of universities and colleges of advanced technology and art and that it would be in the best interests of the country if these so-called students went directly into industry and commerce as soon as they left school. I venture to suggest that we should have a higher proportion of useful work-conscious citizens. We have not, and never have had, sufficient jobs at the level for which many of them think they have qualified.

There is another comment I should venture to make about education. If I have a grumble it is that the so-called 'progressive' ways of teaching which have largely developed since the Second

World War have been a retrograde step. Many parents have misgivings about the decline in standards, coupled with the breakdown of discipline in many schools. Truancy, – a very rare occurrence in any class when I was a boy, – as well as vandalism and arson, have all increased to an alarming extent. Despite two years of extra schooling there is reason to believe that large numbers of children in the 1970s have emerged from a traditional education without a proper grasp of elementary subjects, and this may diminish the contribution that such individuals will be able to make to British society well into the 21st century. I have the impression that children are no longer taught the virtues of hard work, self-discipline, reliability and high standards of achievement. It is a situation which those in authority should tackle with the utmost vigour.

Like most people of my age I have experienced my setbacks, my pleasures and my tragedies. To lose my beloved wife has been my greatest loss of all. Until she became critically ill in June 1974 I felt as active and alert as I had always felt. I had pressed on with all the improvements and additions to our property that we had envisaged from the outset of our moving there early in 1972. The work was practically finished and with no other commitment I had looked forward to easing up and being in my wife's company to a greater extent than ever before. Unhappily it was not to be. In the years that have passed since Freda's death I have tried hard to re-establish myself and will continue to do so, yet I still find it difficult.

Physically I have not much to complain about. I lost two stone in weight and developed a hernia during Freda's illness but I have recovered from the hernia following an operation early in 1975, and I have since regained most of the lost weight. I try to look ahead, but invariably I find myself looking back and I have not found it easy to pick up the threads again in writing this account of my life. Loneliness has been my worst enemy, despite the fact that I still have the great good fortune to have my grown-up son and daughter residing at home. I do, however, sometimes compare and contrast my position with some of my relatives and friends whose circumstances are sadly much less favourable than mine. It is not easy to derive comfort from this, but it certainly helps.

At 'Providence Way' we had perfect seclusion. However, I found it depressing to be there alone and for this reason, coupled with the advantages which would accrue for my son and daughter, we moved to Greater London on 1 August, 1977. In doing so we lost our seclusion and the almost daily pleasure of seeing roe deer and game on our property, with the gorgeous Surrey countryside all around us and Sussex and Hampshire both nearby. But we have gained convenience and accessibility in full measure. I finally decided on Hampstead Garden Suburb in the Borough of Barnet, which has so much to offer. Now I have no problem in attending meetings and keeping in closer touch with friends.

For several years, I was a Council Member of the Institution of Locomotive Engineers, serving on the Establishment Committee and the Finance and General Purposes Committee. The Institution had been in existence since 1911 but on 24 November 1969, it ceased to exist as a separate Institution and became the Railway Division of the Institution of Mechanical Engineers.

Two principal factors prompted the merger. Firstly, the Railway Engineering Group of the

Fig. 20.1 The author's present home: 80 Brim Hill, Hampstead Garden Suburb, London N2

Institution of Mechanical Engineers was duplicating some of the activities of the Institution of Locomotive Engineers. Secondly, young engineers were more inclined to join the Institution of Mechanical Engineers because membership led to the status of Chartered Engineer, whereas the Institution of Locomotive Engineers – despite the excellence of its organization, and the active support of senior railway engineers in Britain and overseas and of engineers in the railway engineering industry generally – was unable to offer this professional qualification.

A Joint Working Party had been appointed to make recommendations for this merger and it will be interesting to give the names of the five engineers who served on it. It was T. H. Matthewson Dick who initiated the merger when he was President of the Institution of Locomotive Engineers. Tommy retired a few years ago when he was Deputy General Manager of the Western Region.

JOINT WORKING PARTY

Chairman
R. C. Bond, a former President of the Institution of Mechanical Engineers and of the Institution of Locomotive Engineers.
Representing the IMechE
Paul Fletcher, Consultant and President of the Institution of Mechanical Engineers 1975–76.
Dr F. T. Barwell, Professor in Engineering at Swansea University.
Representing the ILocoE
T. C. B. Miller, Chief Mechanical and Electrical Engineer of British Railways.
E. J. Larkin, Deputy General Manager, British Railways Workshops.

To the best of my knowledge no one has ever regretted the advisability of this amalgamation.

I have previously referred to a worthy colleague, Frederick B. Illston. On his retirement as Carriage and Wagon Engineer of the Southern Region, he was invited to join De La Rue, the British firm which prints the banknotes for England and many other countries and which is the sole manufacturer of *Formica*. Fred Illston was appointed as the firm's Overseas Sales Manager in the *Formica* Division and in that capacity made several trips abroad. It was a fitting finale for a highly qualified railway engineer. The following piece of verse is his latest Christmas message to me, complete with card, and it was very typical of him, despite his being well into his eighties:

As the years roll by it is sad to relate,
our actions revert to the infantile state;
limbs do not respond as in days of yore,
but still I'm content to crawl on the floor.

I no longer need a brush and a comb,
to regiment the strands that remain on my dome;
nor razor to dispose of superfluous fluff,
for hairs do not grow on fossil-like stuff.

My digestive organs are really tranquil, ·
due to lack of supply of grist to the mill;
in particular, caviare, salmon, and snipe,
but alas! there's no shortage, in general, of tripe.

I greet you gladly at this time of the year,
with overwhelming happiness, health, and good
    cheer;
and hope that the Future will have pleasures in
    store,
far exceeding the memories and joys gone before.
                                        F.B.I.

After six years in the Home Office – in the Police Department, the Criminal Department and the Prison Department – my son, Garth, completed his professional legal qualifications and became a barrister, his name being included in the list of successful candidates published on 2 July, 1975. It was my privilege to be Garth's guest when he was called to the Bar by the Middle Temple on 17 July. It was an impressive ceremony in which for the first time I had the pleasure of seeing Garth wearing the robes of a barrister.

In 1977, after a period as a practising barrister based in common law chambers in the Temple and Lincoln's Inn, he joined C. T. Bowring and Co. Ltd, in the City of London, and was appointed Company Secretary of several subsidiaries in the Bowring Group, which is the largest organization of its kind in the country, handling, world-wide, insurance, credit financing and merchant banking, amongst other things.

It is coincidental that within the space of a few months the two men most involved when railways were nationalized in 1948, and when the wide ranging British Transport Commission came into existence, both died. I refer to the Right Honourable Alfred Barnes and Lord Hurcomb.

Alfred John Barnes was the Minister of Transport in the Attlee Government from 1945 to 1951 and it was he who piloted through the measure nationalizing the railways and road transport. He was the son of an East London docker and was MP for East Ham South from 1922 to 1931 and 1935 to 1955. He was Chairman of the Co-operative Party from 1924 to 1945. He died in November 1974, aged 87. During his term of office as Minister I was one of the party who conducted him around the Derby Locomotive Works.

Lord Hurcomb, GCB, KBE, was the first Chairman of the British Transport Commission. He was educated at Oxford High School and St John's College, Oxford, of which he was made an honorary Fellow in 1938. He entered the Civil Service in 1906 and was appointed to the General Post Office, where, from 1911 onwards, he was private secretary to successive Postmaster-Generals, among them Lord Samuel.

He first entered transport, in which he spent most of his official life, in 1917 when the Ministry of Shipping was formed. After the war he went to the newly formed Ministry of Transport and remained in that turbulent Ministry, first as Director of Finance, and later in higher positions, becoming Permanent Secretary in 1927. When in May 1941, Winston Churchill became Prime Minister and amalgamated the old Ministry of Transport with the Ministry of Shipping to form the Ministry of War Transport under Lord Leathers, Hurcomb took charge of the new Ministry.

When the war ended Hurcomb remained in charge of the Ministry, which dropped 'War' from its title, and was involved almost at once in the task of devising legislation to 'integrate' inland transport, as the political watchword of the day had it, which involved the nationalization of the major part of the transport system of the country. When the Transport Act, 1947, came into force it was Hurcomb who was chosen for the not altogether enviable task of operating the machine which he had played a major part in devising, for he was appointed the first Chairman of the British Transport Commission when it was set up in 1947. He and other members of the Commission paid a visit to the Derby locomotive works following nationalization in 1948 and I was a member of the party which conducted them around.

Following his retirement in 1953 he was able to devote himself to ornithology, nature conservation and fishing, which had always been his main interests away from the office. He died on 7 August, 1975, at the age of 92.

There is one Minister of Transport, Ernest

Marples, who merits special mention. When he died on 6 July 1978, the Press described him as being the most eminent Minister of Transport for 30 years, making reference to the M1, the first motorway, and the introduction of parking meters, traffic wardens and yellow lines. Not least the Press spoke of his support for Dr Richard Beeching, whose sweeping reorganization of British Railways was a landmark in railway history.

In my new home in London I am much more reliant on public transport, and I am reminded of W. W. Maxwell, the member of the London Transport Executive for Engineering. In his Address as the new Chairman of the Railway Division of the Institution of Mechanical Engineers on 26 September 1977, entitled 'In Search of Perpetual Motion' he told his large and appreciative audience that each weekday some two million people travelled on London's Underground and five million on London Transport's buses, and also that between 7.00 am and 10.00 am on any weekday more than a million people entered Central London, over 80 per cent travelling on public transport and only 15 per cent by private car. More precisely, he said that some 300 000 people used road transport, of whom 148 000 travelled in 3200 buses, and 160 000 in 115 000 private cars. These impressive figures certainly make one think. I do not need a car now – my son and daughter will always oblige me – and I am in the fortunate position of holding a BR gold pass and the equivalent for London Transport to help me get around.

I have always kept in touch with most of my relatives and their families, especially my sister and brother. The latter's younger son, Peter, served an apprenticeship in the Derby locomotive works, during which time he made a point of visiting every Running Shed on BR as well as reading every locomotive book available. I have no railway colleague, nor have I ever met a railway enthusiast, whose knowledge of the various classes and workings of steam locomotives throughout BR can compare with his phenomenal store of information in this field. Since his apprenticeship days he has worked in Liberia, for many years as a diesel locomotive maintenance engineer in a supervisory capacity.

My sister's daughter, my only niece, Sheila Margaret, married John Vaughan Simpkinson in 1950 and they have lived in Etwall, Derbyshire, for many years. They have three sons and a daughter, Vicky, who, in 1977–78, was head girl at Derby High School, the school her mother had attended.

I attend, as often as convenient, the meetings in London of the Retired Railway Officers' Society which was founded at the turn of the century and which continues to flourish. Its motto, taken from the works of Dr Johnson, is 'A man, sir, should keep his friendships in constant repair' and is most apt, and it is always a tonic to see old colleagues. I realize that I am growing up because at a recent meeting I spoke to Jack Bellamy, the eldest son of G. S. Bellamy, my pre-war works superintendent at Derby locomotive works (later the Mechanical and Electrical Engineer of the Scottish Region), who had recently retired from a senior operating position at Board headquarters. Such is life!

I always enjoy visiting the two Derby works (and other works) where the present incumbents as Works Managers are Peter Gray (carriage and wagon works) and Charles Garratt (locomotive works). I think of the indefatigable Ernest Pugson, who was at the carriage and wagon works before the Second World War, and of the amiable, if unorthodox, Freddie Simpson at the locomotive works, both in office for many years and both of whom successfully undertook a tremendous amount of pioneering work. I keep in touch with Frederick G. Clements, the current Chief Mechanical and Electrical Engineer of the London Midland Region. The maintenance of the busy electrified main line from Euston to the North is one of his responsibilities. Fred has reminded me that when he was a young man at Horwich works I interviewed him in my office at Derby together with Colonel Harold Rudgard, Motive Power Superintendent of the LMS Railway (subsequently Chief Motive Power Officer at BR headquarters, Marylebone) with a view to our selecting him for transfer to the Running Department. He has certainly made the grade.

Over the years my native town of Derby has frequently been erroneously referred to as the City of Derby. It was therefore very pleasing to me when I heard the official announcement over the radio on Jubilee Day, 7 June, 1977, that the Queen had honoured Derby by raising it to the status of a city to mark her Silver Jubilee Year. It was a signal honour, especially when it was revealed that during the Queen's twenty-five years on the throne she had only granted two previous charters of this kind, namely to Southampton in 1964 and Swansea in 1969.

Whether as a town or a city it has always been a pleasure for me to visit Derby to keep in close touch with my relatives, as well as a wide circle of friends, whenever the opportunity presents itself. I much enjoy attending the Christmas lunch of the former Railway Officers' Mess and the Annual lunch of the Wyvern Club, with its close association with the old Midland Railway. Inevitably as the years pass on age takes its toll and those of us who are privileged to be there get fewer and fewer.

As I draw to the end of my narrative, I would like to include a very personal note. I never thirsted or applied for any office or position. Whatever has come my way has just happened. If I have been moderately successful in any sphere I would put it down to sheer enthusiasm coupled with a determination to see a worthwhile job through to a successful conclusion. It may sound odd to some but I have never smoked and I have never had a glass of beer. Many will think I've missed something. I am not impartial to a glass of wine – perhaps some champagne at a wedding party – and I have kept a variety of alcoholic drinks at home in case any visitor would like some. Despite my lifetime's association with workshops and the kind of vocabulary that one may hear in them as well as elsewhere from time to time, I have managed to live my life without recourse to using any strong language. It may be a small point, but it is sometimes the small things in life which collectively add up to something worthwhile. On the physical side, I can happily say that my general health has been very good, although, of course, I've had relatively minor illnesses like most people.

I would like to conclude my life story on a happy note. As long as I can remember it has been my maxim to make the most of every day. After all, life on this planet is relatively short for all of us and every individual, sooner or later, has his or her problems. There is no escape. Wherever appropriate I've tried to encourage and to give pleasure to those I have met either in business or in other spheres. I hold no grudges against anyone. Fortunately I have a very wide circle of friends, many of long standing. They all make an unconscious contribution to my well-being and I like to think this is mutual. It comes naturally to me to enjoy the company of people drawn from all walks of life. We can all learn from each other, and it does everyone a lot of good to appreciate another's point of view.

In a large organization like British Railways it is quite impossible to keep in touch with all one's former colleagues. I did, however, have the pleasure of attending the Senior Management Mess at Board headquarters as a guest just before Christmas 1977. I had been a founder member of this august body and it was my first visit since leaving twelve years earlier. I observed that, although I knew most of the fourteen officers present, everyone of them had joined the Mess since I left – a gentle reminder that, whoever comes and goes, the job goes on.

It is good to know that British Railways have an unrivalled safety record judged by any standard. The 1976 report of the Chief Inspecting Officer of Railways, published a year later, records that for the first time in railway history no passenger was killed in two consecutive years, the last fatality being in the autumn of 1975. Furthermore, this was the sixth time in this century that there were no passenger fatalities during the year, and the train accident rate fell to 0.84 per million train miles, the lowest figure recorded for several decades.

In 1938, the year of Munich and the year before the Second World War started, Alderman Harold Fern, President of the Fédération Internationale de Natation Amateur and the Honorary Secretary of the Amateur Swimming Association, sent me a delightful Christmas card. It is the only Christmas card I have ever retained and by a stroke of good luck I came across it just at the time I had started to write this chapter. After all these years the wording still appeals to me and in the circumstances I feel I cannot do better than conclude my memoirs by the inclusion of a facsimile of his card and its thoughtful words.

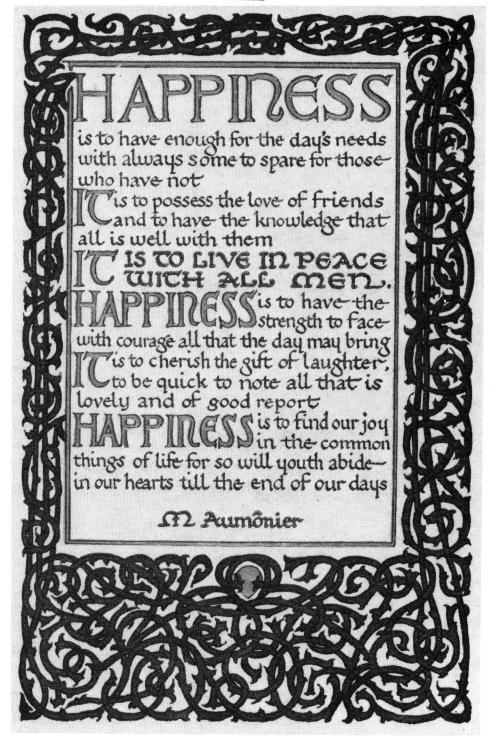

HAPPINESS
is to have enough for the day's needs
with always some to spare for those
who have not
IT is to possess the love of friends
and to have the knowledge that
all is well with them
IT IS TO LIVE IN PEACE
WITH ALL MEN.
HAPPINESS is to have the
strength to face
with courage all that the day may bring
IT is to cherish the gift of laughter,
to be quick to note all that is
lovely and of good report
HAPPINESS is to find our joy
in the common
things of life for so will youth abide
in our hearts till the end of our days

M. Aumônier

BIBLIOGRAPHY

The reader is referred to the following for further information concerning topics covered in this autobiography.

Bond, Roland C, *A Lifetime with Locomotives*, 1975 (Goose and Son)
Bulleid, H A V, *Bulleid of the Southern*, 1977 (Ian Allan)
Cox, E S, *Locomotive Panorama*, Vol. 1, 1965, Vol. 2, 1966 (Ian Allan)
Cox, E S, *British Railways Standard Steam Locomotives*, 1966 (Ian Allan)
Cox, E S, *Chronicles of Steam*, 1967 (Ian Allan)
Cox, E S, *World Steam in the Twentieth Century*, 1969 (Ian Allan)
Cox, E S, *Speaking of Steam*, 1971 (Ian Allan)
Radford, J B, *Derby Works and Midland Locomotives*, 1971 (Ian Allan)
Rogers, H C B, *The Last Steam Locomotive Engineer: R A Riddles CBE*, 1970 (George Allen and Unwin)
Richardson, W Alfred, *Citizen's Derby*, 1949 (University of London Press)

BIOGRAPHICAL PRESS RELEASE ISSUED BY BRITISH RAILWAYS ON 30 DECEMBER 1965

On the Author's retirement from British Rail, the Public Relations Division of BR Board issued the following statement to the Press on 30 December, 1965. It is a concise account of much of his life's work up to that time and crystallizes a good deal of the story which has been unfolded in this book.

RETIREMENT OF MR E. J. LARKIN

Mr Edgar J. Larkin, OBE, MIMechE, MILocoE, Consultant to British Railways Workshops, is retiring on 31 January next, after nearly fifty-two years' railway service.

Biographical Notes

Mr Larkin began his railway career with the Midland Railway Company at Derby in 1914 and was an apprentice in Derby Locomotive Works from 1916 to 1921. His theoretical training was obtained at Derby and District College of Technology. In 1918 he served in the Royal Air Force as a Cadet Pilot.

In 1921 he became a draughtsman in the Locomotive Drawing Office, Derby. In 1930 he became Superintendent of Apprentices in the Locomotive Works, and in 1932 evolved the Progressive System of Workshop Training which has been widely adopted on British Railways. He took charge of the Progress Office . in 1933 and was responsible for locomotive repairs at Derby and Outstation Shops on the Midland Division of the LMS.

In 1934, Mr Larkin was appointed Second Assistant to the Works Superintendent. He introduced a system of Production Planning for the building of new locomotives which was subsequently extended and adapted to the other Main Works of the LMS. He became Assistant Works Superintendent at Derby Locomotive Works in 1940 and was closely concerned with armament and aircraft contracts. In 1942 he was appointed Staff Assistant to the LMS Chief Mechanical Engineer at Derby Headquarters and from 1943 until 1952, acted as Chairman of the CME Sub-Committee and attended the National Arbitration Tribunal and the Industrial Court to give technical evidence on behalf of all the Companies. During this time he put into effect a

scheme he had developed for the establishment of Works Training Schools at seven LM Region Main Works centres.

In 1952 he was appointed Assistant Mechanical and Electrical Engineer, London Midland Region and was Chairman of a number of inter-Regional Policy Committees set up by the BTC for mechanical and electrical engineering activities. During 1955 he was seconded to the Commission to report on the recruitment and training of professional and technical staff in the mechanical and electrical engineering departments to meet the requirements of the British Railways Modernization Plan approved by the Government at £1500 million.

In 1956, Mr Larkin joined a Government delegation to West Germany to compare technological standards and methods of training with those in this country.

He became the first Director of Work Study, British Transport Commission, in 1956. In 1960 he presented a paper on Productivity before the International Railway Congress in Brussels. He was Chairman of the BTC Work Study Development Committee from 1956 to 1962 and of the Headquarters Staff Suggestions Committee of British Railways. He was also the representative of the Nationalized Industries on the British Productivity Council for a number of years.

In 1962 Mr Larkin became Deputy General Manager of the newly-formed centralized Workshops organization of British Railways and was closely identified with the implementation of the Board Plan for rationalizing the twenty-eight Main Works which employed over 60 000 staff. In 1965 he was appointed as Consultant to British Railways Workshops.

Mr Larkin, who was awarded the OBE in 1961, is a Member of the Institution of Mechanical Engineers and of the Council of the Institution of Locomotive Engineers. He is also author of two books entitled *Works Organisation and Management* and *The Elements of Workshop Training*.

Before the war he was a part-time lecturer at the Derby and District College of Technology in Machine Design and Industrial Administration and is a former Vice-Chairman of the Engineering Advisory Committee at the College. He is a former Chairman of the Derby Area No. 1 Hospital Management Committee; a past President of the British Railways (Derby) Swimming Club; and a past President of the Midland Counties Amateur Swimming Association and the Derbyshire Amateur Swimming Association. He was an International Diving Judge and Referee for twenty years.

He is married and has a son and daughter. His son is reading law at Queens' College, Cambridge. His daughter was in the sixth form at Surbiton High School and is now training to become a Secretary.

MISCELLANEOUS FACTS AND FIGURES RELEVANT TO BRITISH RAIL

(Recorded at the time of the author's retirement in January 1966)

Passenger

Total journeys made in the year	928 000 000
Number of trains run each weekday	20 000
Stations	3574
Largest station area:	
Clapham Junction	34½ acres
Largest number of platforms:	
Waterloo	21
Longest platform:	
Manchester (Victoria and Exchange)	2194 ft

Freight

Revenue-earning tonnage carried in the year	240 000 000
Stations	2833
Largest station:	
Bristol (Temple Meads)	15 acres under cover

Locomotives

Steam	2987
Diesel	4811
Electric	277
Total	8075

Coaching vehicles

Passenger carriages	129
Locomotive hauled	12 950
Diesel multiple unit	4109
Electric multiple unit	7148
Total passenger vehicles	24 207
Non-passenger vehicles	8081
Total	32 288
Seating and berth capacity (total)	1 546 391

Freight vehicles
Merchandise:
   Open   112 222
   Covered   92 122
Mineral   357 892
Steel carrying   34 887
Others   14 175

Total   610 998

Route mileage
Electrified   1793
Non-electrified   13 127

Total (all traffic)   14 920

Route mileage (passenger traffic)   10 884

Track miles
Running lines   29 898
Sidings   11 457

Total   41 355

Road motor vehicles
Motor powered   12 912
Trailers   28 589

Ships
Passengers carried   17 818 000
Head of livestock carried   328 000
Motor vehicles carried   1 064 000
General cargo carried (tons)   1 905 000

Structures
Bridges   63 100
Tunnels   1049

Signals and telecommunications
Signal boxes   7912
Track miles with colour-light signals   4407
Track circuits   56 386
Public address installations   636

Steep main-line gradients
Lickey incline (nearly 2 miles)   1 in 37·7
Exeter (between St Davids and Central stations – 7½ chains)   1 in 31·3
Dainton Bank (near summit – 12 chains)   1 in 37

Track

Highest altitude (Druimuachdar)	1484 feet above sea level
Lowest point (Severn Tunnel)	144 feet below sea level
Longest straight (between Selby and Hull, Yorks)	18 miles
Longest stretch of continuous four-track main line (St Pancras to Glendon North Junction, Kettering)	74 miles 78 chains
Number of point heaters (1964)	3084

Longest bridge

Tay bridge	2 miles 364 yards

Longest tunnel

Severn Tunnel	4 miles 628 yards

Stores

Coal used – all purposes (tons)	4 160 500
Coal for locomotives (tons)	3 858 400
Coke (tons)	81 500
Diesel fuel oil – traction only (gallons)	185 267 000
New rails used (tons)	170 000
New sleepers used	2 290 000
Iron and steel scrap salvaged (tons)	750 000

APPENDIX III

THE AUTHOR'S SELECTION OF HISTORICAL EVENTS DURING HIS LIFETIME

1900	30 December	Australian Commonwealth proclaimed.
1901	22 January	Queen Victoria died.
1902	9 August	Coronation of King Edward VII.
1903	17 December	First controlled flight in heavier-than-air machine – Orville and Wilbur Wright in Kitty Hawk. USA.
1904	10 September	*Discovery* returned to Spithead from the Antarctic expedition.
1905	5 September	Peace signed at Portsmouth, USA, between Russia and Japan following heavy Russian defeats.
1906	18 April	Simplon Tunnel opened for railway traffic.
1907	27 January	King Edward VII opened the new Central Criminal Court, Old Bailey.
1908	12 June	Rotherhithe Tunnel opened.
1909	25 July	Bleriot made first cross-Channel flight in 37 minutes.
1910	6 May	King Edward VII died.
1911	22 June	Coronation of King George V and Queen Mary.
	14 December	Amundsen reached South Pole.
1912	14/15 April	*Titanic* disaster off Cape Race; 1517 lives lost.
1913	17 January	Home Rule Bill passed, House of Commons majority 110.
1914	4 August	Great Britain declared war against Germany.
1915	23 April	Germans first used gas on Western front.
1916	15 September	Tanks first used by the British.
1917	26 June	First American contingents arrived in France.
	15 September	Russia proclaimed a Republic.
1918	11 November	Armistice signed by German plenipotentiaries: great jubilation throughout Britain and allied countries.
1919	15 June	First direct air-flight across the Atlantic by Sir John Alcock and Sir A. W. Brown.
1920	13 January	League of Nations came formally into existence.
	14 October	Women graduates admitted for first degrees to Oxford University.

1921	7 February	Sinn Fein outrages in Dublin.
	31 May	Official end of Great War.
1922	29 November	Great find of treasures in tomb of King Tutankhamen near Luxor in Egypt by Lord Carnarvon.
1923	29 October	Turkish Republic proclaimed, Kemal Atatürk first president.
1924	23 April	Wembley Exhibition opened by King George V.
1925	1 December	Summer Time Act made permanent.
1926	6 March	General Strike.
1927	21 May	Lindbergh flies Atlantic alone.
1928	18 July	Women in Britain enfranchised.
1929	10 August	Graf Zeppelin flies from New York to Friedrichshaven in 55 hours.
1930	1 April	End of Board of Guardians.
1931	23 May	Opening of Zoological Gardens at Whipsnade.
1932	19 March	Sydney Harbour Bridge opened.
1933	30 January	Hitler appointed Chancellor by Hindenburg.
1934	28 February	The first vertical bridge in England opened by the Duke of York at Middlesbrough.
1935	6 May	Silver Jubilee of King George V's Accession celebrated.
1936	20 January	Death of King George V at Sandringham and accession of King Edward VIII.
1937	12 May	King George VI and Queen Elizabeth crowned in Westminster Abbey with traditional ceremony and pageantry.
1938	3 July	World Steam Speed record of 126 mph by LNER steam locomotive *Mallard*.
1939	3 September	War declared between England and Germany.
1940	1 June	Bulk of the British Expeditionary Force in Dunkirk safely landed in England. 887 British ships of all types used in the evacuation of 335 000 troops.
1941	1 December	Points rationing scheme came into force.
1942	25 November	German forces retreating before the Red Army offensive at Stalingrad.
1943	27 November	Winston Churchill, President Roosevelt and Marshall Stalin met in Teheran for a four-day conference.
1944	6 June	Invasion of Europe commenced by Allied Forces.
1945	8 May	World War II against Germany officially ended one minute past midnight (Tuesday) VE Day.
	5 August	Atomic bomb first used against Japan, causing widespread devastation.
1946	1 October	Verdict and sentences on Nazi leaders announced.
1947	1 January	British coal industry nationalized.

1948	1 January	British Railways nationalized.
1949	1 January	British Nationality Act came into force.
1950	2 November	Death of George Bernard Shaw, aged 94.
1951	13 July	Foundation stone of the National Theatre laid by the Queen at South Bank, London.
1952	6 February	King George VI died at Sandringham, aged 56.
1953	2 June	Coronation of HM Queen Elizabeth II in Westminster Abbey; ceremony televised.
1954	6 May	Roger Bannister ran the mile in under 4 minutes – the first man in the world to do so.
1955	5 April	Sir Winston Churchill resigned as Prime Minister.
1956	17 October	Queen Elizabeth II opened Calder Hall, the world's first commercial nuclear power station.
1957	4 October	First earth satellite launched by Russia (180 lb sphere, 23 in diameter).
1958	5 August	US nuclear submarine *Nautilus* surfaced after having passed under the North Pole.
1959	10 December	Raising of school-leaving age to 16 recommended by Crowther Report (implemented 1970–71).
1960	17 May	The Queen Mother officially opened Kariba Dam.
1961	12 April	Major Yuri Gagarin of USSR made first space flight.
1962	10 July	*Telstar*, first experimental satellite in space communications, launched – first live television between USA and Europe.
1963	1 August	Under Criminal Justice Act, 1961, minimum prison age raised to 17.
1964	31 July	American *Ranger* 7 hit moon after sending back over 4000 pictures of surface.
1965	22 June	700th Anniversary of British Parliament celebrated.
1966	27 August	Francis Chichester set sail single-handed round the world (arrived in Plymouth 28 May 1967).
1967	3 December	First human heart transplant operation by Dr Christian Barnard at Cape Town.
1968	16 September	Two-tier postal system began in Britain.
1969	21 July	Armstrong and Aldrin of USA first men to land on the Moon (3.56 am, BST).
1970	16 March	Publication of the complete New English Bible.
1971	28 October	House of Commons and House of Lords voted in favour of joining Common Market on terms presented by Government.
1972	30 December	Tutankhamen exhibition in British Museum. 1 600 000 visitors.
1973	5 December	50 mile per hour road speed limit imposed to conserve fuel.
1974	8 November	After 300 years in Central London, Covent Garden market moved to new site at Nine Elms.

1975	3 November	Queen Elizabeth II pressed a button in the control room of the BP Forties field at Dyce, Aberdeenshire, for the formal opening of the first British oil field.
1976	7 August	The hottest temperature recorded in London since records began: 32.3°C.
1977	7 June	Silver Jubilee of Queen Elizabeth II.
1978	2 November	Two Soviet cosmonauts, Vladimir Kovalynok and Alexander Ivanchenkov, returned safely to earth after 4½ months in the orbiting station *Salyut 6*, during which time they were visited on several occasions by space crews and unmanned cargo ships bringing them essential food, fuel, and scientific equipment.

INDEX